GreenSpirit:

Path to a New Consciousness

First published by O Books, 2010
O Books is an imprint of John Hunt Publishing Ltd., The Bothy, Deershot Lodge, Park Lane, Ropley,
Hants, SO24 0BE, UK
office1@o-books.net
www.o-books.net

Distribution in:	South Africa
	Stephan Phillips (pty) Ltd
UK and Europe	Email: orders@stephanphillips.com
Orca Book Services	Tel: 27 21 4489839 Telefax: 27 21 4479879
orders@orcabookservices.co.uk	
Tel: 01202 665432 Fax: 01202 666219	Text copyright Marian Van Eyk McCain 2008
Int. code (44)	
	Design: Stuart Davies
USA and Canada	
NBN	ISBN: 978 1 84694 290 7
custserv@nbnbooks.com	
Tel: 1 800 462 6420 Fax: 1 800 338 4550	All rights reserved. Except for brief quotations
	in critical articles or reviews, no part of this
Australia and New Zealand	book may be reproduced in any manner without
Brumby Books	prior written permission from the publishers.
sales@brumbybooks.com.au	
Tel: 61 3 9761 5535 Fax: 61 3 9761 7095	The rights of Marian Van Eyk McCain as author
	have been asserted in accordance with the
Far East (offices in Singapore, Thailand,	Copyright, Designs and Patents Act 1988.
Hong Kong, Taiwan)	
Pansing Distribution Pte Ltd	
kemal@pansing.com	A CIP catalogue record for this book is available
Tel: 65 6319 9939 Fax: 65 6462 5761	from the British Library.

Printed by Digital Book Print

O Books operates a distinctive and ethical publishing philosophy in
all areas of its business, from its global network of authors to
production and worldwide distribution.

GreenSpirit:
Path to a New Consciousness

Marian Van Eyk McCain (Editor)
with a Foreword by Satish Kumar

Illustrations by Jenny Johnson

BOOKS

Winchester, UK
Washington, USA

CONTENTS

Foreword ... Satish Kumar   1

Introduction ... Marian Van Eyk McCain   5

Part I: Understanding
Understanding the world and our place in it   13
1. Seeing Things Differently ... Grace Blindell   14
2. Gaia Theory and Deep Ecology ... Stephan Harding   36
3. What Are Humans For? ... Brian Swimme   50
4. Falling in Love with Gaia ... Susan Meeker-Lowry   60

Understanding Ourselves
5. The Crack in Everything ... Isabel Clarke   63
6. Reclaiming our Animal Body ... Tania Dolley   76
7. Ecopsychology ... Sandra White, Chris Clarke and Don Hills   85

Part II: Spiritual Pathways   **101**
8. The Great Wheel (About Part II)
   ... Marian Van Eyk McCain   102
9. The Green '-isms' ... Michael Colebrook   108
10. The Four Paths ... Grace Blindell   115
11. Transformation ... June Raymond   127
12. Something is Amiss in the World of Religion
    ... Matthew Fox   130
13. Spirit in East and West ... Jean Hardy   139
14. On Christ ... June Raymond   146
15. Green Buddhism ... Joyce Edmond-Smith   149
16. Green Judaism: Alaskan Salmon Taught Me Bible
    ... Rabbi Jamie Korngold   154

17. The Ecology of Heart: A Sufi Journey
    ... Neil Douglas-Klotz   158
18. On Devotion and Duty: A Pagan View
    ... Emma Restall Orr   164

Part III: Greening Our Culture   **169**
19. The Vital Shift (About Part III)
    ... Marian Van Eyk McCain   170
20. Greening Health: Full-Spectrum Wellness
    ... John Travis and Meryn Callander   172
21. Greening Education (1) The Crisis in Education
    ... Matthew Fox   183
22. Greening Education (2) Touching the Earth
    ... Ruth Meyers   187
23. Greening the Law ... Cormac Cullinan   192
24. Greening Economics: The Post-Corporate World
    ... David Korten   200
25. Permaculture: Bringing Wisdom Down to Earth
    ... Maddy Harland   212
26. Complexity, Form and Design ... Jean Bee   222

Part IV: Walking Our Talk   **233**
27. Walking the GreenSpirit Way: (About Part IV)
    ... Marian Van Eyk McCain   234
28. GreenSpirit in The UK: The Early Years
    ... Petra Griffiths   237
29. GreenSpirit Today ... Marian Van Eyk McCain   246
30. The Theory of Anyway ... Sharon Astyk and
    Pat Meadows   256
31. Simplicity, Activism and the Fourfold Way
    ... Marian Van Eyk McCain   262

About the Contributors   270
Acknowledgments   281

This is a book for anyone who hungers for a spirituality relevant to our times. **Chris Johnstone**, author of *Find Your Power*

Think of 'GreenSpirit' as a vade mecum, namely, those insightful books of guidance known in all the traditions that fit in the pocket and 'went with a person' in the walk through life as a summary of wisdom teachings. GreenSpirit certainly aims to 'walk the talk,' and, while doing so, provides that good companion we all hope to find. **John Grim**, Co-Director, Forum on Religion and Ecology, Yale University

Navigating the most profound transition in the history of humankind will require extraordinary resourcefulness – with a far greater emphasis on spirituality than ever before. 'GreenSpirit' celebrates the diversity and creativity of many of those shaping that greener consciousness. **Jonathon Porritt**, Founder Director, Forum for the Future; Chairman, UK Sustainable Development Commssion

May this treasure trove of a book with its words of wisdom and beauty, and its helpful practical advice, reach many people and guide them into simpler, more meaningful ways of living within the great community of Life. **Ursula King**, Professor Emerita of Theology and Religious Studies, University of Bristol.

'GreenSpirit', with contributions from a host of artisans of cultural trans-formation, skillfully interweaves the strands of our new story, a new consciousness, renewed cultures, and our path to becoming fully human. Marian Van Eyk McCain has crafted an insightful and wide-ranging handbook to the promises and potentials of this new century. **Bill Plotkin, Ph.D.**, author of *Soulcraft* and *Nature and the Human Soul*

Since our thinking and behaviour are underpinned by our spiritual beliefs and understandings, I believe that what we need is a spiritual revolution. And this book is part of exactly the kind of revolution that we need. **John Seed**, Founder and Director of the Rainforest Information Centre

To address the many social and environmental crises we face today, we urgently need holistic, human-scale solutions. 'GreenSpirit' is an inspiring call to reconnect our minds and hearts with practical, grassroots action. **Helena Norberg-Hodge**, Founder and Director of the International Society for Ecology and Culture

Other books by Marian Van Eyk McCain

Transformation through Menopause
Elderwoman: Reap the wisdom, feel the power, embrace
the joy
The Lilypad List: 7 steps to the simple life

Fiction
Apricot Harvest
Waiting a While for Greeneyes
The Bird Menders

"GreenSpirit: Path to a New Consciousness offers numerous healing and inspiring insights; notably, that Earth and the universe are primary divine revelation, a truth to be transmitted to our children as early and effectively as possible."

Thomas Berry
January, 2009

Foreword

Satish Kumar

We Are All Related

I walk in Nature, not as an escape from the strain and stress of urban life, not for entertainment or sightseeing, not even as a scientist looking at Nature as an object of study. I go in Nature as a pilgrim for the renewal of my spirit. Walking in Nature is my meditation and my prayer. The magnificent trees and majestic hills are my temples and cathedrals. I don't look above the sky to seek heaven; my heaven is here on Earth. Being one with Nature, I am enchanted and enlightened.

Walking in Nature came to me very early on in my childhood. My mother was a walker. She would say that if we go in a vehicle or even on an animal like a horse, we are fixed on reaching our destination and we lose our connection with everything on the way. Walking makes the journey itself the destination; there is no destination outside the journey. When you are walking you can look at the flowers and appreciate them. You can look at the bees and learn from them. Nature becomes your teacher, your mentor, your guide and guru.

If you want to learn the lessons of restraint you can learn from the honey bee. As you walk you hear the bees buzzing as they take a little nectar here and a little nectar there, never too much. Never has a flower complained that the honey bee took too much nectar away; so you can learn the lesson of restraint and frugality from the honey bee.

You can also learn the lesson of transformation from the honey bee; what does the honey bee do with the nectar it has taken? It transforms it into sweet, delicious, nutritious, healthy and healing honey. How many humans can do that? Humans

1

take, take and take until Nature is depleted and they make, make and make until Nature has turned into waste and pollution.

From the honey bee you can also learn the lessons of networking. Bees are the greatest pollinators in the world; they connect the plants. They illuminate the interconnectedness and interdependence of all life.

Due to human activity bees are in danger of extinction. Some scientists believe that within a few years all the bees may disappear because of the depletion and pollution of Nature. What will that do to human survival? No bees, no pollination, no plants, no oxygen, no life—no people!

As a pilgrim I can observe Nature, learn from her and connect with her on a deeply spiritual level. I am not separate. I feel myself to be a part of the natural world.

Some environmental academics have come to the conclusion that the beginning of the split between humankind and the natural world is rooted in Genesis where it is stated that humans have dominion over the Earth. Of course Christian environmentalists have challenged this interpretation. Some have even suggested that 'dominion' is the wrong translation. Humans, they say, have no dominion over the Earth; Earth is a 'gift from God' to be cherished and cared for.

Whatever the dispute, the word 'dominion' was planted in the minds of millions of people. Western scientists, industrialists and economists in particular have seen Nature as a resource to be mined for human benefit. They acted upon their belief that the human species is superior to all other species and therefore humans have a right to use the land, animals, forests, rivers and all other natural gifts as they like. Even those who have a benign view of Nature consider humankind to be the stewards of the natural world; humans should look after the Earth and manage it sustainably so that Earth can be the source of wellbeing for present and future generations. Whether dominion or stewardship, human/Nature relationship has been based on an anthropocentric world view. This train of thought dominates much of environmental thinking in the mainstream society as well as in the more established environmental organizations.

However there is a profound undercurrent of thinking represented by deep ecologists which upholds the principle that Nature is not merely a resource for human beings. The value of Nature cannot be measured or determined on the basis of her usefulness to humans; Nature has intrinsic value. Trees, animals, land, rivers and all life, human and other-than-human, has intrinsic value.

Deep Ecology is a radical school of thought, but it is not widely known nor very commonly accepted as yet. Also, Deep Ecology is deep but not deep enough; it accepts intrinsic value but shies away from the notion that life is sacred and that humans need to hold a deep reverence for all life. In other words it lacks a spiritual dimension. Here comes the vision of *GreenSpirit* which complements secular Deep Ecology and could be translated as Spiritual Ecology or Reverential Ecology. *GreenSpirit* attempts to lead us into the greening of the spirit as well as seeing the spirit in the green world.

GreenSpirit is a movement as well as a philosophy. It brings East and West together. Hinduism, Buddhism and Taoism hold a spiritual view of nature. They believe in the unity of all life; human and non-human life are made of the same existential reality, we are all connected, we are all related, there is no separation, there is no dualism. The American Indians, the aboriginal culture of Australia and other indigenous traditions have a similar world view: Nature does not belong to humans, humans belong to Nature, humans *are* Nature, there is no distinction.

For me, God is not a person who created the world in six days in a historical time and then disappeared behind the clouds somewhere away from this world and left us to our fate. For me, God is not a creator in the past. The creator and creation are a continuous process and this process in itself is God. Nature is God. Hindus call creation the Dance of Shiva; the dance and the dancer cannot be separated. We are all dancers and we are the dance; we are all creators and also the creation.

Nature is sacred, Nature is intelligent, Nature is alive. All life has intrinsic value and has a right to live. From this perspective, Deep Ecology and GreenSpirit share a common ground.

I am delighted that Marian Van Eyk McCain has brought many strands of ecology, spirituality and wholeness together. Her book *GreenSpirit: Path to a New Consciousness*, is like Ikebana, the Japanese art of flower arrangement. The essays brought together in this book represent many shapes, colors, forms; they are like beautiful flowers, beautifully composed. I am confident that the book will act like a guide to many who are seeking a right relationship between the human spirit and the natural world.

Satish Kumar

Introduction

Marian Van Eyk McCain

Although human beings have experienced and practiced green spirituality in various forms for millions of years, I used to think it was something I invented.

That is probably not surprising. I was little more than a child—15 years old to be exact—that morning when I first plucked up courage to defy the adults in my family and, instead of accompanying them all to church, spent Sunday morning sitting under a tree.

I have never forgotten the experience of that morning. It was early summer. The sun was shining, the campions and foxgloves were blooming pink against the green of the meadow grass and there were bumblebees buzzing around me as I snuggled into a hollow amongst the tree's roots and leaned my back against its knobbly trunk. From somewhere nearby came the scent of honeysuckle.

Across the fields, I could see the squat, stone tower of the church and I thought of my family sitting inside, on those wooden pews, singing hymns to the God in whom they had tried to persuade me to believe: a God who sat on a tall throne, somewhere above the clouds, surrounded by angels in white robes. And suddenly I knew, with a deep, inner conviction, that there was indeed a God. But it was a nameless, formless God; a God who caressed me with the dappled sunlight that filtered through the leaves, who charmed me with the scents and sounds of summer and who lived in every molecule of everything.

Whatever that God energy was, I knew that I was breathing it. And it was breathing me. It was within me and around me, in the air, the grass, the hedgerows, the birds, the clouds, my blood. It was in everything and it *was* everything, including me.

After that, I never went to the church again. For many years, I continued to refer to what I had experienced as 'God.' But eventually I stopped using the term altogether, as it seemed no longer necessary to do so. By then, like many other people, I had explored various other religions, particularly Buddhism. I had practiced Yoga and meditation, learned about shamanism, paganism, witchcraft, Taoism…seeking, always seeking for some religious tradition into which my beliefs would neatly fit and where I might find a ready-made 'congregation' of like-minded people. But the fit was never quite right. Then in the early 1990s when I was living in Australia, someone invited me to join a new group that was being formed around something called 'Creation Spirituality.'

I had seen this phrase before and dismissed it, assuming that it was something to do with creationism (the denial of evolution). I should not have jumped to that conclusion. It was nothing of the kind. Far from denying evolution, Creation Spirituality celebrates it. This was, in fact, what I had been searching for: an expression of spirituality based on a sense of deep connectedness with the natural world. And when I joined the group, I felt as though, at last, I had come home.

A few years after that, I returned to my native England, and to my delight I found there was a similar group here. The name of the organization and the name of its philosophy are both the same: 'GreenSpirit.'

GreenSpirit, as an organization, is a community of people connected by their way of seeing and experiencing the world around them. These are people who celebrate the human spirit in the context of their place in the natural world and Earth's own evolutionary journey.

For cosmology, as we shall see in the first chapter, plays a huge part in this green spirituality. Humans have always needed their creation stories in order to make sense of a mysterious and awesome universe and nowadays, thanks to science, we have a more amazing and awesome story to tell than ever before.

The radical vision of GreenSpirit brings together the rigor of science, the creativity of artistic expression, the passion of social action and the core wisdom that exists within the spiritual traditions of all ages. Attracting those of many faith traditions and none, GreenSpirit is a network of individuals who believe that human life has both an ecological and a spiritual dimension.

The mission of those individuals, as they band together, is to explore the unfolding story of the universe and to promote common ground between people in the context of this vision. They seek to redress the balance of masculine and feminine in themselves and in the wider culture and to befriend darkness as well as light. And they enjoy creating ceremonies and celebrations which connect them more consciously with the cycle and seasons of the Earth. The need for rituals, rules and celebrations is also, like creation stories, an ancient and persistent need. But as the level of human consciousness expands and evolves, more and more people are becoming disillusioned with the rigidity of society's traditional religious institutions. At the same time, there seems to be an ever-deepening awareness of this need for spirituality in all our lives (as witness the popularity of so-called 'New Age' ideas, worldwide).

This yearning for an authentic and truly meaningful spirituality is happening right alongside the increase in ecological awareness. I believe this is no random coincidence. GreenSpirit is the place where those two things connect: the ecological awareness and the spiritual yearning. When the two come together—the 'greening' of our lives and the longing for those lives to have more of a spiritual dimension to them—a spark is created that lights up the whole sky.

GreenSpirit is not a religion. However it does bear a certain resemblance to religion, in that it has the same three main aspects one would find in most religions: a body of wisdom, a sense of the sacred and a community of like-minded people. Unlike most religions, though, it has no standard set of ritual practices. Neither does it have a priesthood. People can be members of GreenSpirit and continue to practice whatever religion they feel at home in—or none at all.

I suppose what unites this group of people could best be described as an attitude—a particular kind of orientation to life, to the world, to the universe in which we live and of which we are all a part. It is like a new pair of spectacles. You look through them and you see the same world that was always there yet now it all looks different. Because to see the world through GreenSpirit eyes is to see everything as ecocentric (Earth-based) rather than anthropocentric (human based). This is a very big and very significant change. Most of society and most of its institutions—including most of its religions—remain stubbornly and arrogantly anthropocentric. This is one of the reasons why so many things have gone so badly wrong. We have put our human needs above the overall needs of the planet.

Not that we are any more innately selfish than any other animal. Let's face it, beavers would probably chop down every sapling from here to the horizon if they had the opportunity to do so, and feel no guilt about it. But because our clever human brains have given us the power to override all those natural checks and balances that have kept any one species—including beavers—from upsetting the system, we pose a greater threat to that system than any other creature before us, as we are now beginning, belatedly, to realize.

Since the world's resources are finite, we cannot continue to grow and multiply and consume without destroying everything and thereby destroying ourselves. So even from a purely pragmatic point of view, our behavior and our ways of thinking need to change if our species is to survive. Only by changing the way we see the world and by changing the way that we have been relating to our fellow creatures and to the Earth can we hope to prevent ourselves from damaging the planet's ecosystems beyond repair and sending our own species—as well as so many others—to extinction.

To live in the world from a GreenSpirit orientation is to see oneself as being *of* the Earth rather than *on* it and to see the planetary ecosystem as a whole (rather than humans) as being of central importance in everything and at all times.

But a GreenSpirit way of seeing the world is not based purely on the pragmatic need to develop a sustainable way of life for humans in order to prevent ecological collapse. It grew out of a hunger of a different kind. That is the hunger for meaning, for a deep sense of connectedness like the one I felt that long-ago Sunday morning, for a spiritual dimension to everything we do and feel and experience. Only when that deeper meaning is restored to our lives can we ever feel completely whole and happy. And only then can we do our part to change things for the better, working from the heart rather than the head, doing our part from passion and love of the Earth rather than from duty, fear, coercion or political correctness.

Many people may not even realize they have lost this sense of meaning and connectedness, so immersed are they in their world of objects, of concepts, of trivial preoccupations and mass-produced entertainment and so caught up are they in their frenetic, modern lifestyles. It is only when we slow down and look more deeply into ourselves that we might notice a hunger there for something we can scarcely name.

That hunger can assume strange forms in some people, such as alcohol or drug abuse. It is like a treasure hunt in which the seeker has been tricked into seeking treasure in all the wrong places. The same applies to most other addictions, including the addiction to consumerism which our Western societies now have in epidemic proportions.

This hunger for lost connectedness can also find us looking longingly at some of the world's last remaining indigenous peoples and imagining that in them small reservoirs exist of some primordial wisdom that we lost touch with a long time ago. This may or may not be so—we tend to sentimentalize such things—but at least we are on the track of something important. For that wisdom we find in so many indigenous cultures, is often about the bond between humans and the Earth. But although a study of other, more Earth-based cultures might give us clues as to the direction we need to take in reclaiming our lost sense of the sacred, let's not look back wistfully and romantically at some imagined golden past. The green spirituality described in this book is one designed for now, for the twenty first century and for the future. Our species may have come dangerously close to destroying our world through our ignorance, our greed, our misunderstanding of the true nature of our beingness, but finally we are beginning to understand what we need to do to put ourselves back on course and steer ourselves *forward* to safety, to sanity, to right relationship with the universe that birthed us.

In Part IV of the book you will find more details about GreenSpirit as an organization. However, the main thrust of the book is to describe, from as many viewpoints as possible, what this green spirituality is and how it can be used by anybody, anywhere, as a compass for both the inner and the outer journeys through life.

Following this Introduction, the book is divided into four parts. In the first, entitled 'Understanding,' we shall be looking at the various threads which have created the weave we call GreenSpirit.

The first is cosmology. In describing this, we shall be drawing on the work of Thomas Berry and Brian Swimme, co-authors of *The Universe Story*, that masterful telling of the tale of our existence, from the 'Big Bang' onwards.

Another major thread is the one referred to earlier: Creation Spirituality. In other words, a spirituality centered on the beauty and mystery of the world we see around us, rather than on some imaginal realm of gods and angels. Here we shall be turning to the thought and writings of Matthew Fox, the iconoclastic Christian priest who became unpopular with the Vatican for his insistence that the concept of 'original sin' needed to be replaced by one of 'original blessing' and who eventually left that church to become an Episcopalian instead.

A third thread is the thread of Deep Ecology: a way of appreciating the Earth and all its life forms by acknowledging their intrinsic value, as opposed to measuring their value on the basis of their usefulness—or otherwise—to human beings.

Then there is Gaia Theory: the discovery that our planet Earth, far from being merely a lifeless rock with a thin covering of air and water and life clinging to it like lichen on a stone, displays all the attributes of a living organism, including the ability to self-regulate.

Lastly, there is Ecopsychology. This is a way of understanding ourselves and our psyches in terms of our relationship with Nature, both around us and, just as importantly, within us.

In the second part of the book, 'Spiritual Pathways,' we examine the ways in which all these ideas fit together with some of the traditional religions and how each of those may be practiced from a GreenSpirit orientation.

Part III, 'Greening Our Culture,' is concerned with how we might bring—and indeed are already beginning to bring—GreenSpirit thinking to bear on the different institutions and sectors of human society, such as law, medicine, education, politics, economics, design and so on.

Finally, in Part IV, 'Walking our Talk,' we discuss the practicalities of living a GreenSpirit lifestyle. This is a lifestyle in which ecologically-minded behaviors such as simple living, 'downshifting,' recycling, frugality and so on all flow from a pure and boundless love of the Earth rather than from fear or because some individual, institution or government tells us it is the right thing to do.

We look at the history of GreenSpirit as an organization, what it provides for its members now and how the reader may link up with the services and opportunities it offers to people who wish to become part of our ever-widening spiritual community. Like planets in a solar system, this is a community which in turn is part of a larger one, in a web of relationships that spans the globe. Here, as we listen to people describing their experiences of GreenSpirit, it becomes clear how well and how satisfyingly it stands alone as a form of spirituality that lacks nothing and requires no compromise, no translation of language and no special props or dedicated buildings.

You will hear many voices in this book. Some of the contributors are already well-known names, some not so well-known. A number of the essays included here are extracts from longer works or are transcripts of talks given at GreenSpirit events over recent years. Some are adapted from writings previously published in the GreenSpirit Journal or in the form of booklets printed by GreenSpirit Books. Some of the work is brand new and written especially for this book. Together, this collection of writings presents, for the first time in one volume, a comprehensive picture of GreenSpirit both as an organization and as a philosophy of life. From these pages you will discover what GreenSpirit is, what it stands for and how it can provide a way out of our current dilemmas and into a joyous, sustainable, peaceful and harmonious future.

Part I: Understanding

"It's really simple. Here's the whole story in one line.
This is the greatest discovery of the scientific enterprise:
You take hydrogen gas, and you leave it alone, and it turns into
rosebushes, giraffes, and humans."

– Brian Swimme

Understanding the world and our place in it

1. Seeing Things Differently

Grace Blindell

Our journey towards understanding

Throughout the brief span that the human species has been upon this beautiful planet our interpretation of our relationship with the natural world—the animals, plants, trees, the elements of wind, water, air and earth, as well as the sun, moon and stars—has shifted, both consciously and unconsciously. Running parallel have been humankind's developing and shifting attempts to define, explain and understand the great mystery of creation itself.

If we were to let our minds drift both back in historical time, we would see an extraordinary panorama. We would see tribal deities concerned with small groups of people, we would see pantheons of gods, each with their individual responsibilities. We would see deities of place, mountain, river, sea, and sky. We would see goddesses concerned with fertility and the seasons. We would see a deep reverence for the natural world.

Slowly, not necessarily everywhere, we would be able to discern shifts towards a single deity and the influence this had upon human attitudes. Concepts of justice as well as punishment, forgiveness as well as revenge, would begin to be seen.

We are now aware of this slow evolution of human interpretation and explanation to ourselves of 'how things are.' Through the eyes of GreenSpirit, no one step invalidates a previous awareness, although our human history is tragically marked by the false assumption that each new, wider understanding must demolish all that went before.

The aim of this chapter is to put GreenSpirit in its context within the natural progression of human awareness. Although there is always a danger of our wanting to be the one true and final 'revelation', giving in to our human desire to 'be right' and to 'have the answer', to take that stance would be to follow the old path to division and antagonism. One of the great 'certainties' that underlies the new, wider vision that inspires GreenSpirit is its embrace of the Whole. Both the evolving human understanding together with the evolving natural world are seen as an ongoing but unfinished journey, our 'enlightenment' today a part of an ongoing and unfolding universe. This in no way belittles any part of the journey; each understanding, each awareness is a vital link in an evolving Whole. The new, wider vision of GreenSpirit must therefore be willing to accept both knowing and *not knowing*.

To look at one example, we turn to humankind's view of the place of the sun. When it was postulated that the sun did not do what the evidence of our eyes told us that it did, but first that the Earth was round and later that the Earth rotated and orbited the sun, what a terrifying shift that demanded of our interpretation of our place within the visible universe. Gone was the comfortable security of a flat Earth, with 'God' in (his) abode above, and the devil and (his) domain below, the sun placed in the sky by 'God' and journeying its everlasting 24-hour odyssey from east to west, then plunging through the dark underworld to reappear daily in the east, the stars fixed and permanent as a sort of back-drop. Instead came this terrifying reversal of all that certainty. What must it have been like to have been at the center of all that upheaval?

And yet...what really happened? We were simply being impelled towards a widening of our horizons. Nothing had really changed, our planet had been circling the sun for 4,500,000,000 years, the Earth had been revolving on its own axis 4,500,000,000 years. The change that was being demanded was a change in our human perceptions, an abandoning of the cozy security of the earlier cosmology to something less clear-cut, more mysterious, wider, more awe-inspiring, but nevertheless a reality that had always been so.

We live in and are part of an evolving and ever-expanding universe, and evolution is a continuous process. Nor is it the physical world alone which is in the process of change; this process includes also consciousness in all its forms. Bede Griffiths (the Christian/Hindu mystic who died in 1993) on being asked: 'Is the universe going somewhere?' replied, 'Yes, towards consciousness.'[1] Thus has the conscious awareness of the human race gradually moved, shifted, changed and evolved, in an ongoing attempt to orient and define its place within — and its relationship — with the perceived world in both its natural and sacred dimensions.

We do not all need to be scientists, nor do we need to be cosmologists, but we do need to know our own human cosmic story. Only when we know that story do we begin to understand our place within it. So let us turn briefly, now, to the changes and challenges that arose in the twentieth century, and which continue to confront us in the twenty first.

The challenge of the twentieth century...and beyond.

"We simply have to explore the religious implications of Quantum Theory and the Big Bang origins of the universe."
– Walter Schwarz. Former Religious Editor of The Guardian newspaper.

GreenSpirit rests firmly upon the new understanding of the nature of reality that emerged during the twentieth century, and upon the subsequent shifts and movements that have developed in the light of this wider awareness.

In this chapter I invite you, the reader, to enter into a simple, but accurate, presentation of these new insights, and respond with your whole humanity—not only the intellect, but with your spirit, your emotions, and that deep instinctive 'knowing' which lies buried within our human species. To quote Lorna Marsden, a respected Quaker thinker:

"The spiritual life, the life of imagination and the heart is an endowment of humanity that is primal. It works against the elevation of the use of reason beyond the borders of reason's competence."[2]

Brian Swimme, in a lecture given at the Institute in Culture and Creation Spirituality in Oakland, California, said this:

"We had the mind once to comprehend… we have drowned that in a pursuit of the knowledge of how/why, and now we have lost that ability, buried under words, numbers, measurements. We now have the story, but without the mind to comprehend fully…our technological mind is incapable of appropriating the news."

GreenSpirit recognizes this deep split that has been created within the human mind by our mechanical western pursuit of the how/why and seeks to heal that split. Not by going back, nor by denying the intellect, but by seeking a synthesis between these two equally needed parts of ourselves.

The two discoveries that have changed our understanding of the nature of the universe—and thus of who we are and our place within that universe—in a fundamental way are these: firstly what is loosely called the 'Big Bang' origin of the universe, and secondly what is equally loosely referred to as quantum physics. To enter into the reality of the meaning of these revelations far more is required than the workings of the human brain. The human being possesses so much more: vision, imagination, intuition, as well as a deep, shamanic ability to 'know.' These are our inheritance, and it is this quality of knowing that is evoked by the wonder of the new story.

As the nineteenth century faded and the twentieth dawned, we lived, or thought we did, against a backdrop of an unchanging and stable universe. It is true that the idea of evolution—that is to say, of ongoing adaptation—had entered our consciousness, but that idea was exclusively confined to the biological world.

Yet within a few decades that stable and unchanging universe had become an expanding and evolving one, and not only that, it had become a universe with an identifiable beginning, and one that would finally end.

The new telescopes built through this last century, first on mountain tops and now launched on satellites, have seen further and further into space, observing events that happened longer and longer ago, from which the light is only now reaching us. We are seeing how, countless millions of years ago, the universe was a frenzy of wild activity, galaxies colliding as they condensed from a maelstrom of turbulent gas; we are seeing how, many millions of years before that, the earliest stages were completely calm, an almost featureless cloud of shining concentrated incandescence where only the tiniest ripples hinted at the creative emergence to come later. Theoretical calculations then take us further back still, over the 300,000 years of this cloud's lifetime, which our telescopes cannot penetrate, to the unimaginable earliest events that both brought forth the physical patterns that shape our material world, and also determined the precise chemical composition of that cloud, so crucial for the evolution to come. This is 'Big Bang Theory,' strangely named for such a calm and seemingly featureless beginning.

Nothing that the human species has had to comprehend in its brief span on this planet compares with the challenge of this new revelation. We are the first generation of humans to know, at a concrete and factual level, the story of the universe, and to face its implications: that this is also our own story. Nor is this new understanding some sort of optional extra that we can opt out of under the pretext 'I am not a scientist,' 'I am not a cosmologist' or even 'I am not religious.' This vast, all-embracing, new understanding literally contains everything within its unfolding.

Here the same staggering new knowledge is being described by Brian Swimme and Thomas Berry in their book *The Universe Story*.

"...a momentous change in human consciousness...a change of such significance in its order of magnitude that we might think of it as revelatory, meaning by this term a new awareness of how the ultimate mysteries of existence are being manifested in the universe about us."[3]

From that first primordial flaring forth until this present moment, every star that has been born and died, every whirling galaxy and every atom, every life form that has come and gone, every earthworm and every cabbage, all the great forests that have covered the planet, each unique sunrise and sunset, dance and rhythm, music, art and poetry, all human emotions, all human spirituality, the questioning human mind, the rise of consciousness—all, without exception, are an inseparable part of the ongoing story.

Ernesto Cardenal in his narrative poem 'The Music of the Spheres' evokes the grandeur and the magic of the place of the human within this unfolding cosmos:

Suppose reader, we want to see the star HD193182,
The star could not see its beauty
Unless we did.
We are the star seeing itself.
Born in its fire

and cooled to be able to think and see.
Protons, neutrons, and electrons
are the human body, the planet, and the stars.
From the unconscious consciousness came,
So in us the planet loves and dreams. [4]

Yes, we are indeed not a separate species objectively surveying the universe, but the universe itself reflecting upon itself.

Yet we cannot hope to grasp the true depths of meaning within this story until we find again within ourselves that quality of imagination which is our human inheritance. Not lost, but overlaid with the deadening dust of undiluted mechanical science. In *The Universe Story,* Brian Swimme and Thomas Berry warn against seeing only the scientific mechanistic story. They say:

"This story incorporates the human into the irreversible historical sequence of universal transformations. The important thing to appreciate is that this story…is not a story of a mechanistic, essentially meaningless universe but the story of a universe that has from the beginning had its mysterious self-organizing power that, if experienced in any serious manner, must evoke an even greater sense of awe than that evoked in earlier times at the experience of dawn breaking over the hills, of the night sounds of the tropical rainforests, for it is out of this story that all of these phenomena have emerged."[5]

What about the second of these shifts in our understanding, quantum physics? In quantum physics we are no longer faced with the solid facts of Newtonian science which assumed that complete understanding of the nature of the physical world could be reached by reducing everything down to its smallest 'building blocks.' During the twentieth century scientists tried to do just that, following the simple theory that once we had broken down the elements of matter into their smallest particles then we should understand not only the nature of matter but the nature of the universe itself.

Alas, the quest was like peeling layers from an onion, where each layer revealed a further one below, until the last 'ultimate layer,' if such a thing there was, was seen to be far beyond the capabilities of experimentation to probe, even if the entire energy output of the Earth was harnessed in the attempt. But in the course of this hunt came an apparent paradox. Even at the first stages of the onion peeling, when science uncovered the electrons that spray the pictures onto our television screens and the photons (particles of light) that are manipulated in the night-time viewing devices of the modern soldier, these objects— electrons, photons, and the many others later to join them— seemed sometimes to behave as particles, and sometimes as waves.

Dana Zohar, in her book *The Quantum Self* says:

"The most revolutionary statement that quantum physics makes about the nature of matter, and perhaps of being itself, follows from its description of the wave/particle duality, the assertion that all being at the sub-atomic level can be described equally well either as solid particles, like so many billiard balls, or as waves, like undulations on the surface of the sea… it is the duality itself which is most basic. Quantum 'stuff' is essentially both wave-like and particle-like simulta-neously." [6]

So the stuff of the universe, the stuff of which we too are fashioned, is both solid and firm, possible to pinpoint in space, and at the same time, subtle, wave-like, rippling, interpene-trating, and impossible to pinpoint in space.

This coexistence of waves and particles was fully understood at the new, intellectual level through work by the Cambridge physicist Paul Dirac in the 1940s. But the intellectual struggle is only one aspect of the challenge of quantum physics. As humans we are called to go beyond the intellectual, responding as well with that other part of ourselves, which can rise to transcend paradox and live wildly with mystery and uncertainty. It is that part of ourselves that knows what Schrödinger, one of the founders of quantum theory, called its greatest revelation: interconnectedness—a key concept—which I need to describe in a little detail.

It was predicted in the 1930s but only experimentally verified by the French physicist Alain Aspect in the 1980s. He carried out experiments on pairs of photons (particles of light) which were produced from a common source (a tube of fluorescent dye) and which then travelled to opposite sides of the laboratory. He found a wonderful synthesis of freedom and relatedness: the two particles responded unpredictably, but in a way that was determined by whatever contexts they were placed in, and in a way in which the two particles harmonized their free responses. They behaved as if they continued to share a common source for their ongoing creativity.

What quantum theory presented in stark, unavoidable form, the rest of science woke up to as something that had been overlooked but was now obvious. Of course the whole universe is interlinked by fields that never wholly fade, however far they penetrate! Of course most systems are poised to respond unpredictably to the subtlest influence from the most distant star! Of course! But how are we to respond to disclosures that challenge us to open up to the deeper intuitions of our hearts?

Charlene Spretnak in her book *States of Grace*, pinpoints our dilemma very accurately (and amusingly) when she says:

"Insistent on avoiding any metaphorical mumbo-jumbo, so abhorrent to the modern mind... they (the scientists) seem to place their faith in declaring a directive to society that is almost charming in its naiveté. Everything is composed of a subatomic flux of wavelets and particles, chaos and pattern, boundaries are fluid. Possibilities are endless. Unrelated separateness is an illusion. Interconnectedness is reality. Process is all. Revise your perceptions, concepts, and life accordingly. Any questions?"

Just a few. Charlene Spretnak continues:

"Since modern socialization has taught us to deny subtle perceptions that do not fit with a rationalist, mechanistic model of existence, how are we supposed to instantly develop our atrophied sensitivity in order to grow in awareness of the intricate, moment-to-moment dance of creation, disintegration and recreation?" [7]

A dilemma indeed, for we are (at present) out of balance, our rational and intellectual side having been raised to the status of final arbiter. How do we redress the balance?

"The shift into the New Story is just this…seeing differently." ~ Matthew Fox.[8]

How do we begin 'to see things differently'?

TOWARDS SEEING DIFFERENTLY.

I shall lure myself into this new way
Slowly, subtly,
And with cunning.
I shall take myself by surprise
And trick myself towards
That teasing boundary

One way or another.
Too long have I lived
This side of the frontier
Kow-towing to the Single Straight Line,
Whilst over there
Flutter the many-dimensional
Butterflies of paradox.
I shall walk daily
Along that tremulous meridian
And learn . . .
I shall lay my ear
To the pulse-beat of the planet
And know. . .
I shall dwell
Within the inner and outer together
And see . . .
That my end is my beginning,
That all things are connected,
That there is no longer
I and Thou,
Nor I and It,
Only the One.

So let us look at those subtle shifts that are taking place today. The Quaker writer quoted earlier (Lorna Marsden), describes these changes as: "...the opening of horizons towards the unification of knowledge."

These movements can be seen as the breaking down of ancient barriers as well as the widening of narrowly held concepts, so that the separate and seemingly irreconcilable parts come together to make a balanced whole.

These movements come from different starting points and have a bewildering variety of names. However, they have two immensely important things in common. Firstly, they are grassroots in their origins. Secondly, in every case they expose to the light previously divided—or even buried and denied—aspects of a whole. This coming together of hitherto opposed facets, this joining of polarities, is a profound indication of the compelling urge towards wholeness from which there can be no turning back. These movements we now see all around us.

The rise of feminism asserts the need for balance within a society predominately male dominated. Off-shoots of this embrace the retrieval of the feminine aspect of the Divine, the rediscovery of the Goddess, and last but by no means least it releases men from the stultifying impositions of patriarchy.

The revolution we see within medicine with the rapid spread of alternative approaches to healing which look beyond the symptoms to the context of the illness or complaint, is again indicative of the growing drive towards seeing the whole rather than the parts.

What is loosely described as the 'green' movement comprises a wide spectrum, and yet without exception it is grassroots in its origins. Greenpeace, Friends of the Earth, animal rights movements, the concern for organic farming, environmentalist movements, the concern for endangered species and for rainforests, Deep Ecology, one and all, and many more acknowledge our interconnectedness and interdependence with the planet.

Within the realm of psychology there is a trickle-down effect to more individual attempts to deepen our understanding of our own personalities and our 'shadow-sides,' Jungian theory, Humanistic and Transpersonal Psychology, Ecopsychology and Psychosynthesis, to name just a few.

The tentative rapprochement between the leading representatives of the various religions is only a shadowy reflection of the global spread of interest and cross-over taking place among ordinary people. Without doubt this can be seen as an awakening of 'spirituality' at the expense of allegiance to a creed or guru.

The Quaker Universalist Group basis which states "We believe that no one faith can claim to have a monopoly of the Truth" could perhaps sum up this more open approach.

Finally, and noticeably in those countries where a Western colonial attitude has despised and belittled the native wisdoms and spiritualities, there has been a renaissance of those suppressed wisdoms. Parallel with this has been a recognition from the predominately Western cultures that indigenous peoples have much to teach us, and that learning is a two-way process.

There is clearly a paradigm shift under way, and an increasingly holistic vision lying behind each fragment of this mosaic. Consciously or unconsciously, the human race is being propelled towards recognizing its absolute interconnectedness with the whole. As Diarmuid O'Murchu said in 1993:

"(We) belong to this community of Earth and share in its spectacular self-expression. This is the setting that seems to be implicit in the movements towards ecological integrity in this late twentieth century…"[9]

And according to Thomas Berry and Brian Swimme we have a special role to play, thanks to the evolution of our capacity for self-reflection:

"It is the special capacity of the human to enable the universe and the planet Earth to reflect on and to celebrate, not simply the present moment but the total historical process that enables this moment to be what it is."[10]

Changing our perceptions

"One of the major shifts in consciousness required for our time is that we belong to the evolutionary co-creative process, and it is in rediscovering our mutual interdependence ... that we reclaim our spiritual identity."[11]

Spirituality is a human attribute, an innate quality within us which responds and always has responded to the ultimate Mystery of Being. Spirituality expresses itself both within and without formal religion. This expression has had different emphases throughout human existence; nevertheless, its core has always been an awareness of inclusion and interconnectedness, thus bringing together the bits and pieces which often dominate our lives, blinding us to their ultimate wholeness. GreenSpirit articulates how this innate human spirituality reflects and is immediately 'at home' within the wider understanding of the journey set out in the foregoing pages.

Let us now examine four dramatic shifts in perception which come from a wider, inclusive vision. Old, deeply embedded cultural attitudes and assumptions are transformed, once we look through the wider lens of the new vision. I will describe in turn a new concept of the sacred; the change from a human-centered to a cosmic-centered viewpoint; the transformation of the Christian idea of original sin which has been so influential in our Western culture; and finally the healing of the wounds inflicted by dualistic thinking.

(i) The Sacred.

Firstly, we can no longer draw a line of distinction between what we consider 'sacred' and what we consider to be 'inanimate matter.' GreenSpirit sees the whole of creation as sacred. One of the definitions found in the dictionary of the word 'sacred' is 'worthy of, or regarded with reverence and awe.' It is in this sense that the word is used here, thus the reader may fit comfortably anywhere along the spectrum of religious or non-religious belief.

The now undisputed fact that we—the human species and

our planet Earth—belong within the context of an evolving universe demands the deepest reverence and awe. Who are we? A universe that has moved inexorably, over vast unimaginable periods of time from pure energy to matter, and (on this planet) from matter to life, and finally from life to conscious self-awareness, is the milieu in which we now find ourselves. This milieu holds within itself a revelatory new understanding of the place of the human. Within this context the human becomes the self-expression and the self-awareness of the universe itself. In his book *Reclaiming Spirituality* Diarmuid O'Murchu says:

"The consciousness we possess as human beings... needs to be freshly understood as an integral dimension of the intelligence that permeates all life in the universe." [12]

And Matthew Fox points out that either everything is sacred or nothing is.

(ii) The Cosmos.

Secondly, we must shift away from our anthropocentrism. Throughout human existence our interpretation of who we are and our relationship with both the created world and the Divine has been entirely from a human-centered perspective. Until now we have known only our own story. With the New Cosmology we find ourselves plunged into a new story, wider, more magnificent, and also more terrifying than any we had previously imagined. Our human-centered viewpoint is now too narrow and too limited for we are part of an ongoing and evolving whole. What changes does this wider cosmic-centered picture make to our understanding of what it is to belong to the human species on planet Earth? I shall mention three.

We have to look again at the value systems by which we order our lives. Justice, the ecology, even language, need to reflect this new, cosmic dimension. For greater detail along these lines see 'Conditions of the Ecozoic Era' in Thomas Berry's *Befriending the Earth*. In his words:

"It is amazing that we should be so sensitive to suicide, homicide, and genocide and have absolutely no moral principles for dealing with biocide or geocide. Over-concerned with the well-being of the human, we feel it is better that everything is destroyed than that humans suffer to any degree." [13]

We are both power-less and power-full
Set against the incomprehensible vastness of the universe, the human species, living out its short lifespan on planet Earth, can seem ridiculously small and insignificant. Yet the same scenario changes when we recognize that the growth of life and the emergence of consciousness on planet Earth is the one known instance where the universe itself has evolved to a form of conscious self-awareness. Thus the human, with its consciousness and its gift of choice, holds both the power to create and the power to destroy. Paradoxically both views are true.

We are peripheral and we are central
Further, and again paradoxically (for the willingness to embrace paradox is truly a part of this new way of seeing), we are no longer, in the earlier narrow sense, the center of the universe.

Nevertheless, in the light of our interdependence and inter-connectedness within the whole, irrevocably all that we are, do, think or feel affects everything else.

"When we try to pick out anything by itself, we find it hitched to everything else in the universe...No particle is ever wasted or worn out, but eternally flowing from use to use." [14]

"The universe is like a raisin cake in the oven, it expands from every place and angle." [15]

RAISIN CAKE

If I go anywhere in the universe,
Southend, The Pleiades, Tierra del Fuego, Mars,
No matter where, it is the same.
I gaze out into 'all that is'
And from that place 'all that is'
Flares outwards.
The expanding universe blossoms from every point.
Ergo ... the centre is everywhere.
Thus ... the wild-flower meadow and the dried-out dust-bowl,
The spring-budding chestnut and the felled rain-forest
Are also that centre.
Like a pebble dropped in a pond
All energy, all despair, all beauty, all pain,
All fear, all love, ripples outwards, affects all.
You ... me ... them ... both periphery and centre.

(iii) Sin

The third approach challenges the Christian doctrine of original sin. As Matthew Fox explains in the introduction to his book *Original Blessing*:

"The fall/redemption spiritual tradition is not nearly as ancient as the creation-centered one. The former goes back principally to St Augustine (354–430AD)...The Creation Centered tradition traces its roots to the 9th century BC, with the very first author of the Bible, to the Psalms, to the Wisdom books of the Bible, to Jesus, and much of the New Testament." [16]

It cannot be emphasized enough how widely this darkened view of original sin has cast its shadow. We all carry its scars whether Christian or not. Guilt, unworthiness, the rejection of the body as being a source of sin, the suppression of spontaneous creativity, all these and more spring from this doctrine which has dominated our Western culture for centuries.

A spirituality that is centered in creation looks to the real beginning, that cloud of shining incandescent radiance, the origin of all that now is. 15,000,000,000 years later a creation-centered spirituality cannot look at the astonishing emergence of a self-aware form of life on this small planet and accept that this particular life-form is singled out to be 'born in sin.' This rejection of the doctrine of original sin does not in any way deny the reality nor the existence of what might be called 'the negative.' There remains an inescapable tension between good and evil, light and dark, creation and destruction.

(iv) Beyond Dualism.

Since GreenSpirit turns away from a fragmented view of reality to one which embraces the wholeness of creation, there comes a recognition of the rifts that have been created by our dualistic way of describing the world. We all tend to see things in terms of opposites and set these opposites in fixed contra-position to each other. Thus, religion is set against science, reason against intuition, the human against the natural world, spirit is seen as opposite of matter, and so on. However, in grasping the concept of the whole we begin to see that these so called opposites are, as it were, two sides of the same thing. Beyond dualism there is the coming together of polarities, the reconciliation of opposites. Instead of either/or there is both/and. These opposites that our dualistic mode of thinking has made us so comfortable with turn out to be the necessary co-relatives of each other. Like concave and convex, each defines the other, and without the one the other would be unknowable.

In the beginning there was nothing,
No-thing – nothing.
And from the nothing there came
Longing. A great desire, yearning,
Yearning for its opposite.
For in order to define the One
The existence of the other is necessary.

(From a longer narrative poem 'The Story')

To sum up, it is vitally important that we are aware of the mind-set within which we live, and to recognize how this mind-set has determined cultural attitudes and assumptions. We need to acknowledge also, whether we like it or not, how deeply these assumptions are embedded within our own psyches.

As Einstein is often quoted as saying, it is impossible to solve a problem from the same mind-set which created it in the first place.

However, once we can stand back and begin to see things from the new, wider perspective, then these old, outworn attitudes begin to lose their foothold within our minds. The many-dimensional butterflies of paradox beckon us. Certainty is out—yes. Mystery, challenge, the pain and the wonder of being are ours (as they have always been), but now we know the context and essence of our 'Being.' Our context? A universe emerging into self-awareness. Our 'Being'? An expression of that emergence.

The inclusive journey: Spirituality and Science
Out of this human quest have arisen what may loosely be called the 'great religions' as well as the native spiritualities. Teilhard de Chardin in his comprehensive story of the evolving universe, *The Phenomenon of Man,* [17] shows its development to be both psychic and material, in other words both spiritual and physical. In the same way that every living form that has emerged since the

dawning of the universe is an integral part of that emergence, so too is every new insight, every intimation of our deep interconnectedness, every vision of our human destiny. Thus we must embrace the recognition that the emergence of the differing religions is an equally valid part of the ongoing but unfinished journey of human consciousness within the evolving universe.

It is not the purpose of this chapter to analyze and define the deep insights pertaining to each individual religious revelation. The meaning of the word 'revelation' given in the dictionary is 'the act or process of disclosing something previously secret or obscure, especially something true.' It is in this sense that I use the word here. Thus the new understanding brought to us through science is equally a revelation, previously unknown but nevertheless true.

"I consider that our new understanding of the universe is a new revelatory experience...it is the way the divine is presently revealing itself to us."[18]

Over the centuries the world's religions have accumulated much in the way of 'clutter,' some valuable, some not. However, when we look with the eyes of wisdom at the simple revelation in the original message, we will recognize, without exception, that the underlying message offers an illumination, opening up a shaft of light upon our understanding of the nature of the Ultimate Reality, God, the Ground of our Being, or whatever name the reader feels most comfortable with.

The time-developmental, evolutionary universe within which we now see ourselves poses no threat, any more than did the heliocentric revelation mentioned earlier. The only change forced upon us by discovering that the sun did not orbit the Earth as we had supposed, but vice versa, was a widening of the context within which we interpreted the world and our place in it.

Similarly today, it is only our understanding of the context of our being that is being challenged.

"There is always the mystery of things, and the mystery of existence can be given the name divine, it can be called God, or immanence, or whatever one wishes, we must admit the mystery of things."[19]

And the 'mystery of things' in this new and wider context is that we are a part of an unfolding that is greater and more mysterious that we had ever imagined.

All human insights and revelations which have guided the human venture are inextricably themselves a valid part of the ongoing unfolding. So our challenge now is to find that 'more expansive role.' Trusting that deep intuitive knowing that is ours we shall be enabled to let fall away the impedimenta and clutter that have accumulated over the centuries within our chosen spiritual path, and embrace again the profound insights which lie at the center of each one of these revelations. For it is within these understandings and perceptions that the new validity—and the more expansive role—lie.

Faith and doubt are not polar opposites; to trust one's uncertainty needs courage. This is the sort of faith which trusts itself to a venture so awe-inspiringly vast that its unfolding to the here and now has taken 12,000,000,000 years. Yet that small act of faith, in itself, becomes a contribution and a reinforcement of that very unfolding. A human expression of the consciousness of the universe becomes an integral part of that unfolding. Everything, spiritual and material, is a part of the whole.

Notes
1. Griffiths, B. The Viriditas Lecture, The Institute in Culture and Creation Spirituality, Oakland CA, 1991
2. Marsden, L. 'People and Planet, the Spiritual Dimension,' *The Friend's Quarterly*, November 1991

3. Swimme, B and Berry, T. *The Universe Story* (Harper San Francisco, 1992) Ch.12, p.223

4. Cardenal, E. *The Music of the Spheres*, trans. Dinah Livingstone, (Katabasis, 1990)

5. Swimme, B and Berry, T. *op. cit.* Ch.12, p.238

6. Zohar, D. *The Quantum Self*, (Bloomsbury, 1990) Ch.2, p.9

7. Spretnak, C. *States of Grace* (Harper San Francisco, 1991) Ch.1, p.21

8. Fox, M. Lecture, The Institute in Culture and Creation Spirituality, Oakland, California, 1991

9. O'Murchu, D. *The New Cosmology*, (unpublished, 1996)

10. Swimme, B and Berry, T. *op. cit.* Epilogue, pp.264-7

11. O'Murchu, D. *Reclaiming Spirituality* (Gill & Macmillan, 1997) Ch.3, p.41

12. —. Ch.6, p.99.

13. Berry, T. *Befriending the Earth* (Twenty-Third Publications, 1991) Ch.4, p.100

14. Wolfe, L.M. (Ed.) *John Muir: Son of the Wilderness* (University of Wisconsin Press, 1973) p.123

15. Swimme, B. Lectures at The Institute in Culture and Creation Spirituality, Oakland, CA, 1991-2

16. Fox, M (1983) *Original Blessing* (Bear & Company, 1983) Introduction, p.11

17. Chardin, Teilhard de. *The Phenomenon of Man* (Harper, 1961)

18. Berry (1991) *op. cit.* p.16

19. Berry (1991) *op. cit.* p.19

The material in this chapter was adapted from Grace Blindell's popular booklet *What is Creation Spirituality?* published by The Association for Creation Spirituality in 2001.

All poems in the text without specific attribution are by the Author.

Understanding the world and our place in it

2. Gaia Theory and Deep Ecology

Stephan Harding

The word 'ecology' comes from biology, where it is used to refer to the ways in which living things interact with each other and with their surroundings. Ecologists go out in the field to quantify Nature, to collect numbers which are then entered into computers to tease apart the complex interrelationships in the living world. These activities are supported and justified by the concept that our universe is merely a dead machine, and therefore ultimately predictable and controllable by humankind. One of the most brilliant popular expositions of this scientific attitude is *The Blind Watchmaker*, by Richard Dawkins, which describes the blind, unconscious process of natural selection which, we are told, has made all the wonderful creatures, or rather 'mechanisms' around us.[1]

But running parallel to this mainstream mechanistic view there has been another — increasingly marginalized — view, that our universe is an organism, a living being. In this view, the 'machine' description of our world is considered inadequate when applied to living things. It is quite clear that machines don't arise from eggs or seeds, that they don't rebuild their own parts right down to the molecular level, nor can they convert fuel into their own substance, as living beings do. The human heart, for instance, acts like a pump, but unlike a man-made machine, it is a pump that grows and repairs itself.

Gaia Theory: Earth as a living organism
Recently the view of our Earth as a living organism has staged a

major revival in the Gaia hypothesis originated by James Lovelock with the help of evolutionary biologist Lynn Margulis.[2] Put simply, the theory proposes that that a life-like quality emerges at the level of the Earth from the interactions of living beings with each other and with non-living parts of the planetary system (the rocks, atmosphere and oceans). This lifelike quality is the Earth's ability to regulate essential characteristics of its surface, such as the average temperature, the salinity of the oceans, and the mixture of gases (such as oxygen and carbon dioxide) in the atmosphere over thousands of millions of years within the narrow limits that life can tolerate.

Scientific orthodoxy rejected the Gaia hypothesis when it was first formulated since it seemed impossible to imagine how this emergent self-regulation could come about as a result of the conventional interactions between life and its non-living environment. This was a useful criticism, and to explore it, Lovelock and his colleague Andrew Watson developed a mathematical model called Daisyworld.

Daisyworld is a simplified planet which, like our own, circles around a sun whose output of energy is ever-increasing. Scattered on the rich, moist soil of Daisyworld are the seeds of two species: dark and light daisies. At first, Daisyworld's sun produces so little energy that it can't warm up the planet to the point where the soil is warm enough to trigger the germination of daisy seeds. But after some time the soil becomes warm enough for daisies to germinate, and both light and dark daisies appear. Because of their shade, the dark daisies are able to absorb the sun's energy more effectively than the light ones, which reflect solar energy back to space. Dark daisies take over the planet because they are able to warm themselves more than their light competitors, and so produce more offspring. As a result, Daisyworld darkens. The dark daisies have warmed themselves and the entire planet.

As the sun gradually and smoothly increases its output of

energy, light daisies gain more and more of a foothold since by reflecting solar energy back to space they cool both themselves and the planet. An astronomer observing Daisyworld through a telescope as its sun brightened would witness first bare ground, then a sudden explosion of dark daisies, then a mixture of dark and light daisies with light daisies gradually taking over, then light daisies on their own, and then the sudden demise of light daisies.

An extraordinary emergent property arises in Daisyworld as a result of the interactions between solar energy, surface temperature and the populations of the two daisy species: the system regulates its temperature within the narrow limits that daisies can tolerate despite an ever-brightening sun. By means of this example, Lovelock and Watson showed that self-regulation could in principle emerge completely automatically at the planetary level without the need of mystical forces or some sort of Gaian consciousness.

Critics point to the simplicity of Daisyworld, which they say cannot tell us much about the vastly more complex real world. They ask for real life examples of Gaian self-regulation. Although Daisyworld does in fact capture some essential characteristics of the real Earth, it is important to answer the criticism by taking a brief look at how the Earth regulates temperature by adjusting the level of carbon dioxide in our atmosphere and by seeding clouds.

The natural source of atmospheric carbon dioxide is volcanic activity. One way in which it is taken out of the atmosphere is through the weathering of silicate rocks such as granite and basalt. Water reacts with the rocks in the presence of carbon dioxide, which is taken out of the atmosphere and locked up with calcium from the rocks to form calcium bicarbonate that is eventually washed into the sea. Life isn't needed for the weathering reaction to happen, but bacteria and plant roots in soils greatly increase the rate of the process by actively pumping carbon dioxide out of the atmosphere into the soil, and by physically breaking up the rocks into many small fragments. Once in the sea, the calcium bicarbonate is absorbed by various minute marine algae (in particular the coccolithophores) which use it to make exquisite shells of chalk. These rain down to the bottom of the ocean when their tiny occupants die, thus safely locking away carbon that was in the atmosphere in massive deposits of chalk and limestone and thereby cooling the Earth. Plate tectonics eventually melts some of the chalk, releasing carbon dioxide back to the atmosphere via volcanoes. Mathematic models suggest that this is the self-regulating feedback that has kept the Earth's temperature within habitable limits over geological time periods.

Coccolithophores also help to produce clouds. When they die, they emit a sulphurous gas called dimethyl sulphide (DMS), which rises up into the air above the ocean surface. Here the DMS is oxidized, forming minute droplets of sulphuric acid. These droplets act as nuclei on which water vapor can condense, thereby seeding dense white clouds that cool the Earth by reflecting solar energy back to space. It is possible that this is another self-regulating feedback that regulates the Earth's temperature. Furthermore, some of these clouds rain sulphur onto the land surfaces, which helps the land vegetation to grow and hence absorb carbon dioxide from the atmosphere via photosynthesis.

These examples demonstrate that living beings have a major part to play in shaping the environment, in part through the absorption of carbon dioxide and by seeding clouds. All around us, plants and animals recycle the essential components of our lives: water, nutrients and gases, in a complex and creative evolutionary process. Gaia theory teaches us that we can no longer see the Earth through the lenses of separate scientific disciplines. It gives us a view of the Earth as an organic whole that has important implications for the way science is conducted and taught.

Gaian perception: seeing the world as a whole

To understand Gaia, we must let go of the mechanistic, compart-mentalizing conditioning imposed on us since childhood by our culture. From an early age nearly all Westerners (and especially young scientists) are exposed to the concept that life has come about due to the operation of blind, meaningless laws of physics and chemistry, and that selfishness underpins the behavior and evolution of all plants and animals. A child's mind becomes totally ensnared by this style of intellectuality, so that the intuitive, inspirational qualities of the mind are totally ignored. The mind's intuitive ability to see each part of Nature as a sub-whole within the greater whole of the Earth is destroyed by this sort of education. The result is a totally dry, merely intellectual ecology, not a genuine perception of the dynamic power, creativity and integration of Nature.

A Gaian approach opens new doors of perception and opens up our vision of the interdependence of all things within the natural world. There is a symphonic quality to this interconnect-edness, a quality which communicates an unspeakable magnifi-cence. When you stand on a sea-cliff in winter, watching masses of grey cloud rolling in from the Atlantic, a Gaian view helps you understand the clouds in their global context. They have formed due to massive climatic forces and have manifested within a small part of the whole—the part you happen to be standing in. The water in the cloud is circling through the water cycle, from rain to river to sea to coccolithophores to clouds again. As you experience this dynamic, ever-shifting reality, you may suddenly find yourself in a state of meditation, a state in which you lose your sense of separate identity, and become totally engrossed in the life process being contemplated. The contemplated and the contemplator become one.

From this oneness there arises a deep appreciation of the

reality of interdependence, and from this comes the urge to be involved in opposing all sorts of ecological abuses. Here arises the feeling that what is happening in evolution has great value and a meaning impossible to articulate or to detect via reductionist scientific methodology. This highly developed sensitivity, this experience of radical interconnectedness, is the hallmark of supporters of the Deep Ecology movement, and is the basis for the elaboration of any ecological philosophy, such as the pioneering work of the Norwegian philosopher, the late Arne Naess, who first coined the term 'Deep Ecology.'

Deep Ecology

In the 1960s, having read Rachel Carson's book *Silent Spring* [3], Arne Naess was moved to apply his formidable philosophical skills to understanding the ecological crisis and its resolution. Since becoming the youngest ever professor of philosophy at the University of Oslo whilst still in his twenties, Arne Naess revealed his brilliance by studying and writing extensively in many fields, including semantics, philosophy of science, and the works of Spinoza and Gandhi. But Naess was much more than an academic. His approach to ecology bears the stamp of his life's experience as a philosopher in the truest sense, as a lover of wisdom, and as a lover of mountains. A key influence in his long life was his deep relationship to Hallingskarvet, a mountain in central Norway, where, in 1937, he built a simple cabin at the place called Tvergastein ('crossed stones').

To understand what Arne Naess means by Deep Ecology it helps to imagine this place: high up, totally isolated, with commanding views of landscape down below. There he lived, looking out on that vast, wild panorama, reading Gandhi or Spinoza and studying Sanskrit. In this inhospitable retreat, under snow and ice for most of the year, where only lichen and tiny alpine flowers grow, Arne Naess spent a total of more than ten years, watching, climbing, thinking, writing, and adoring the mountain. It is at Tvergastein, with Arctic storms threatening to blow away his roof, that most of his important work in Deep Ecology has been done.

For Arne Naess, ecological science, concerned with facts and logic alone, cannot answer ethical questions about how we should live. For this we need ecological wisdom. My own contribution to Naess's insight is that there are three dimensions of depth in Deep Ecology: deep experience, deep questioning and deep commitment. These constitute an interconnected system. Each gives rise to and supports the other, whilst the entire system is what Naess would call an 'ecosophy,' an evolving but consistent philosophy of being, thinking and acting in the world that embodies ecological wisdom and harmony.

Deep experience

Deep experience is often what gets a person started along a deep ecological path. Aldo Leopold, in his book *A Sand County Almanac*, provides a striking example of this. For Leopold, the experience was of sufficient intensity to trigger a total reorientation in his life's work as a wildlife manager and ecologist. In the 1920s, he had been appointed by the US Government to develop a rational, scientific policy for eradicating the wolf from the entire United States. The justification for this intervention was that wolves competed with sport hunters for deer, so that fewer wolves would mean more deer for the hunters.

As a wildlife manager of those times, Leopold adhered to the unquestioning belief that humans were superior to the rest of Nature, and were thus morally justified in manipulating it as much as was required in order to maximize human welfare.

One morning, Leopold was out with some friends on a walk in the mountains. Being hunters, they carried their rifles with them, in case they got a chance to kill some wolves. It got around to lunch time.

"We were eating lunch on a high rimrock, at the foot of which a turbulent river elbowed its way. We saw what we thought was a doe fording the torrent, her breast awash in white water. When she climbed the bank toward us and shook out her tail, we realized our error: it was a wolf. A half-dozen others, evidently grown pups, sprang from the willows and all joined in a welcoming melee of wagging tails and playful maulings. What was literally a pile of wolves writhed and tumbled in the center of an open flat at the foot of our rimrock.

In those days we had never heard of passing up a chance to kill a wolf. In a second we were pumping lead into the pack, but with more excitement than accuracy; how to aim a steep downhill shot is always confusing. When our rifles were empty, the old wolf was down, and a pup was dragging a leg into impassable side-rocks.

We reached the old wolf in time to watch a fierce green fire dying in her eyes. I realized then, and have known ever since, that there was something new to me in those eyes— something known only to her and to the mountain. I was young then, and full of trigger-itch; I thought that because fewer wolves meant more deer, that no wolves would mean hunters' paradise. But after seeing the green fire die, I sensed that neither the wolf nor the mountain agreed with such a view." [4]

Perhaps it is possible to understand what Leopold means when he says that the wolf disagreed with such a view, but how could a lifeless, inert mountain possibly agree or disagree with anything? What could Leopold have experienced in that pivotal moment in his life? Clearly, he is using the word 'mountain' as a metaphor for the wild ecosystem in which the incident took place, the ecosystem as an entirety, as a living presence, with its deer, its wolves and other animals, its clouds, soils and streams.

For the first time in his life he felt completely at one with this wide, ecological reality. He felt that it had a power to communicate its magnificence. He felt that it had its own life, its own history, and its own trajectory into the future. He experienced the ecosystem as a great being, dignified and valuable in itself. It must have been a moment of tremendous liberation and expansion of consciousness, of joy and energy — a truly spiritual or religious experience. His narrow, manipulative wildlife manager's mind fell away. The mind which saw Nature as a dead machine, there for human use, vanished. In its place was the pristine recognition of the vast being of living nature, of what we now call Gaia.

Notice that the experience was not looked for, expected or contrived. It happened spontaneously. Something in the dying eyes of the wolf reached beyond Leopold's training and triggered a recognition of where he was. After this experience he saw the world differently, and went on to develop a land ethic, in which he stated that humans are not a superior species with the right to manage and control the rest of Nature, but rather that humans are 'plain members of the biotic community.' He also penned his famous dictum: "a thing is right when it tends to preserve the integrity, stability and beauty of the biotic community. It is wrong when it tends otherwise."[5]

Naess emphasizes the importance of such spontaneous experience. A key aspect of these experiences is the perception of gestalts, or networks of relationships. We see that there are no isolated objects, but that objects are nodes in a vast web of relationships. When such deep experience occurs, we feel a strong sense of wide identification with what we are sensing. This identification involves a heightened sense of empathy and an expansion of our concern with non-human life. We realize how dependent we are on the wellbeing of Nature for our own physical and psychological wellbeing. As a consequence there arises a natural inclination to protect non-human life. Obligation and coercion to do so become unnecessary. We understand that other beings, ranging from microbes to multicellular life-forms to ecosystems and watersheds, to Gaia as a whole, are engaged in the process of unfolding their innate potentials. Naess calls this process 'self-realization.' For us humans, self-realization involves the development of wide identification in which the sense of self is no longer limited by the personal ego, but instead encompasses greater and greater wholes. Naess has called this expanded sense of self 'the ecological self.' Since all beings strive in their own ways for self-realization, we recognize that all are endowed with intrinsic value, irrespective of any economic or other utilitarian value they might have for human ends. Our own human striving for self-realization is on an equal footing to the strivings of other beings. There is a fundamental equality between human and non-human life in principle. This ecocentric perspective contrasts with the anthropocentric view which ascribes intrinsic value only to humans, valuing Nature only if it is useful to our own species.

Deep questioning

The new sense of belonging to an intelligent universe revealed by deep experience often leads to deep questioning, which helps to elaborate a coherent framework for elucidating fundamental beliefs, and for translating these beliefs into decisions, lifestyle and action. The emphasis on action is important. It is action that distinguishes Deep Ecology from other ecophilosophies. This is what makes Deep Ecology a movement as much as a philosophy. By deep questioning, an individual is articulating a total view of life which can guide his or her lifestyle choices.

In questioning society, one understands its underlying assumptions from an ecological point of view. One looks at the collective psychological origins of the ecological crisis, and the related crises of peace and social justice. One also looks deeply into the history of the West to find the roots of our pernicious anthropocentrism as it has manifested in our science, philosophy and economics. One tries to understand how the current drive for globalization of Western culture and of free trade leads to the devastation of both human culture and Nature.

This deep questioning of the fundamental assumptions of our culture contrasts markedly with the mainstream shallow or reform approach. This tries to ensure the continuance of business as usual by advocating the 'greening' of business and industry by incorporating a range of measures such as pollution prevention and the protection of biodiversity due to its monetary value as medicine or its ability to regulate climate. Although Deep Ecology supporters often have no option but strategically to adopt a reform approach when working with the mainstream, their own deep questioning of society goes on in the background. This may subtly influence the people with whom they interact professionally.

While they were camping in Death Valley in 1984, Arne Naess and George Sessions devised the Deep Ecology platform, also known as the eight points of the Deep Ecology movement.[6] These are meant to act as a sort of filter for the deep questioning process. If you can largely agree with the platform statements, (which are presented here in a concise re-wording) you fall within the umbrella of 'the Deep Ecology movement' and you can place yourself within the ranks of its supporters. The platform is not meant to be a rigid set of doctrinaire statements, but rather a set of discussion points, open to modification by people who broadly accept them.

The Deep Ecology Platform

1. All life has value in itself, independent of its usefulness to humans.
2. Richness and diversity contribute to life's well-being and have value in themselves.

• 3. Humans have no right to reduce this richness and diversity except to satisfy vital needs in a responsible way.

4. The impact of humans in the world is excessive and rapidly getting worse.

5. Human lifestyles and population are key elements of this impact.

6. The diversity of life, including cultures, can flourish only with reduced human impact.

7. Basic ideological, political, economic and technological structures must therefore change.

8. Those who accept the foregoing points have an obligation to participate in implementing the necessary changes and to do so peacefully and democratically.

Deep commitment

Finally, we come to deep commitment, which is the result of combining deep experience with deep questioning. When an ecological world view is well developed, people act from their whole personality, giving rise to tremendous energy and commitment. Such actions are peaceful and democratic and will lead towards ecological sustainability. Uncovering the ecological self gives rise to joy, which gives rise to involvement, which in turn leads to wider identification, and hence to greater commitment. This leads to 'extending care to humans and deepening care for non-humans.'

No student of ecology is ever introduced to this new mode of holistic discipline in our schools and colleges. There is no culture of experiencing oneness with the natural world. All one does on an ecology field trip is to collect and measure. Deep contemplation of Nature is considered to be at worst a waste of time, at best something to do during one's spare time.

It can be argued that many truly great scientists had this connection, this sense of the greater whole of which they were a part. Without educating this sensitivity, we churn out scientists without philosophy, who are merely interested in their subject, but not thoroughly awed by it. We churn out clever careerists, whose only concern is to make the grade, be the first to publish, be the first to be head of a department, or to split the atom.

It is this kind of training which leads to the mentality responsible for the massive social and environmental mistakes of Western-style development. Trained to shut down our perception of the world so that we see it as a mere machine, we are perfectly free to improve the clockwork for our own ends. There is no moral impediment to building huge dams which flood vast areas, or to logging old growth forests, or to sanctioning economic growth at all costs, or to altering the genetic make-up of any organism for our own ends.

Gaian perception helps to remedy this great mental and spiritual plague, the Western malaise which is now claiming millions of victims, human and non-human, throughout the world.

Gaian perception connects us with the seamless nature of existence, and opens up a new approach to scientific research based on scientific intuitions arising from scientists' personal, deep ecological experience. When the young scientist in training has sat on a mountain top, and has completed her first major assignment to 'think like a mountain,' mechanistic thinking will never take root in her mind. When she eventually goes out to practice her science in the world, she will be fully aware that every interconnected aspect of it has its own intrinsic value, irrespective of its usefulness to human beings.

Notes

1. Dawkins, R. *The Blind Watchmaker* (W.W.Norton, 1996)
2. Lovelock, J and Margulis, L. 'Atmospheric homeostasis by and for the biosphere: The Gaia hypothesis' *Tellus* 26 (1) 1974, pp. 2–10
3. Carson, R. *Silent Spring* (Houghton Mifflin, 1962)

4.   Leopold, Aldo. *A Sand County Almanac* (Oxford University Press, 1949) p.138

5.   *ibid*. p.262

6.   Sessions, G. (Ed.) *Deep Ecology for the Twenty First Century* (Shambhala, 1985)

Understanding the world and our place in it

3. What Are Humans For?

Brian Swimme

Every now and then we are struck by a fact that causes us to stop and reflect upon the whole moment we live in and this happened to me very recently. I was reading that the average American citizen is responsible for a ton of waste a week and I had to stop and think about that. When you add together all the waste that comes from the manufacturing processes and the extraction processes, it adds up to a ton. What struck me as so surprising was that I had no idea I was generating a ton of waste a week. And because so much of my work is focused on the health of the planet I thought, *Gee, if every week I'm producing a ton of misery for the Earth, how much positive am I producing a week to match that?* I had this horrifying thought that at the end of my life it may turn out that that ton a week I was producing was the major impact of my life. We have this underlying view of the Earth and the universe as being sort of neutral, composed of mechanistic processes that we can manipulate to make various things. So if our entire civilization is organized around that point of view and we work at it hard, study, go to university and so forth, I guess it's not surprising that we would get good at producing lots of things and make ourselves ignorant of the full cost of that.

It is a moment, then, to ask ourselves a fundamental question: is it possible that we have a fundamentally mistaken orientation to the universe and to what it means to be human in the universe? Is it possible we've made a fundamental mistake and our way forward includes at least, in part, reflection on this cosmological or primordial question: what's the nature of the universe? What's our role in the universe?

Our whole civilization has become very good at making things and extremely good at getting us to buy them, but once we've done this, no-one gave us any help on what to do with all this junk we bought as the years went by. The idea of recycling, the idea of cutting back, has nothing to do with our economy. So what has happened is that springing up all over the landscape — at least in the USA — are self storage units. I read a report that the self storage enterprise is growing faster than computers, growing faster than aerospace. It's exploding.

The universe is 13,700,000,000 years old. 13,700,000,000 years ago, the universe came into existence and began to complexify. Try to take that in. It's hard. We just discovered it. So you might begin to suspect that maybe we are here for something more important than buying and storing all these consumer items. Maybe a 13,700,000,000 year process might have prepared us for something deeper than that. What is it? How do we find our way into a more appropriate understanding of what it means to be human?

My suggestion is that if we reflect upon the universe itself we can get some clues. You can get clues from lots of different places. Obviously you can look at various traditions and so forth, but usually when you look at traditions, whether it is religious traditions, scientific traditions, philosophical traditions, you end up listening to other humans. It's important to listen to humans but what if we just listen to the universe as a whole? Would we get maybe a sense of what we're here for, of what's going on, what's the nature of our moment?

Here's an approach to the universe that is focused on this question. The universe goes through massive transitions. It is a story, a development, a process, not just a place. So it's a story with some major moments and these, I think, speak to *our* moment.

For instance the universe begins as light and particles and it is completely determined by the light at the beginning of time. Light determines the nature of the universe. But as the universe expands out it cools and enables the matter to begin to show its own potentiality. So, after several hundred thousands of years, the matter actually develops into the start of the galaxies. Within 1,000,000,000 years, maybe even 200,000,000 years, the universe has changed, from just particles into galaxies: the first macro transition.

The second in our own particular lineage would be here on the planet Earth. Earth starts off with molten lava and an atmosphere and forms of light, very early on. But maybe 3,900,000,000 years ago, life began. That's just immediately when you think in terms of 4,000,000,000 years of the Earth; right away life began. But life was negligible; it didn't become a planetary power until another 1,500,000,000 years later when the Earth began to organize itself as a planet. This is the Gaia hypothesis coming from James Lovelock and Lynn Margulis but it is the dawning realization that the actual physical nature of the atmosphere, the physical nature of the water was being determined in part by the self organizing dynamics of the planet as a whole so that you start off with life and water and minerals and you arrive at a moment of Gaia organizing itself. Gaia has its own stages it goes through. The point I'm trying to get across here is that something that was quite negligible in the beginning—the cells of life—developed and became a planetary dynamic. I think our way of understanding our moment is along these lines. Something that was negligible in the past has now become so powerful that it is a partner to the planetary dynamic, namely the human. And if you think of the human you get a sense of the journey we have taken. If you go back and see what we were like at the beginning. You know, the human story. It's actually hard to mark off and say "This is the start of the humans," because we do blend seamlessly into this creative event called universe. But one way to identify an important moment was when we began to walk on two legs which is around 4,000,000 years ago. So some anthropologists think of that as the start of the hominid line, the start of what would lead to *Homo sapiens*.

If you can just bring that into your imagination for a second. Just imagine the first hominids—Australopithecines—that are standing up on two legs. Can you imagine how unimpressive they would be? They haven't developed any facility of walking on two legs, they are stumbling around and they have a brain the size of a small coconut. They don't stand out. If you're examining the African biome and you're going through a look at the species and you're from Andromeda galaxy you would barely even notice them. But they had a power, a new power they were bringing into the universe. We call it the human imagination. With this power, humans would soon figure out how to employ fire for their own benefit. And then they would draw the animals into their agenda, through domestication. Soon the winds and the rivers would become part of the human tool kit. And then even the DNA itself would be appropriated for our purposes.

So here we are at this moment. We are the species that has drawn in all the powers of the universe and is changing the fabric of the planet as a whole. The sun has been burning for 5,000,000,000 years. Never once was there a species on this planet that drew the power of the sun into its own agenda. In a certain sense it's magnificent. In another it's so overwhelming because what does it mean to have done this?

Here is my way of summarizing our challenge. We've drawn in all the powers of the universe to use for the old projects of humanity, the projects that are no longer viable. We have all the powers and are using them for challenges that we don't even have any more.

William James, one of the finest American philosophers and psychologists, when he was thinking about our moment and wondering how we can escape the scourge of militarism, said, "What we need is a project, a creative project that takes us beyond warfare." His suggestion was that we wage warfare on Nature, to use all that energy to confront Nature.

So our current situation is that, for instance, we are affecting the carbon cycles. Without the humans, this amazing, intricate Gaian system processes 2,000,000,000 tons of carbon a year in amazingly elegant and intricate ways. We humans are adding 6,000,000,000 tons of carbon. So we are adding the 6,000,000,000 tons of carbon pursuing microphase agendas, outdated challenges. We are pursuing projects that no longer make sense for this power. Another way to say it is that we have developed planetary power but we are using it for a microphase project. What is a *macro*phase project, what is *macro*phase wisdom that would enable us to proceed in a way that would be a blessing for the Earth, rather than degradation?

Here's my suggestion. In terms of thinking about how we move forward my first suggestion for you is that we need to find ways of contacting the universe. When I say universe, unfortunately there is a connotation of vast, vast, far away galaxies and so forth. I mean universe as anything around us. Everything in the universe is infinite and intimate, both. Therefore there is a way in which the immensities of the universe are also intimate, intricate, immense, vast, everything, no matter what we look at. So it is this first step. We are living inside a civilization that has surrounded us with artifice, contraptions, commodities, stuffed garages, useless superficial distractions. That is where we live, in this web. So the first step is this. Find a way to contact the primordial powers of the universe as they appear in the wind or in the flower or in the sunshine. Find a way to contact with the hope *simply of a moment of astonishment.* Maybe the role of the human depends upon such moments.

The universe is just chock full of creative potentiality and creativity. There are fires of creativity everywhere and it's not that we have to somehow learn to be creative; everything that *is,* is creative. It's that we have to learn to participate with the creativity that is at the base of all matter.

When I was studying galaxies, 20 years ago, one of my professors made a statement that told me something very, very important. We were looking at the elegance of the galaxies. One of the images is to imagine all the universe as all these particles and then the galaxies come fluttering into existence— 100,000,000,000 snowflake-like galaxies flutter into existence. That process is so elegant we couldn't articulate it, we couldn't even speak it with our mathematics. And so the professor said, "Well, if there are no galaxies in the universe that would be really easy for us to explain." And I thought *well then if you use the word 'intelligent' what does it best describe?* What connotations come to mind when you think of the word 'intelligent'—Einstein, Mozart? Sure. But shouldn't 'intelligent' be used to describe a universe that can create 100,000,000,000 galaxies? Or should it be used just for the humans who can't yet figure out how the universe did this?

So rather than thinking of the universe as a neutral place, a background, a gravel pit, begin to think of it as a place of intelligence and beauty and music.

For humans, music has to do with a certain kind of vibration in the air and is opposed to cacophony, which is a different kind of vibration, so that music moves us and has a coherence and a harmony and a depth and powerful things happen when we are around music. The same thing with the universe. There would be a number of different vibrations passing through it and some of these would cohere and amplify and powerful things would happen around them and the size of the galaxies would depend on the form of the music that was passing through. Another way to say it would be to talk about the vibrations and fluctuations that are passing through the Milky Way galaxy. These clouds of gas are just hanging there, they've been hanging there for a million years and then suddenly the wave comes through. The wave is going to activate particular stars depending upon the nature of the music so it would be along those lines, the wave, the fluctuations, the vibrations are at the root of the structures that come forth.

Take, for example, a spiral galaxy. We have now discovered that the 'arms' of a spiral galaxy are actually giving birth to the stars themselves. We first thought of those arms as being made of matter, and just twirling around, like one of those spinning objects. But actually after we looked at it more carefully we realized that's impossible. The gravitational dynamics really don't work out. What has happened is that an immaterial wave is passing through the galaxy and as it passes through it ignites the stars so these are massive stars that are exploding, have very short lives and then the wave will go on and activate other parts of the galaxy. The stars themselves don't sweep along and make the arc of the arm.

Now why I find this so thrilling is that we begin to realize the galaxy is not simply a conglomeration of stars; it's rather a system that is organizing itself. Some physicists think of a galaxy as something like a cell. It somehow 'knows' what it's about and gets to the work of giving birth to itself.

Think how our Earth differs from the moon. All of the material of the moon, the thousands of minerals, are identical with the Earth. But look at the difference. It is the same matter but it is the conditions of the planet that enable Earth to come alive and begin this process of unfolding. Within the framework of Gaia Theory we see that the temperature of the Earth has been controlled by the Earth itself so that the temperature early on was very, very hot and only bacteria could live there but Earth itself lowered the temperature until a certain critical point and then all of a sudden the eukaryotes—the more complex forms of cellular life—came forth. Then, as these co-evolved with the planet, the temperature was carried still lower and suddenly you had multi-cellularity and plants and animals. The multi-cellular plants and animals could not have existed in the previous eras. This is the part that is thrilling, to begin to speculate on, to reflect on. Earth altered herself so that her deeper treasures could begin to unfold through these great ages of Gaia. Not as we thought before, accidentally, but rather as part of the self-organizing nature of our planet.

I think that kind of delicate, elegant creativity that we talk about at the birth of the universe is happening right now. Our challenge is to find a way to participate with it as opposed to explaining it, find a way to participate with it so our lives become a chord of the music.

If you look back in time to the birth of the universe, it's plasma, just particles, it's a big gluey mass of all these interactions taking place. We know now that the order that's happening there already contains life. That's the astonishing thing we are discovering: that the intricacies found at the beginning of the universe contain life, potentially. They're not alive but that ordering has the possibility of life.

So there is layer after layer after layer of beauty in the universe and as it comes to a certain level of complexity it is then able to show another dimension of beauty. Before that beauty begins to express itself in an explicit form, it lives within us in a form as music and dream. That's the way in which the universe's heart or its yearning presses into subtle spaces of human consciousness and so we are haunted by that; we are driven in a certain sense to give voice to it and to bring it into an embodied form.

If you really work physically hard, digging soil and putting it in a wheelbarrow, you are really tired at the end of the day. Now if you can imagine 6,000,000,000 people doing that every day for 10,000 years, that wouldn't be enough work to move the Earth an inch. Yet *something* is really moving the Earth. Just imagine if we had the task of moving the Earth around. It's overwhelming. But you will have noticed that animals are never really exhausted because they take naps. The point is, it's effortless for the Earth because it's responding to attraction. The universe works through effortlessness. The galaxies just flow along their trajectories because of the way in which allurement is drawing them.

So I think that to be human is to be fascinated in a particular way. We need to sort through the specious forms of allurement, the specious forms of attraction that relate to someone else's project, of greed, mediated by the advertisers. As we sort through, we come to a childlike, mystical thrill of life, a zest for being and the pursuit of that is a form of effortlessness.

There are, of course, obstacles that one meets in the pursuit of allurement but the first question is what is it that draws you deeply? I'm convinced that if we humans could reflect deeply on that, beneath rational consciousness, just allow ourselves to feel what fascinates us, we would be drawn right out of our militarism, right out of our consumerism.

In the United States the food that is advertised the most is the worst for you. You see my point? We're trying to get ourselves to do things we hate. That's the point of advertising. And —this goes back to my comment about animals—we valorize exhaustion in a strange way. We think we're just building machines but when the machine becomes the view of the universe it becomes the view of the human and then a good human is a good machine. As you know, what is valued in our society is someone who is productive, productive like a machine, working a certain number of hours, no breakdown, etc. So my point is that if, like the indigenous people, we regarded exhaustion as a form of human sin, we would then be on the road to responding to the deep allurement that is drawing us moment after moment after moment. Then we, too, would be part of the creative, effortless music of the universe.

This chapter is based on a talk given at a GreenSpirit event in London in 2003.

Editor's Note: Brian Swimme has asked me to mention to you that the talk was originally accompanied by slides of a series of awesome pictures taken by the Hubble Space Telescope. These made his explanations of, for example, spiral galaxies, even more meaningful. You can find pictures from the Hubble Space Telescope on the Internet at http://hubblesite.org/

Understanding the world and our place in it

4. Falling in Love with Gaia

Susan Meeker-Lowry

My personal introduction to the Gaia Hypothesis was in November 1985. It was my second visit to the Chinook Learning Center, an intentional community and educational center on Whidbey Island in Washington State, USA, founded by former residents of Findhorn. I was participating in Chinook's conference, 'For the Life of the Earth,' to learn about new projects and to share ideas.

I arrived a bit late for the first gathering on Friday evening and Thomas Berry, author, priest, and cultural historian, had just started speaking. His eyes twinkled with good humor and he was full of energy and passion as he spoke of the importance of integrating ecology and spirit into politics, economics...and everything else. His wasn't simply an intellectual understanding of the topic. I could tell he felt the magic of the Earth in every cell of his body. It wasn't just what he said, it was how he said it. I was entranced.

One of the topics he discussed was the Gaia Hypothesis. My heart immediately embraced the idea. As Thomas spoke, the pieces fell into place. He put words on what I'd known intuitively all my life. Tears came to my eyes, hope grew in my heart, and my mind reeled with the implications. I thought about the role love plays in the healing process, how it works miracles, speeding recovery from illness and nourishing the spirits of people and animals alike. 'Healing the Earth' was a common phrase, but it seemed so arrogant. How could we possibly heal the Earth? But, if the Earth is alive then love is an important part of the healing process. And if love is part of the healing process then we can make a difference. What we do and how we do it matters. We may be David acting against a powerful Goliath, but we have Gaia, a living being, on our side! Nothing has been the same for me since.

There are many books available designed to help us reconnect with Nature and our human nature as well. Some are intellectual and theoretical, others are experiential, and still others read more like stories. While I know it takes more than a book to change someone, I also know that a good book read at the right time can touch us and make a difference. Sometimes the right words—like Thomas Berry describing the Gaia Hypothesis all those years ago—help us articulate a feeling or confirm an intuition.

But our minds and intellects can take us only so far. To understand Gaia, to let her into our lives, we must fall in love with the Earth. It's that simple. We must love the Earth with the same passion and concern and fierceness that we love our children, our parents, our lovers, our mates. As anyone who has ever fallen in love knows, logic and reason having little to do with it. Sometimes we resist, but it happens anyway. Sometimes the object of our love seems totally wrong to others, but it doesn't matter. We love regardless. And the love we feel for our children is totally unconditional. This is the way we must love the Earth because this is the kind of love that changes everything. When we love someone we want the best for them. We make mistakes, yes, but once we realize what we have done, we try to do better next time.

When we love someone, we don't deliberately set out to destroy or undermine them or jeopardize their chances at life. When they are hurt we yearn to hold and comfort them, and we know that our love makes a difference. Sometimes love is all there is, and it's enough.

The best way to fall in love with the Earth is to experience her.

On a basic level, of course, every breath we take connects us to the Earth. So does the food we eat, the water we drink and bathe in (and flush down the toilet). The leather in our shoes, the cotton or wool or silk of our clothes, the paper we take notes on, etc. The point is to increase our awareness, to remind ourselves often of how we depend on the Earth, how we couldn't survive without her. Remember — we live *in* Gaia. We eat, sleep, read, take the bus, drive our cars, and dispose of our trash *in* Gaia.

The implications of Gaia Theory are immense and touch every aspect of human behavior, from science to politics to commerce to social services. Nothing is exempt. We are coming full circle. In the beginning, gods and goddesses reigned and myth and stories explained the meaning of life and guided human behavior. As our knowledge of Nature and the human body expanded, life was reduced to its material parts and the magic, the indefinable essence of being alive, was discounted and even feared. Science became the new god and the goddess was banished. Gaia helps us integrate the stories of the ancients with the stories of modem science into a cohesive whole and restores wonder and magic and mystery to our lives. The path to Gaia Theory may have been scientific inquiry, but the path to Gaia is through the heart.

This is an extract from a longer article entitled 'Gaia in Our Hearts,' first published in *Spirit of Change* magazine in Jan/Feb 2002.

Understanding Ourselves

5. The Crack in Everything

Isabel Clarke

How come human beings are so clever, and at the same time, so stupid? This question is vital to the joint survival of ourselves and our planet as we know it. Our cleverness is obvious in the way we have used our ability to control our environment to our own ends; to eliminate so many uncertainties and discomforts from our daily life. Our stupidity is evident in the way that this activity has increasingly entailed devastating side effects for the planet on which we—and more importantly, our descendants— depend for sustenance and survival. We love our children. So how come we are content to condemn them and their children to a ruined Earth?

Something is the matter with the way we relate to our planet, to our descendents and indeed, to ourselves and each other. An international conference to tackle climate change seems to illustrate this only too clearly. No-one can now dispute the facts, but can we get together and agree an immediate way forward, without feeling taken advantage of, without trying to score points? So far, the only way to avert deadlock has been to delay any real steps towards the declared goal.

The general irrationality of human behavior has been noted from the time of Plato (and no doubt, before). Recent understanding of the way in which the brain is wired up enables us to get some sort of a handle on this. We fail to act in straightforward, rational ways, because our rational, logical, faculty is only one part of the complex apparatus that is a human being, and it is not necessarily the most important part, or the one that is in charge.

Blaming the crocodile

Matthew Fox blames the 'reptilian brain' for our failures. I think he has grasped some of the argument, but only some. You could say that he has taken hold of one leg of the crocodile. By 'reptilian brain' he is referring to the inner and lower regions of our brain that govern sleep and waking, rapid response to danger, emotions and arousal.

Parts of this apparatus do indeed have a lot to answer for. When the 'rapid response' department picks up a hint of threat, it galvanizes our bodies into action, flicking the series of switches that transforms the human being from a calm, relaxed state into either a would-be prize fighter or a quivering jelly. The problem is that for most perceptions of threat in our current society, it is hard to say which of these two responses is the more potentially disastrous (though I would suggest the fighter). Worse, memory serves up all the nastiest things that have ever happened throughout our lives to date and produces them at such moments as if they were current, as this particular mode of processing does not appreciate niceties like time. This is also an effort—at one time adaptive but nowadays usually counterproductive—to keep us safe, by reminding us of all possible dangers.

So, is the solution to try and transcend our animal inheritance and move into the higher realms of the neocortex? I would argue: no. It is the human capacity for logical thought and individual self consciousness that enables us to develop the technology that can wreck the planet, and then to retreat into the cocoon of individuality to enjoy the fruits of our efforts, while the future burns and drowns. The neocortex has a lot to answer for as well.

We need to understand the brain better; its limitations as well as its achievements. The problem is the gap between these two systems of processing described above—the so called 'reptilian' and the neocortex; the emotional and the logical; the fact that they developed separately; that they represent evolutionarily different parts of our history; and that they sometimes cooperate well and at other times they do not speak to each other. We need to understand this gap. Research into the interconnections within the brain over the last three decades gives us a fairly clear picture of the way in which these two parts of our makeup are essentially distinct.

"There is a crack in everything; that's where the light gets in" (Leonard Cohen)

Detailed cognitive experimentation suggests that the human mind works by different bits (subsystems) passing information from one to another and copying it in the process. In this way, each subsystem has its own memory. Different systems operate with different coding, for instance, verbal, visual, auditory. There are higher order systems that translate these codings, and integrate the information. The crucial feature of this model is that there are not one but two meaning-making systems at the apex. The verbally coded **propositional** subsystem gives us the analytically sophisticated individual that our culture has perhaps mistaken for the whole. However, the wealth of sensory information from the outside world, integrated with the body and its arousal system is gathered together by the **implicational** subsystem, which looks after our relatedness, both with others and with ourselves. The implicational subsystem is on the lookout for information about threat and value in relation to the self. We are, after all, social primates, and where we stand at any one time in the social hierarchy is crucial for our wellbeing, if not, normally, for our survival. We experience 'where we stand' in the form of our current emotion, be it happy contentment, vague apprehension or seething anger.

We are unaware of this 'crack' between our two main subsystems because they work seamlessly together most of the time, passing information between them, so that we can simultaneously take the emotional temperature and make an accurate estimate in any situation. This starts to break down in states of very high and very low arousal. To be human is to know what it is like to be in a flap, and unable to think clearly—a state that Daniel Goleman describes as 'emotional hijacking'[1]—because the body has switched to action mode in response to perceived threat, and fine grained thought goes out the window. In our dreams, and on falling asleep, we enter another dimension where logic is totally absent. The application of certain spiritual disciplines, or certain substances, can effect this decoupling between the two subsystems in waking life, so affording a different quality of experience where the sense of individuality becomes distorted or merged into the whole.

Relationship and the Implicational Subsystem

I would argue that the implicational subsystem, the older part of our makeup that we share with our non human ancestors, regulates our relatedness, and so the web of connection mentioned earlier. It is porous to other beings; studies in group process, and the therapeutic concept of transference, illustrate the subtle blending of people in relationship. I suggest that this extends to non human creatures (our tribal ancestors, as well as pet owners, would vouch for this); and beyond or within to the Earth and God, Goddess etc. Furthermore, this relationship is reciprocal. The quality of our relationship with important others, including the Earth and the non human creatures helps to create us. For instance, where we treat the Earth, non human creatures, or vulnerable people(s) with exploitation and contempt, this eats away at our own integrity, and our unavoidable involvement in a society which does this is a continuous sore deep within our being. We are created at the same time as we create.

Understanding Spirituality

This model says quite a lot about human beings: that they are inherently unstable taken in isolation: that they are continually in flux and subject to the moral quality of their relationships, for instance. It also offers a way of understanding spirituality which makes it integral to the experience of being human. To return to the subsystems, I hypothesize that we encounter a 'spiritual' quality of experience when the implicational subsystem is in the ascendant but without the dominance of self focused emotions. This allows a state of being in relation with the whole, whether mediated by, say, an experience of Nature, or a more abstract experience of God or the ultimate. This experience is generally received as ecstatic and awe inspiring in the short term. Because it implies loss of the ability to get one's bearings in a grounded fashion, it is not a good state to spend too long in. I like to use the term 'transliminal' to describe this state, as it is free of the baggage of other descriptors (mystical, psychotic etc.) The ability to pass both ways across the threshold (or 'limen') determines the difference between a beautiful experience and a nightmare world where there are no boundaries and therefore no safety.

In this attempt to explain our proneness to breakdown, the fascination of the spiritual and the obstinate imperfection of our institutions, political and other, I have stuck closely to theories that come from information processing. These processing systems link the various bits of the brain that we know govern different functions, so that it is obvious that the propositional subsystem will utilize circuits from the neocortex, whereas older and deeper brain regions such as the limbic system and amygdala (the 'reptilian' brain referred to by Matthew Fox) will be more important for the implicational subsystem. Because of the complexity of the connections (and because of bias in what I know about), I am not grounding my claims in neuroscience, only in cognitive science.

Implications of this model

Among the far reaching implications of the model I am presenting is the notion that there is a horizon beyond which science in its exactitude will not reach. Analytical certainty is the domain of the propositional subsystem: art and the spirit of the implicational. These represent two ways of knowing accessible to human beings, each with its own logic. Science deals in 'either/or,' religion and art in paradox and 'both /and.' Both are great sources of knowledge and wisdom, but each is incomplete because, as an instrument of apprehension, we are incomplete. In the same way that dancing a new theorem in physics would be an inefficient (albeit delightful) means of exact communication, so building complex and exact theories of spiritual reality are necessarily speculative. There is no way of verifying them, or deciding between them, so they are artistic rather than scientific. Possibly their function is to assuage our human anxiety when faced with the vast mystery of what we can never fully know, but which fills our world with wonder.

The result of all this is that not one of us really knows who we are, because 'who we are' keeps changing. Our self-conscious individuality is rooted in that verbally based, logical, propositional subsystem (the 'head' bit). However, the other part, the implicational subsystem (the 'heart' bit) which connects with our bodies and our emotions, gives us everything that makes life feel worthwhile. This part does not make sense in a purely individual way. Our emotions are designed to manage relationship, and this part of ourselves is rooted in relationship. In a very real way, we *are* relationship. Not just the obvious relationships—all relationships.

This is where our connection to ecology comes in. Right at the heart of our being.

Let me explain. Several schools of psychotherapy are based on the idea that we carry inside ourselves internalized patterns of relating which play out in whatever situation we find ourselves. One of the founding mothers of psychoanalysis, Melanie Klein, identified this role of relationship. She called such internalized relationships 'objects,' leading to the somewhat obscure term 'object relations theory.' Freud's concept of transference is another example of the same phenomenon. One of the therapies I use, Cognitive Analytic Therapy, brings these ideas together in the useful concept of internalized 'Reciprocal Roles:' repeating patterns of relating that originate in the past, but can be spotted and so revised in the present. The character of these patterns determines the character of the person. Someone who is contemptuous of everyone does not come across as very lovable. We make ourselves by the way we relate.

Another clue to the centrality of relationship to our being is the way that losses shake us to the foundations. People often arrive in the acute mental health hospital where I work as a clinical psychologist because they have lost partners, parents or just jobs. The fabric of their being is disrupted by this and they need time and assistance to recover. Our relatedness is the foundation of that 'heart' part of our being. This is most obvious in the case of those close to us. The ecopsychological perspective recognizes that this relatedness extends far beyond the obvious family and friends; our relationship with those other beings with whom we share the Earth, the animals, and with the very ecosystem and the Earth itself, is knitted into the fabric of our being. The character of that relationship lies at the heart of who we are, but paradoxically, we lose part of our individuality when we really embrace relationship. That is how we breathe and grow. The tragedy is that we are currently locked into a relationship of reckless greed and exploitation with this wider reality. I would suggest that this damages us as much as it damages the planet. It causes deep pain that is hard to bear.

The Role of Addiction

Human beings are also adept at finding ways of blocking out pain: ways that cause even more damage. We call it addiction. Matthew Fox really put his finger on this aspect when he identified the role and extent of addiction in our society in his book *Original Blessing*. [2] Addiction to alcohol, drugs, self harm, eating disorders and eating—all the obvious ones—are rife all around us. Fox added many of the seemingly harmless pastimes and lifestyle features of our society to the list of addictions: shopping, TV and cars, for instance.

As we know, these are all features of the reckless consumption which is consuming the planet in its relentless conversion of the precious and limited resources of the Earth into toxic waste. Interesting from the psychological point of view is what this culture of addiction does to us as human beings. Addiction is about shutting off, limiting and narrowing down, as a defense against feeling; against really living. The heroin addict's life is reduced to obtaining the next fix, and all values of relationship and morality are jettisoned in that frantic quest.

In this respect, spirituality is the opposite of addiction. Spirituality is about opening out, receptivity, allowing oneself to be vulnerable. So, why are people so easily persuaded to retreat into this self-limiting, sterile place (persuaded because this situation is clearly in the interests of global capital)? I return to the earlier argument that relationship, and therefore emotion, feels so dangerous precisely because it penetrates to the core of our being. In my hospital work, I need a way of making sense of the instability of human beings, and their proneness to escape into addiction. All the main mental health problems or diagnoses can be understood in terms of the drive to escape from emotional pain and uncertainty; from insecurity and uncertainty about the self into the false certainty of symptoms. The consumerist, materialist addictions also give us that false sense of security. They secure the present at the cost of the future.

I have painted a pretty bleak picture. The genius of Matthew Fox's prophetic writing is that, as well as making no bones about what is wrong, which is the duty of any prophet, it gives us a vision and hope to take us forward.

In *Original Blessing*, Fox was making the bold claim that Christianity had lost its way and betrayed its roots. He was appealing to an older tradition to bring it back on track. At the heart of his critique was the argument that the idea of 'original sin' was a distortion of the true tradition, introduced by St. Augustine in the fourth century CE. Fox appealed to the gospels, to the Hebrew prophets and to mystical writers such as Meister Eckhart and Hildegard of Bingen (among many others) to restore the original vision. According to this vision, creation was not flawed and sinful, but good and bountiful. Justice for the disadvantaged and marginalized was at the heart of morality, not the search for individual purity.

In the light of the great challenge of our age, the peril of the planet, ecological justice needs to take pride of place.

The Importance of the 'Four Ways'

(Editor's note: we shall be looking at these four ways again in more detail in Part III of this book, 'Spiritual Pathways')

Matthew Fox set out a program for people to follow in order to get back to this original vision. He took the medieval mystics' idea of following specific paths of instruction: 'viae' — the Latin for ways. He came up with his Four Ways. First was the *Via Positiva* which mobilizes the individual towards God through the wonder of creation. The painful encounter with the brokenness of creation, the *Via Negativa* follows naturally from this. Accessing these depths opens humanity to its innate creativity, the *Via Creativa* — which is a mark of our godlike quality; awakening creativity in the individual — is the catalyst that enables the person to engage with others in justice work to transform the planet, which is the *Via Transformativa*.

I will now use Fox's Four Ways to suggest a way out of the mess we humans have made of our relationship with the planet. To understand this psychologically, I will draw out the concept of our two distinct ways of processing, arising from the two completely different systems in our brains as described above. These distinct systems translate into distinct ways of being. I will emphasize relatedness and how relatedness invites us beyond the individual to a place of wonder and vulnerability.

As noted earlier, addiction is about closing down; shutting off. Fox's Four Ways are all about being open, being vulnerable. In terms of the two types of processing, it means leaving the apparent safety of our individuality and opening ourselves up in relatedness.

The first way, the *Via Positiva*, is about the immediate response to the wonder of creation; its intricate beauty and commanding majesty. This is the response that calls the individual out of the sterile cocoon of his or her individuality to respond to the whole. Defensiveness and self interest fall away, and joy and generosity take their place. However, simply reveling in beauty and awe could turn into shallow pleasure-seeking: say a long holiday in a destination only reachable by a planet-destroying plane ride. It is the deep and sacrificial response of love that makes possible the rest of the journey through the four ways. This response opens the individual in vulnerability. Again, that closed off individuality is dissolved by entering into the divine sea of love. Love opens the door to the *Via Negativa*: to the darkness of both suffering and letting go. This is the opposite of the darkness of the blocking out of the outside world, the escape into addiction. Love entails responsibility for the beloved. It opens the eyes and the heart to the damage that we are doing in our greed and stupidity. The courage to enter that darkness, and the strength to let go of the addictions that are ruining the planet, and preventing us from being truly ourselves, is the mark of the *Via*

Negativa. It also means the courage to risk losing our 'selves' in the sense of the self as identified with the verbal, logical, side of our being. Making those sacrifices enables us to connect both with the wider reality beyond us and with ourselves.

This conjunction puts us in touch with the wellspring of creativity that can flow between our being and the being of the universe. In the *Via Creativa*, the dance of the Four Ways takes us back into the individual in order to unlock the enormous potential that might otherwise remain shut up within. Taking the risk of losing our selves, we can indeed gain the whole world. Releasing this creativity opens the way for the fourth and the most powerful *Via* of all: the *Via Transformativa*, the one with a key to our current dilemma.

This is a model of flow: flow between the individual and the whole, flow of the individual into the whole and the whole into the individual. It is a hopeful model: one that moves away from the restricted, addicted, mode of being that traps us in our limited individuality, limits our vision to immediate comfort and interests, and cuts us off from the wonder that catches us when we lift our eyes to the whole. It is also a vision that calls for real risk and real sacrifice. In the case of the *Via Transformativa*, it also calls for action.

Taking his cue from Thomas Berry's concept of 'the great work' [3], Fox dignifies this action with the idea that by working towards the good of creation, and against ecological destruction, we are participating in the work of continuous creation; we are participating with that which some people choose to call 'God.'

In line with the psychological model of the person that I have sketched in above, where a part of each one of us is composed of relationship, and flows in and out of the whole in that relationship, 'God' can be seen as a name for the furthest and deepest reach of that web of relationship. Names and conceptualization belong to the other part of our being, the part that pins things down. In my understanding, 'God' is way beyond the grasp of that part. It is something we can only feel, as feeling is our way of 'knowing' relationship.

Walking the Walk

What matters here is that by doing something quite humble, like keeping a household going—cleaning, caring and cooking wholesome food, operating in as authentic a way as possible in a twisted societal order—we are part of that continuous process of creation. Fox develops this theme further in another book of his: *The Reinvention of Work* [4] Through our meeting with the pain of all beings in the *Via Negativa*, our creativity is awakened and we gain the courage to stand up for that authentic path. For some this might mean overt action, such as taking part in political demonstrations or working for justice. For some it will be supporting organizations and others who also walk this path. This is a collective and a communal redemption. Alone we are nothing.

GreenSpirit is one of many organizations working in this direction. In many ways, its orientation is profoundly ecopsychological. Its emphasis on the centrality of spirituality in the work of justice and Earth healing encourages us to engage in this work with the heart as well as the head: to embrace that vulnerability that will enable us to open the part of ourselves that exists in connection into fuller relationship with the other creatures and the Earth. This is both sacrifice and enlargement of our being, and so a truly spiritual way forward.

However, GreenSpirit does not ditch the intellectual, the 'head' part of our being. In this, it is true to the spirit of balance, which I see as essential to any success in the perilous enterprise of being human. It respects the latest findings of science, the fruits of that analytical neocortex part of our thinking apparatus, as well as honoring the older, 'heart' part of the human being. In engaging the 'heart' as well as the 'head' with the work of transformation, the dangerous vulnerability that this entails is not ignored. GreenSpirit approaches this encounter in a spirit of joy and love, not guilt and fear. These are enabling and opening emotions and will assist what is necessarily a risky enterprise.

The use of ritual and sharing are important elements in moving in safety from the confines of the individual to the embrace of the whole, and they play an important part in the life of GreenSpirit as an organization.

What I have been doing here is attempting to offer an understanding of the human being, in relation to the whole. My hope is that this insight into the human mind from cognitive science can inject a little humility into our understanding of ourselves, and our place in the order of things, in relation to the Earth, the non human creatures and those who come after us. We have achieved much in terms of technology, security and comfort for the privileged, but at a price that could cost us our beautiful home, the Earth, and destroy the habitat of those other beings with whom we share it. As more and more wars are waged to secure the raw materials needed to maintain our reckless lifestyle, we need a new vision and a new direction. The logical arguments about global warming and loss of diversity are not enough. People hear them, and emotionally shut off from them. We need to harness the power of the transliminal and the numinous if we are to escape from the blind alley down which we are heading.

Notes

1. Goleman, D. *Emotional Intelligence* (Bantam, 1997)
2. Berry, T. *The Great Work* (Crown Publications, 2001)
3. Fox, M. *Original Blessing* (Bear & Company, 1983)
4. — *The Reinvention of Work* (HarperSanFrancisco, 1994)

Understanding Ourselves

6. Reclaiming our Animal Body

Tania Dolley

You do not have to be good.
You do not have to walk on your knees
for a hundred miles through the desert, repenting.
You only have to let the soft animal of your body
love what it loves.

These lines from Mary Oliver's well-loved poem[1] encapsulate for me the essence of relationship to my body. They remind me about my 'animal body' and connect me to a tangible 'felt sense' of my embodied self. Reconnecting with a deep sense of acceptance in this way subtly changes my relationship to my inner self or soul. It seems to call my spirit back into my body, eliciting a sense of 'rightness' as I feel an inner shift and the recognition of "Ah yes, this is how it's meant to feel."

So often it seems that the journey of spirituality can, inadvertently maybe, lead us to recreate or exacerbate splits in us—mind ('good') versus body ('bad'): spirit ('good') versus matter ('bad')—seemingly a legacy of traditional Christian orthodoxy which taught that the body and its needs and impulses are the 'root of all sin.' This has generated a sense of shame and 'disowning' of our physical selves, experienced particularly perhaps by women in our culture. For me, spirituality is intrinsically about a journey towards wholeness ('(w)holy-ness'), which includes a process of healing the inner splits that divide and separate us from all aspects of our selves, from God or Spirit, as well as from the Earth.

One expression of how we, in the industrialized world especially, have lost connectedness with our embodied, 'earthy' selves can be seen in our dysfunctional relationship with Nature and our attitudes and behavior towards the Earth. We have abused our 'Earth body,' Nature, just as we also often neglect or deny the needs of our own bodies, not least through the relentless demands and stresses of complex modern working lifestyles. For many of us, our lifestyles impede a natural, daily rhythm that could otherwise allow us to honor the needs of both body and soul. Just as in our fast-paced culture we expect endless productivity from our personal bodies, even driving ourselves to exhaustion as we squeeze more out of ourselves, so we seem to expect a never-ending provision of resources from the Earth.

Yet we ignore the wisdom of the body at our peril.

I had a humbling experience of this, following an accident when my car skidded on wet mud and flipped over. It happened so fast, I had scarcely realized what had occurred before registering that I was unhurt. After extricating myself from the vehicle, grateful for being alive and safe, I told myself that there was therefore no need for any trauma reaction. Observing my good fortune to have escaped unscathed, a policewoman inquired why I was not upset, as would be expected. Advising me not to be surprised if shaking and crying hit me later, she mused that maybe I would be lucky and not suffer from shock. I concurred, naively assuming that because my psychologically-trained rational mind knows about trauma reactions, there was no need for me to have one on this occasion. So I didn't.

Several weeks of feeling unwell then ensued. I eventually consulted my GP, anticipating a flea in my ear for wasting her time with such a vague malaise. To my amazement she immediately pronounced that I had classic symptoms of a condition common in people who had experienced no shock after an accident. Explaining how the normal adrenaline response instead becomes suppressed and chronic, she assured me it should pass in a few weeks and prescribed some rest.

Feeling very relieved and grateful for her insightful diagnosis, I retired to bed with a good book: 'Waking the Tiger' by Peter Levine.[2]

It was fascinating to learn, from reading this, how animals and humans respond physiologically to traumatic experiences and how our 'animal body' naturally responds to a threatening situation regardless of what our rational mind may think. The nervous system's response to danger is hard-wired in the reptilian (instinctual) and mammalian limbic (emotional) parts of our brain that we share with other animals. A threatened human or animal must discharge the adrenaline mobilized to negotiate danger, for example by shaking or trembling, or it will succumb to trauma as the residual energy persists in the body creating a variety of unpleasant symptoms.

While animals instinctively discharge this energy, humans are less adept at this and when confronted with a life threatening situation, our rational brains may become confused and override our instinctive impulses.

Levine described precisely my attitude following the accident, explaining that while our highly evolved neo-cortex (rational brain) cannot override the fight, flight or freeze response to danger, it allows an overcontrol which interferes with the instinctual responses generated by our older (evolutionarily) reptilian brain that are necessary for return to normal functioning. I felt rather chastened, realizing that it would have been much healthier to allow my body's natural adrenaline response, and disconcerted at my mind's power in overriding this. I realized that in order to heal more quickly I needed to listen to and connect with the feelings and sensations that my animal body had registered, but my rational mind had not. I had to allow my body to 'speak' and tell its own story of the accident and release its trapped shock energy. In processing the experience in this way with the assistance of a colleague, I quickly felt back to normal.

Whilst our hunter-gatherer ancestors lived closely with the natural world and survival depended on powerful instinctive physical responses to danger, survival in modern life depends more on our ability to think. Levine suggests that consequently most of us have become separated from our instinctual selves and our human animal nature, and in so doing, we alienate our bodies from our souls, and also from the Earth. Certain spiritual and therapeutic practices thus aim to facilitate awareness of our bodies.

Buddhist teacher and psychologist Jack Kornfield[3] mentions James Joyce's Mr. Duffy who "lived a short distance from his body," as do many of us. He explains how meditation practice may involve opening up to physical (as well as emotional) pain as we re-engage with neglected physical aspects and loosen tightly-held muscular patterns.

Wilhelm Reich[4] suggested this 'body armor' develops as a defense against emotions and prevents the free flow of energy. Reich saw the mind-body split as causing us to destroy each other and our planet, so his therapeutic work aimed to help reunite mind and body.

Many body-focused therapies view the body-mind-spirit as a whole system and recognize the importance of integrating memories held on a cellular level. Eugene Gendlin[5] views the body as a 'biological computer' storing a vast amount of information which it can instantly deliver as a "holistic, implicit, bodily sense of a complex situation"[6]. Gendlin emphasizes that this bodily awareness or 'felt sense' is a physical, not mental, experience and is more accurate than rational thought. He suggests this inner sensing is a vital ingredient of successful therapy and as change occurs, a 'felt shift' is experienced.

Similarly, Carl Rogers' term 'organismic experience' refers to that sense of bodily knowing beyond intellectual understanding.

Rogers describes a 'fully-functioning person' as being congruent with this organismic experience or bodily felt sense, and open to "the sensory and visceral experiencing which is characteristic of the whole animal kingdom."[7] Western culture does not generally teach us to experience and 'be with' ourselves in this manner; we are used to living in a disconnected way that does not embrace our felt sense and ignores this natural human capacity.

Does our cultural world view and Western lifestyle then somehow keep us feeling separate from our own body, as well as from the Earth body and a felt sense of the interdependence of all life? This was brought home to me many years ago with a powerful experience in the Amazon rainforest. Being in this awesome wilderness environment, I suddenly found myself feeling as if I were a jungle animal, tangibly experiencing my 'animal body' for the first time. It was an almost overwhelming sense of being part of the jungle, as if my body was merging with that of the forest around me as physical senses of which I had never been aware sparkled into life. I could scarcely feel where 'my' body ended and the forest began. All my senses alive and tingling, it felt as though I was thinking and feeling through my skin, experiencing my surroundings directly though my physical body. Swimming in the river, with the sweet, warm water caressing my skin I felt immersed in the womb of Mother Nature.

It was an extraordinary and deeply moving experience that stirred my soul in a new way. The profound sense of reconnection, with my body and with wild Earth, of becoming 'embodied,' seemed to touch and reawaken a long-forgotten reality in the depth of my psyche. I sensed that a 'missing piece' of my self not previously encountered in my Western upbringing and academic education had finally slotted back into place. Although I had some experience of connection with Spirit, this 'body awakening' was different. It felt like a deeper integration of all aspects of my being.

Perhaps in the jungle I had also encountered my 'ecological

self,' that Deep Ecologist and philosopher Arne Naess[8] postulates. Wondering whether the experience of feeling 'embodied' and 'ensouled' in this way somehow arose from being in the unique Amazon environment, I was heartened to find that my newly-discovered animal body responded similarly back in the woods and forests of England.

In re-inhabiting our body or becoming fully embodied we can re-embrace that aspect of ourselves which has grown out of the Earth, quite literally; every atom and molecule that makes up my body is derived from the food and water and air that has sustained my life, and is inextricably entwined with the whole web of life on this Earth and cosmos beyond.

Some of the practices of Deep Ecology and Ecopsychology seek to help us reconnect with this truth in a tangibly felt, embodied way, and the Universe Story[9] and 'Deep Time' meditations can facilitate this awareness. In reconnecting with our body, can we then reconnect with Nature and the Earth that nurtures us, directly experiencing our interconnectedness with all life and with our deeper Self or Spirit—even perhaps a mystical oneness with all that is?

Connecting to our 'ecological self,' an expanded sense of self that includes an identification with all beings and the biosphere as a whole, often precipitates 'passionate engagement' in environmental action motivated not by duty, but by love for the web of creation. Conversely, cutting off from our embodied felt sense disconnects us from feelings, and the reality of our interconnectedness. This may serve to numb us to the pain we might otherwise feel about the destruction of our beloved planet's habitats and the suffering caused to other Earth communities by our industrial-growth society and highly consuming lifestyles.

This theme of listening to the body seems to echo the process of listening to our inner Self, the whispers of Spirit or our 'inner voice,' and extends also to listening to the Earth 'body.' Joanna Macy observes that:

"We are living cells in the living body of Earth. Our collective body is in trauma and we are experiencing that. Even though we try to suppress it or drown it out or cut a nerve so we don't feel it, the collective plight exists at some level of our consciousness...We need to listen to ourselves as if we were listening to a message from the universe...There is no private salvation."[10]

Perhaps my experience of suppressing my body's natural response to a trauma somehow reflects how we relate to our collective body in trauma. Chellis Glendenning[11] suggests that one response to the trauma of living in a technological society that disconnects us from the natural world may be dissociation, whereby we split our consciousness and repress our experience, shutting down our full perception of the world. Denial is another form of dissociation that protects us from painful feelings and trauma. The collective denial of how our way of life is affecting the Earth allows us to avoid experiencing fear and pain about what is happening to our planet, and to continue ignoring the reality of our destructive behavior.

As Kornfield notes,[3] problems also arise when denial of our full humanity—and this includes our body—is built into a spiritual view. The denial of ordinary human longings is a form of idealization prevalent in many spiritual traditions which advise against personal needs and desires, he suggests, so that the ideal of otherworldly perfection risks translating into repression. This can result in cutting us off from our own experience.

Spirituality is not about being 'above' the mere physical, human reality of our lives; rather, it is about embracing it, including and 'being with' all of our experience in a process of integration towards becoming whole.

An embodied spiritual practice can facilitate healing the splits and help us open up to parts of our selves, our bodies and our feelings that we have rejected or denied, so that we can reconnect with the wholeness of our human animal nature. The felt sense, as a means through which we experience ourselves as organisms, offers a way we can learn to hear the Earth 'speak,' to listen to our instinctual voice and learn again to trust the wisdom of the soft animal body. When we embrace the reality of our experience, whatever this may be, we open to a deeper connection with our bodies, with Nature and with Spirit. Energy flows and we become more fully alive. As we reconnect, a felt sense of care for ourselves, for others, and for the Earth may arise naturally. Through this process of embodiment and integration of all parts of ourselves, we may then reclaim our whole human animal nature and our connection with the Earth.

Notes

1. Oliver, M. *New and Selected Poems, Volume One* (Beacon Press, 1992)
2. Levine, P. *Waking the Tiger: Healing Trauma* (North Atlantic Books, 1997)
3. Kornfield, J. *After the Ecstasy, the Laundry* (Rider, 2000)
4. Reich, W. *Character Analysis* (Orgone Institute Press, 1949)
5. Gendlin, E. *Focusing* (Bantam Books, 1981)
6. Gendlin, E. *Focusing-oriented Psychotherapy* (Guilford, 1996)
7. Rogers, C. *On Becoming a Person: A Therapist's View of Psychotherapy* (Constable, 1967) p.105.
8. Naess, A. 'Identification as a source of deep ecological attitudes.' In Tobias, M. (Ed.) *Deep Ecology* (Avant Books, 1985) pp. 256-270
9. Swimme, B and Berry, T. *The Universe Story* (Harper San Francisco, 1992)
10. Macy. J. Interview by Karla Arnes, *Wild Duck Review*, 1995, II(1) 1- 3. cited in Conn, S. 'Living in the Earth: Ecopsychology, Health and Psychotherapy,' *The Humanistic Psychologist*, 26, 1998 pp. 1-3

11. Glendinning, C. 'Technology, Trauma and the Wild,' in Roszak, T, Gomes, M & Kanne, A. (Eds) *Ecopsychology : Restoring the Earth, Healing the Mind*. (Sierra Club Books, 1995)

'Reclaiming Our Animal Body' was first published in GreenSpirit Journal, vol. 10,1 Spring 2008.

Understanding Ourselves

7. Ecopsychology

Sandra White, Chris Clarke and Don Hills

"Our planet is in danger. ... (The facts and figures) are so real as to test all our capacities of denial, almost impossible to integrate into the *reality* of the humdrum of our daily lives. They took on reality for me when I first participated in actions to protect some of the remaining rainforests near my home in New South Wales, Australia. Then I was able to embody, to bring to life, my intellectual knowings in interaction with other beings—protesters, loggers, police and with the trees and other inhabitants of these forests. There and then I was gripped with an intense, profound realization of the depth of the bonds that connect us to the Earth, how deep are our feelings for these connections. I knew then that I was no longer acting on behalf of myself or my human ideas, but on behalf of the Earth . . . on behalf of my larger self, that I was literally part of the rainforest defending herself."[1]

What is Ecopsychology?

John Seed's description of a critical moment in his shift in consciousness is an evocative example of ecopsychology's main ideas and will no doubt strike a chord with anyone interested in green spirituality.

This relatively new field is being developed through a wide range of perspectives and techniques and for the past three years our organization, GreenSpirit, in the UK, has been conducting its own explorations of what ecopsychology is and how its ideas might best be communicated.

A starting point for us was to find the points of difference between ecospirituality and ecopsychology, for they both emphasize the unity and value of all and "place psyche (soul) back into the natural world"[2]. Ecopsychology, however, also unfolds the *human* dynamics that are linked with the ecological crisis. For example, it considers how consumerism may be rooted in our loss of soul, our culture's loss of contact with the unified whole, so that when we try to fill our world with poor substitutes we become addicted rather than feel satisfied. In this chapter, we aim to give a taste of the concepts, experiments and experiences we have engaged with, share some of the tentative conclusions we have drawn and show how we have put some of it into practice.

One aspect of ecopsychology is to think about not only 'where are we?' but also 'how did we get here?' and, in tracking the history of ideas, propose an analysis of what the path of Western-style evolution has cost us. A strong theme takes into account the psychological impacts of the 'myth of progress' which has under-pinned the evolution of our industrial and technological civilization over centuries and resulted in a collective mindset which experiences itself as separate from and superior to the rest of Nature. This, perhaps, is best encapsulated by Freud's description of the task of civilization:

"... its actual raison d'être, is to defend us against nature. We all know that in many ways civilization does this fairly well already, and clearly as time goes on it will do it much better. But no one is under the illusion that nature has already been vanquished; and few dare hope that she will ever be entirely subjected to man. There are the elements which seem to mock at all human control; the earth which quakes and is torn apart and buries all human life and its works; water, which deluges and drowns everything in turmoil; storms, which blow every-thing before them. ... With these forces nature rises up against us, majestic, cruel and inexorable; she brings to our mind once more our weakness and helplessness, which we thought to escape through the work of civilisation."[3]

With his evocation of 'our weakness and helplessness,' Freud also identified a critical characteristic of the modern mind—our desire to separate ourselves from our inherent vulnerability. Our vulnerability to what, may we ask? Elsewhere, Freud made clear the parallels between the tumult at the depths of the human mind and that within Nature, when he described the task of psychoanalysis as "to strengthen the ego, ... to widen its field of perception and enlarge its organization, so that it can appropriate fresh portions of the id...it is a work of culture not unlike the draining of the Zuider Zee."[4] In short: "Where id was, there ego shall be."[5] Freud's articulations reveal the degree to which the collective Western human project has become one of conquest, without and within.

We could say that ecopsychology brings new questions and propositions to our psychological understanding of what it means to be human in the twenty first century; here are just a few:

- What are the psychological implications for us as a society and as individuals if our project is to eliminate 'the enemy' without and within?
- How have centuries of believing in separation and superiority shaped our modern psychologies?
- If humanity is, instead, embedded in the web of life, what does this mean for individuals' ability to lead happy lives and achieve their full potential?
- If the destruction that human civilization is wreaking on the rest of life on our planet reflects the ways in which we are destroying aspects of our inner psychic lives that we have defined as 'the enemy,' how can we bring about change in this

collective trend?

- Given what John Seed has described as "...the *reality* of the humdrum of our daily lives," how can we integrate moments of connection, insight, and spiritual awakening into mundane existence, so that we can construct our lives and our work differently, at both the level of society and the individual level?

At its heart, ecopsychology recognizes that, because humanity is an expression of Nature, the living system of Earth makes its own contribution to the work of addressing such questions. One way it does this is by holding up a mirror to ourselves and this can have transformative power. For instance, during the cooperative inquiry described later, one of us connected with the slow silent being of a beech tree and as a result found the same silent being-ness in himself, leading to a new inner freedom. Another way Nature helps is in its examples—mirrors to ourselves if we choose to think of them as such—of where it is possible to live abundantly within finite, local ecosystems, like lakes and forests, where species only grow to the size that their habitats can support and every part of the system experiences and expresses abundance without impinging on any other part.

Intrinsic to this are the dual and connected principles of relativity and relatedness. Lakes and forests show how the closeness of the different species and intensity of their interactions provide the basis for each individual species to grow to the maximum size the ecosystem can sustain relative to everything else in the same ecosystem. While this may happen for them at an instinctual, rather than conscious, level, the contrast is sharp with the separated, individualized lives of many of us in modern industrialized society, where there is not the same consistency of interactions to foster our sense of relativity. This is not to romanticize community or to deny death or the real competition for food; it is, rather, to examine some consequences of how modern life is structured and its psychological impacts.

Ecopsychology equally emphasizes relatedness and the kind of relationship in which we are ourselves changed as we change the other—one of the hallmarks of genuine relationship—extending this to the 'other than human.' With the intense quality of individualism our culture fosters, we risk losing this capacity too. All these, and many other aspects are often summed up in the concept of the *ecological self*. Experiencing a human-human relationship, particularly a relationship of love, is a both/and event. I am one with the person I love, and at the same time that person is wonderfully themselves, wonderfully other than I. So each of our selves is enlarged, while each retains its being. This is how we grow our selves; in a sense, we *are* our relationships. Ecopsychology proclaims that this is even more true of the human–Nature interaction, so that our self is ecological. When we open our selves to the other-than-I of a bird or a tree we first feel empathy and honor, but then we feel also identification, which Arne Naess took as the defining quality of the ecological self.[6] Jung gave a flavor of this experience:

"At Bollingen I am in the midst of my true life, I am most deeply myself...At times I feel as if I am spread out over the landscape and inside things, and am myself living in every tree, in the splashing of the waves, in the clouds and the animals that come and go, in the procession of the seasons." [7]

The paradox is striking, in that when he is most deeply himself he also is inside everything else. One aspect of the field of ecopsychology is that it is developing practices which promote this paradoxical experience, so that its implications can then be absorbed and integrated into daily life.

Ecopsychology in GreenSpirit: the first steps

Ecospirituality and Deep Ecology have for many years been

developing techniques for growing the ecological self, and GreenSpirit adopted these long before they were assimilated into ecopsychology. One such was the 'mirror walk' first introduced by Joanna Macy in 1991.[8] So, when in 2005 this chapter's authors proposed to plan a large residential ecopsychology gathering, the idea was well received. We wanted to bring together ecospiritualists, ecopsychologists and ecoactivists, to exchange resources and see if a more coordinated, cohesive approach between these constituencies might accelerate the cultural change that is needed if the worst manifestations of ecological cataclysm are to be averted. A 'visioning' event was held, inviting 18 people from the three sectors to help us to conceive what such a gathering needed to contain and a representative working group started to meet to take things forward.

We agreed at the outset that we would practice the process which we intended to offer to the larger gathering, that of coming together from our different perspectives and learning about ecopsychology through our structured engagement with the Earth community at intervals in the course of our work. But it took us a long time to learn, the hard way, how necessary it was to take this intention seriously. For several meetings we went round in circles, knowing that successive plans arrived at by a largely intellectual process were inadequate, realizing that there was a key to be grasped, but seeming unable to find it. We did well in listening to and addressing our different perspectives as human beings, seeing the dynamics between us as a microcosm of the larger system but, by definition, this kept us within the human frame. The breakthrough occurred when we went out together onto Southampton Common and then separated to spend an agreed period of time alone, being receptive to whatever we might experience. As we opened ourselves to the life around us, trees, squirrels, crows, and people too, 'had their say' in our deliberations through their presence and their individuality. Each of us let go of our human preoccupations and expanded to a realization of what we were about. The event we were considering needed to be grounded in participants' awareness of the reality of the Earth community.

As it turned out, some informal market research then revealed that the sort of gathering that was required in order to fulfill our aims would not be economically feasible in the time available, but we now had the impetus to explore ecopsychology in a quite different way. We needed to examine what was going on when we used varied tools to encounter the more-than-human world to grow in empathy and identification with other beings: what helped and what hindered this growth? Was this the key, not only to our particular tasks, but to how industrialized humanity might re-learn how to live in harmony with the Earth? So we adopted a well tried method for investigating subjective experience, a version of what John Heron and Peter Reason have called 'cooperative inquiry.'[9]

The four of us convened a new group for four residential meetings of 24 hours, enjoying the hospitality and beautiful surroundings of Douai Abbey. For the first, we were eight, and thereafter seven and, again, we invited people of diverse backgrounds and interests. Our cooperative inquiry entailed four stages making up a cycle: (i) formulation of a question and procedure of investigation; (ii) engagement in a practice with attentiveness to what happens; (iii) sharing the experience with our colleagues by expressing it in non-verbal means; (iv) joint reflection on the outcome, making sense of it and revising the formulation or posing a new one. At each of our meetings, we passed through several of these complete cycles and a stage (ii) always spanned the period between meetings, so that our 'homework' consisted of engagement in the chosen practice. The non-verbal element in the research was crucial. Rather than imposing linear thought on the experience immediately, we held back the words, sharing our experience with each other through bodily actions or painting. Only when we had thus each witnessed and participated in the others' experiences, drawing upon the body's intelligence and the imagination, did we jointly reach for the appropriate words and concepts to make sense of what we had found.

Often a cycle would branch off a previous one to explore a particular aspect of the process rather than directly engaging with Nature, as in the following example, the third inquiry cycle. Here, we posed the hypothesis 'We can intuit empathy with the whole, through the human,' which arose out of our recognizing ourselves as a group of people already empathically connected with Nature and also the previous cycle in which we had explored how fear can cut across our ability to feel connected with other people and behave in connected ways. The main action we would undertake as 'homework' would be to do regular meditations in which we would extend our empathy to widening circles of people, observing our feelings and also observing them when watching/listening to radio or TV news reports. We recognized, however, that we needed a 'taste' of empathy before parting and so did a group 'sculpt,' evoking that quality towards each other. Once reunited at Douai Abbey, we began by physically modeling and expressing through mime and movement our experiences of this inquiry which, for many of us, had been challenging. Holding in mind visual symbols, making a ritual practice of empathy, embodying expressions of empathy, and maintaining 'the right psychic diet'—feeding our sense of our own core validity from which we could honor others' core validity—were all helpful in meeting the challenges and developing our practice.

In discussion we encountered the concept of 'woundedness' and how this interacted with our ability to empathize, sometimes facilitating empathy and sometimes preventing it.

What strikingly came out of this, and many other cycles, were the ways in which blocks within ourselves (which we may consider as 'woundedness') simultaneously prevented us from relating openly to humans *and* to the other-than-human. Realizing and understanding a block in our human connections led to the realization of a block in our other-than-human connections, and vice versa. Partly drawing upon the transformative experience of being with the beech tree mentioned earlier, in one strand of our discussion we recognized how Western culture privileges 'doing' over 'being' and, in effect, denies the intrinsic value of simply being human. Individual moments when we felt denied by other people provided a concentrated dose of this cultural norm, causing acute, personal pain, out of which blocked, rather than connected, behaviors arose. This means that healing individuals, healing society and healing our relationship with the whole Earth community cannot be separated—indeed, Alastair McIntosh calls for 'cultural psychotherapy' and has articulated elements of an imagined '12-step program' to this end[10].

Expressing the diverse faces of ecopsychology

GreenSpirit additionally decided that the Spring 2008 issue of the Journal would be devoted to ecopsychology and we were able to publish an issue with careful presentations of the full diversity of the subject and make these presentations available on our website also.

A further unfolding of GreenSpirit's understanding of ecopsychology was in the construction of its 2008 Annual Gathering. Our challenge: how to give a group of 30 or more members a practical experience of this many-stranded process and convey a flavor of the experiences that had been so meaningful and transformative for us? We wanted to experiment with how the ideas of ecopsychology could guide a nourishing event for a larger group of humans in a setting with plenty of access to the wider Earth.

Two central components were soon agreed: an introductory talk about ecopsychology, given by Tania Dolley, making explicit what we were doing; and an extended period (an hour and a half) of individual engagement with the other-than-human world, leading into a process that provided a taste of our cooperative inquiry, expressing in non-verbal ways what that engagement had felt like, before analyzing any practical learning from the experience that we might want to take forward into our lives once home.

An important organizing idea also emerged: the interplay of different layers of community. Many would be arriving as individuals (though the organization also had many existing links of friendship), and we would assist them in forming a temporary community, with the addition of more family-sized groupings—'home groups'—within which the whole experience could be discussed in safety. At the same time as this human community was forming, it would be discovering its roots in the wider-than-human community. Then towards the end there would be a turning to two more permanent communities: the geographical or workplace ones of our everyday lives, and the larger membership of GreenSpirit.

The particular components of the program embodied these ideas. At the first plenary session, for example, people not only publicly introduced their own human selves, but also introduced a place that they felt connected to, invoking that place and feeding their connection with it by inviting the spirit of it to join us through that simple act of naming it. This was remarkably effective: the next time you found yourself next to that person, you thought , "aha! Norfolk marshes," or "yes, the South Downs." We had started to grow a communal ecological self, which we would remain in touch with when, at the end of the gathering, we all returned to these beloved places.

Moving between the individual and different sizes of home groups or other subgroups was key to the effectiveness of the solo experiential session outdoors which was at the heart of the event. Before launching out for the solo, ad hoc groups gathered around four magnificent old trees and used some observation techniques for opening to the natural world and using our body-senses, learning the wisdom of the body, rooting ourselves in our sensory experiences. This enabled us to engage with the more-than-human world from a different place when we were on our own for an extended period. Participants were asked to 'hold onto' the experience, not rushing to put it into words over lunch, so that after lunch within the security of home groups we could explore it in drawing, movement or modeling clay. In this way we made something more available to our understanding and integrated the whole experience into ourselves, and secured its meaning through a sharing, both non-verbal and verbal, with a secure 'family.'

We also wanted the human group, the temporary organism we would become for the weekend, consciously to experience and express its biodiversity as a microcosm of the whole. The ritual on the Saturday evening was co-created with contributions from individuals previously discussed during the home group meetings. This provided a vivid and profound celebration of individual talents and our interconnectedness, perhaps best exemplified by the two poetry readings which were accompanied by members of the whole group enacting what they heard while the poems were recited, becoming wind and trees and water and creatures and sound, bringing the outside in and experiencing within ourselves the not-human.

The transition from this temporary community to awareness of the wider communities to which we would be returning was made through a 'snowballing' exercise on the final day, in which groups were accumulated and stuck together like the process of building a snowman. First individuals recalled their inner experience of the weekend and particularly the solo time outside, then they shared its meaning with a random other person, then these pairs joined up to fours to start thinking about its implications for their lives in their home communities, then these joined into eights to do some practical brainstorming, reported back in plenary, for its relevance to GreenSpirit.

Many people, like Denise Moll below, reported that their time alone in Nature was powerful and reconnected them with experiences, emotions, qualities and ideas which they had been missing and for which they hungered.

"First, after gathering round a tree with a group, with some beautiful words read out, written by Tania Dolley, I walked, reminding myself to slow down and see where my steps took me. I had a vague idea of going to look at some sheep I saw in the distance, but I never found them. Instead I turned off the drive and cut off left across a field of vivid green grass, sparkling with dewdrops, gently swaying in the wind, the 'Indian summer' sun warming my skin.

Eventually I was drawn to sit on a clump of old straw and this is where I chose to 'be with nature' and see what came to my eyes, ears, nose, breath and heart. My body gradually relaxed. I 'let go,' gazed around, absorbed…:-

- Senses and heart savored a great Stillness all around…deep resonance with all that is…beauty beyond words.
- Looking around with my glasses on, then taking them off and being surprised to see that dewdrops on the blades of grass had turned into little sparkling stars shimmering, shining, symbolizing for me a great joy in being. Looking with a sense of wonder at these sparkling stars, I noticed some had turned green and gold—a result of Brother Sun of course, but would have gone unnoticed by me in ordinary circumstances.
- My ears registered many sounds, not shattering the glorious peace because they blended: different cries and calls of birds, a hum and whizz of insects, wasps. Droning of an aeroplane far up beyond me, invisible to the eye…reminding me how much human beings have 'put' into the atmosphere, some

would say unnecessarily, others seeing benefits for modern travelers, in opening up a greater world. It is excess that is the trouble, not balance, and being able to STOP when that is required.

- My nose drank in soft smells of early autumn, a scent of grass and trees and a faint tinge of smokiness, which suggested to me the season was in process of changing, and that I needed to change with it and not resist its offerings, even the shorter days and long nights of darkness.

- Balmy air filled my nostrils with a sense of delicious aroma, while soft wind played with my hair and grasses, and tree branches gently swayed. There was such a feeling of Oneness I drew in my breath and exhaled slowly, savoring the air and soft caresses from the sun-filled field.

- My fingers gently stroked a blade of grass; it felt like velvet. A single blade of grass, symbolizing all grass everywhere, like an individual symbolizing humanity. I was filled with awe.

- Spiders' webs: how *do* they make these amazingly delicate structures without any regard for where (or they would know most would be destroyed). Here in the field, dew bedecked and softly shining, many had been created—no sign of the 'architects,' but perhaps they were in hiding waiting, watching...

- Brown mounds of molehills suggested a presence of living beings just beneath the surface; leaves falling lightly, soft hues of changing colors; an enormous oak just behind me signifying strength, stability, on-goingness, offering shade and shelter—a haven for birds to rest and flit from branch to branch.

- A soft grey bird's feather lay cradled in a little group of grass; nearby prickles warning not to touch. I reflected that nature is both nurturing, healing, soft and ruthless with its spikes and stings and unforgiving harshness. Wild creatures, big and small, sometimes prey on each other—'survival of the fittest'—and rough vegetation elbows out the delicate flower, areas grow into uninhabitable wildernesses. Was it always like this? Could all of nature live in harmony?

I felt a kind of unforced peace, a consequence of being as open-hearted as I knew how to the present moment. I knew I had some thorny issues to return to in my life on the morrow, but living in the moment in this idyll was easy and would strengthen and nourish me to face what had to be faced. The only way this peace of mind could have been disturbed was if I chose to disturb it with uncontrolled thoughts. It was bliss, pure bliss. You cannot give bliss to another; it's a personal journey, though seeing another's bliss can sometimes encourage your own.

There is an ebb and flow of life which comes and goes whether we like it or not. To acknowledge and move with this flow is what will cause the least upset to psyche and lives.

Thank you, GreenSpirit, for giving me this opportunity. And it is a gift that can be used again and again!"

The snowballing exercise was explicitly designed to support the integration of these experiences, first into conscious under-standing and then into practical commitment, and we have since heard from one colleague that he now regularly participates in land maintenance with a residential community local to him. This is ecopsychology at its best: accessing our interconnection with the whole and the psychological healing and wellbeing it brings, reflecting upon that experience and integrating it into our lives.

We in GreenSpirit will continue to explore ecopsychology and contribute to the development and dissemination of its ideas, bringing to bear our perspectives on the place of humanity within the emerging universe.

Notes

1. Seed, J. 'To hear Within Ourselves the Sound of the Earth Crying' in Seed, J., Macy, J., Fleming P., Naess A. (Eds) *Thinking Like A Mountain* (New Society Publishers 1988) p. 6

2. Fisher, A. *Radical Ecopsychology: Psychology in the Service of Life* (SUNY Press, 2002); from a review by Almut Beringer in *Human Ecology Review*, Vol. 10, No. 2, 2003, pp. 187-8

3. Freud, S. *The Future of an Illusion* (W.W. Norton, 1961) as quoted in Dunann Winter, D. *Ecological Psychology: Healing the Split between Planet and Self* (Addison Wesley Longman 1997)

4. Freud, S. *New Introductory Lectures on Psycho-analysis* (W.W. Norton 1933)

5. *ibid..*

6. Naess, A. 'Identification as a Source Of Deep Ecological Attitudes' in Tobias, M. (Ed.) *Deep Ecology* (Avant Books, 1985) pp.256-270

7. Jung, C.G. *Memories, Dreams and Reflections* (Fontana Press, 1993) p.252 and in Sabini, M. (Ed.) *The Earth has a Soul: the Nature Writings of C G Jung* (North Atlantic Books, 2005) p.14

8. Macy, J. and Young Brown, M. *Coming Back to Life: Practices to Reconnect Our Lives, Our World* (New Society Publishers, 1998) p.88

9. Heron, J. and Reason, P. 'The practice of cooperative enquiry: research 'with' rather than 'on' people,' in Reason, P and Bradbury, H (Eds) *Handbook of Action Research: Participative Enquiry and Practice* (Sage, 2001) pp.179-188

10. McIntosh, A. *Hell and High Water: Climate Change, Hope and the Human Condition* (Birlinn Limited, 2008) p. 210

Part II: Spiritual Pathways

"The Miracle is not to walk on water. The miracle is to walk on the green Earth, dwelling deeply in the present moment and feeling truly alive."

– Thich Nhat Hanh

About Part II

8. The Great Wheel

Marian Van Eyk McCain

Most, if not all, of the world's human societies have some sort of creation myth: some story about how the world came to be, how it works, and what their part in it might be. Now, as we have seen in the first part of this book, that great human adventure we call science has given us a broader, deeper understanding—of the universe, of this little corner of it that we call Earth and of the inner workings of our own selves—than was ever possible before. It has given us a new story. However, as Thomas Berry and Brian Swimme point out in their book *The Universe Story*:

> "(It is not) the case that this story suppresses the other stories that have over the millennia guided and energized the human venture. It is rather a case of providing a more comprehensive context in which all these earlier stories discover for themselves a new validity, and a more expansive role."[1]

Most of what we learn about religion when we are children is merely its outer surface. And millions of people are content to remain on the religious surface their entire lives. Those who are not often refer to themselves as 'spiritual seekers.' I, too, used to call myself a 'spiritual seeker.' I spent several decades exploring, studying, learning, reading, thinking, meditating, trying out various practices and trying to piece together a set of beliefs that felt right for me. And over those many years of exposure to dozens of different religions, belief systems and spiritual traditions I came to think of it all in the shape of a giant cartwheel.

At the very hub of the cartwheel is what Aldous Huxley referred to as 'The Perennial Philosophy' which is common to all cultures and all religions.

"...the *metaphysic* that recognizes a divine Reality behind the world of things and lives and minds; the *psychology* that finds in (one) something identical with divine Reality and the *ethic* that places (one's) final end in the knowledge of the Immanent and Transcendent Ground of all things." [2]

It can be reached from any point on the rim of the wheel by following the spoke to its mystical heart where practitioners of every tradition have discovered, each in their own way, the ultimate oneness of everyone and everything.

Every religion and spiritual belief has this mystical heart. We can discover it in the words of Jesus Christ if we know where and how to look for it. From there we can trace it through the writings of the Christian mystics such as Julian of Norwich, Meister Eckhart and Hildegard of Bingen—and more recently Teilhard de Chardin and now Matthew Fox. It finds beautiful expression in the Sufi tradition at the mystical heart of Islam and in Buddhism it stands out particularly clearly in the sayings of the Zen masters. In Hinduism, we find it in the non-dual philosophy of Advaita Vedanta and it appears again in the Hasidim of Judaism.

But it is a big wheel and its spokes are long. Out on the rim of the wheel is where all the misunderstandings occur. Millions spend their lives out on that rim, yelling at, glaring at—or at best simply tolerating—people somewhere else on the rim because their beliefs are different. Wars are waged around that rim. Christians on one side of the wheel and Moslems on another have been battling for centuries because their particular versions of the 'truth' are so different. But someone who has gone to the mystical heart of Christianity and another who has gone to the mystical heart of Islam will hold hands at the hub and see the divine in each other and in everything. As will, for example, a Pagan, a Buddhist, a Hasidic Jew and a shaman, if they have truly penetrated to the core and found love there and oneness and the 'peace that passeth all understanding.'

The Sufi poet Rumi said it best, I think:

"Out beyond ideas of wrongdoing and rightdoing, there is a field; I'll meet you there."[3].

Sadly, many of the spokespersons for the various spiritual traditions whose task it is to pass on those traditions to others are as far out on the rim of that wheel as anybody else. Which is why, as Matthew Fox claims in his provocative chapter, 'something is amiss in the world of religion.'

Baron Friedrich von Hügel, the Roman Catholic theological thinker and author who died in 1925, wrote of three elements of religion: the *historical/institutional element*, the *scientific/intellectual element*, and the *mystical/experiential element*. It is the first—the historical/institutional element—that holds sway on the rim of the cartwheel, where people align themselves unquestioningly with the dogma they have been given. The second element—the scientific/intellectual—is the process of moving away from the rim of the wheel and along one of the spokes by means of questioning, experimenting, searching for ultimate truth. Some find what they seek within their own traditions. Some find it elsewhere. And some turn away, disillusioned, from any kind of spiritual path. Those who are able find a satisfactory answer, whether within their own tradition or in some other form of spirituality, may then move towards von Hügel's third element—the mystical/experiential . For in his view, the essence of all religion is, as he described it, "the mystical adoration of the infinite by the individual." So, as Jesus instructed:

"Let him who seeks, not cease seeking until he finds, and when he finds he will be troubled, and when he has been troubled he will marvel ..."[4]

This is where we reach the hub. This is where we marvel. I once heard Brian Swimme say that one of our important roles, as humans, in the evolution of consciousness on this Earth, is to be astonished. "To provide a space for the universe to become astonished with itself."

There are many who, having reached that hub, no longer feel the need to align themselves with any religious or spiritual institution at all but whose daily lives are permeated with spirituality. Yet there are also many others who continue practicing within one of the main faith traditions, either the one they were brought up in or another which feels like a better 'fit,' whilst understanding them in a new and deeper way.

This second part of the book, 'Spiritual Pathways,' begins with a chapter by Michael Colebrook on 'The Green '-isms," the aim of which is to demystify some of the terminology one often hears in discussions of comparative religion. Like for instance, what is the difference between 'pantheism' and 'panentheism'?

Next, Grace Blindell describes for us Matthew Fox's 'four paths' of Creation-centered spirituality' referred to earlier by Isabel Clarke. These are four distinct paths that a personal, spiritual journey can take and we are likely to take all of them at one time or another. They are: *Via Positiva*, the spirituality of joy: *Via Negativa*, the spiritual path of facing despair: *Via Creativa*, the spirituality of creativity and *Via Transformativa*, the journey towards spiritual transformation. This last is then expanded in a brief essay by June Raymond.

Matthew Fox himself gives us his thoughts on the state of the world's religions today and the significance of Thomas Berry's teachings in providing us with an Earth-based alternative. Jean Hardy then gives a brief overview of the world's spiritual traditions in her chapter 'Spirit in East and West.'

Despite the shortcomings of the various institutions which purport to represent the world's main religious traditions, despite the bloodstained history of religious conflict caused by ignorance and misunderstanding around the rim of the 'great wheel,' there is still treasure at the heart of every tradition. This is one reason why many people are able to retain their allegiance to the institutions yet follow their own brand of green spirituality at the same time. For example, when Thomas Berry urges Christians to 'put the Bible on the shelf,' he is speaking not about turning one's back on the wisdom of Christ but about stripping back the accretion of over-literal, patriarchal, misinterpretations of Christ's message that has taken place over the last 2000 years. For it is the institutions themselves that have distorted the wisdom of the great teachers, particularly Christ and Mohammed, and used it to exacerbate divisiveness between individuals, tribes and nations.

So in this next section of the book, we hear June Raymond telling us why she remains a practicing Christian, Joyce Edmond Smith talking about 'Green Buddhism,' Rabbi Jamie Korngold on Green Judaism, Neil Douglas-Klotz on Sufism and Emma Restall Orr on Paganism.

The wheel's rim, as we all know, is thickly populated. The world is full of people who claim Christianity as their religion yet rarely heed Christ's message. It holds many Moslems with whose interpretation of Islam their revered Prophet would disagree. There are many token Buddhists, many Hindus who understand very little of their ancient heritage, and even some Pagans whose behavior at times belies their professed respect for the Earth. But the writers who speak here for some of the world's great wisdom traditions have all moved into von Hügel's third element. They have all reached the hub of the wheel. And as you will see, they have all found treasure there.

There are, of course, numerous spiritual traditions not represented in this book. There simply would not be room to include them all. The aim of this section on spiritual pathways is purely to show by example how GreenSpirit can encompass—and be enriched by—other stories, other traditions, other forms of wisdom. And how anyone, anywhere, can reach this new, 'green' consciousness from any point on the 'great wheel.'

Notes
1. Swimme, B. and Berry, T. *The Universe Story* (Harper, 1992) p.238
2. www.religiousworlds.com
3. Jalal al-Din Rumi (translated by Coleman Barks)
4. *The Gospel According to Thomas: The Gnostic Sayings of Jesus* (Harper, 1959) 80:14

9. The Green '-isms'

Michael Colebrook

This chapter provides an introduction to a number of belief systems relevant to GreenSpirit and which have acquired names ending in -ism and each of which deserves at least a chapter in its own right, if not an entire book. All that is attempted here is a very brief outline together with some indication of their interrelationships.

In nearly all the modern translations of the Bible, verse 1 of Psalm 121 is presented in the form of a rhetorical question; the New English Bible has:

I look up toward the hills,
From where does my help come?
which is answered in verse 2:
My help comes from the Lord,
the Creator of heaven and earth!
In contrast to this, the older King James Bible has:
I will lift up mine eyes to the hills,
From whence cometh my help.

It is a complete sentence with no question mark. This provides scope for an interpretation that help can come directly from a contemplation of the hills. In this reading, verse 2 becomes a gloss on verse 1 as opposed to providing a resolution to the posed question.

It would seem that the recent translators are keen to emphasize the transcendent nature of the divine and to stress the separation of the creator from the created natural world. The alternative interpretation, on the other hand, carries the impli-cation that the divine can be considered as, in some undefined sense, present within the created order. This belief system is known as 'panentheism' (from the Greek: *pan* 'all,' *en* 'in' and *Theós* 'God': 'all-in-God'ism.) The divine is seen as both within creation—immanent—and also beyond and above creation—transcendent[1].

This view has clear implications for the form of the relationship between the human and the divine. Also, the world can no longer be viewed as the stage on which the human drama is acted out in response to the transcendent presence of God; it is legitimate to turn to the hills for help.

There is fairly wide range of beliefs that can be embraced under the umbrella of panentheism. At one end, the immanence of God is pictured as taking a purely spiritual form and confined to humans, as the Quakers put it, "there is that of God in everyone." At the other end of the spectrum of panentheism the immanence of God is interpreted as implying that the whole universe, the entire created order, is a physical manifestation of the divine as well as a spiritual one. The theologian Sallie McFague employs the image of creation as 'the Body of God'[2].

Here, panentheism almost merges with 'pantheism,' the belief that God and creation are synonymous. In spite of this apparently precise definition, in practice, pantheism tends to become a label attached to a variety of views that the divine and the natural are at least interdependent and at most identical. Thus John Scotus Eriugena (c.810-877):

"Ultimately, God and creation are one and the same....Since Nature, the Creator of the whole universe, is infinite, it is confined by no limits above or below. It encompasses everything itself, and is encompassed by nothing."

And D.H. Lawrence (1885-1930):

"There is no god

apart from poppies and the flying fish,
men singing songs, and women brushing their hair in the
sun."

Pantheism is a subtle and intuitive expression of feeling that does
not lend itself easily to precise philosophical analysis. [3]

There is a purely secular mode of pantheism in the form of
'naturalism' which holds that all phenomena can be explained by
natural causes, with the implication that the supernatural does
not exist. Naturalism has emerged as an understandable
metaphysical extension of the developments of modern science
where there is a widespread belief (or at least hope) that the
formulation of a 'theory of everything' is within the realm of the
possible.

A strict naturalism carries the implication of a purely natural
state of humanity which many find hard to accept. In the Western
cultural tradition there has been and still is a widespread belief
that humans are qualitatively different from the rest of creation.
A human-centered view of the world emerged very strongly in
the Renaissance. Pico della Mirandola in his *Oration on the
Dignity of Man* (1486) put these words into the mouth of God,

"Neither an established place, nor a form belonging to you
alone, nor any special function have We given to you, O
Adam, and for this reason, that you may have and possess,
according to your desire and judgment, whatever place,
whatever form, and whatever function you shall desire. The
nature of other creatures, which has been determined, is
confined within bounds prescribed by Us. You, who are
confined by no limits, shall determine for yourself your own
nature, in accordance with your own free will... I have placed
you in the centre of the world..."

In a more up-to-date formulation, paragraph 299 of the

Catechism of the Catholic Church states:

"The universe, created in and by the eternal Word, the 'image of the invisible God,' is destined for and addressed to man, himself created in the 'image of God' and called to a personal relationship with God."

This very human orientated view has a name, it is known as 'anthropocentrism' and it has both religious and secular expressions. It is a widely held view and is influential in nearly all aspects of Western culture.

From an anthropocentric viewpoint the rest of creation is of a lesser form of existence, it is 'destined for and addressed to man.' Humans have the right to explore and exploit the rest of the natural world as they see fit. A very successful method of exploration within the sciences has been the process of taking things apart to see how they work and to find out what they are made of. The method has been so successful that it is tempting to carry the idea further and to believe that things *are* what they are made of. This belief is known as 'reductionism.' While reductionism may not be an inevitable consequence of anthropocentrism it would appear that it has grown from the same roots. Marcus Chown has pointed out in a recent book that the entire human race would fit in the volume of a sugar cube.[4] What he means is that if all the fundamental particles in all the people in the world were squeezed tightly together they would occupy the volume of a sugar cube. The implication is that humans and indeed all living things are simply collections of fundamental particles. The Nobel laureate and physicist Stephen Weinberg says:

"All the explanatory arrows point downward, from societies to people to organs, to cells, to biochemistry, to chemistry, and ultimately to physics."[5]

He also says: "The more we know of the cosmos, the more meaningless it appears."

There has been a reaction against such extreme reductionism. Phillip Anderson claims that:

"The ability to reduce everything to simple fundamental laws does not imply the ability to start from those laws and reconstruct the universe. In fact, the more the elementary particle physicists tell us about the nature of the fundamental laws, the less relevance they seem to have to the very real problems of the rest of science."[6]

There is no way that the sugar cube of so-called fundamental particles could be reconstructed into the human race.

Without denying the methodological value of reductionism as a useful and successful way of finding out about the world, recent developments in systems theory have focused on emergent properties, where wholes are held to be more than simply the sums of their parts, where sets and collectives of entities exhibit properties that are not predictable from any knowledge of the properties of the individual entities. As D. H. Lawrence puts it:

"Water is H2O, hydrogen two parts, oxygen one, but there is also a third thing that makes it water and nobody knows what that is."[7]

'Emergentism' claims that a living organism is more than a collection of fundamental particles. No knowledge of the fundamental particles, however extensive, could be used to predict the emergence of life. Life is something entirely new and the result of inherent processes that can be recognized as creative. Emergentism involves a layered view of nature, with the layers arranged in terms of increasing complexity and where each possesses its own fundamental attributes and in many instances its own science, from molecules, to water, to living things, to forests, to the Earth.

Lee Smolin[8] suggests that in spite of the efforts to separate the sciences from all forms of religious belief, classical science and orthodox Christianity share a belief in a form of transcendence, of something outside the physical universe. For the sciences this has the form of universal laws related to a fundamental theory. For the orthodox Christian it has the form of a divine creator and sustainer.

Panentheism and emergentism represent a move in the opposite direction, emphasizing the inherent properties and potential *within* a physical universe that is intrinsically evolutionary and self-creative. Stuart Kauffman[9] has provided a very persuasive account of emergentism as opposed to reductionism. Thomas Berry claims that:

"The earth, within the solar system, is a self-emergent, self-propagating, self-nourishing, self-governing, self-healing, self-fulfilling community."[10]

The cosmologist Carl Sagan suggests:

"A religion old or new, that stressed the magnificence of the universe as revealed by modern science, might be able to draw forth reserves of reverence and awe hardly tapped by the conventional faiths. Sooner or later, such a religion will emerge."[11]

The recognition that the universe is inherently creative and self-organizing in the form of a cascade of emergent entities capable of producing the utterly marvelous world we live in, coupled with a panentheistic view of divine activity and involvement, may provide the basis for the kind of religion that Carl Sagan is seeking.

Notes

1. Peacocke, A. *Evolution, The Disguised Friend of Faith* (Templeton Foundation Press, 2004) pp. 97-109
2. See http://home.utm.net/pan/panorama.html
3. McFague, S. *The Body of God* (SCM Press, 1993)
4. Chown, M. *Quantum Theory Cannot Hurt You* (Faber and Faber, 2007)
5. Weinberg, S. *Dreams of a final Theory* (Random House, 1994)
6. Anderson, P. 'More is Different' (http://www.cmp. caltech.edu/~motrunch/Teaching/Phy135b_Winter07/MoreIs Different.pdf)
7. Lawrence, D.H. *Pansies* (Martin Secker, 1929)
8. Smolin, L. *The Life of the Cosmos* (Weidenfield and Nicolson, 1997) p. 198
9. Kauffman, S. *Reinventing the Sacred* (Basic Books, 2008)
10. Lonergan, A. and Richards, C. (Eds) *Thomas Berry and the New Cosmology* (Twenty-Third Publications, 1988) p. 108
11. Sagan, C. *Pale Blue Dot* (Ballantine Books, 1997)

10. The Four Paths

Grace Blindell

This chapter will clarify what have come to be known as 'the four paths of Creation Spirituality' which Isabel Clarke referred to in Chapter 5. These were first set out by Matthew Fox in his book *Original Blessing*. Primarily they need to be understood as 'enablers.' Enabling us to see through 'different eyes.' For as William Blake said, 'The eye altering alters all.'

> "Ideas remain impractical when we have not grasped, or been grasped by them. When we do not get an idea we ask 'how' to put it into practice, thereby trying to turn the insights of the soul into actions of the ego. But when an insight or idea has sunk in, practice invisibly changes. The idea has opened the eye of the soul. By seeing differently we do differently. The only legitimate 'how?' in regard to these psychological insights is: 'How can I grasp an idea?'"[1]

Our task is to enable our new understanding about the nature of the universe to bear upon our whole selves, not just upon our intellect so that we can carry 'seeing differently' into all walks of our daily lives.

Creation Spirituality does not lay down rules of 'thou shalt' or 'thou shalt not,' instead it offers paths and insights. These spiral from one to the other, enabling a transformed and deeper understanding of what it is to be both an emerging consciousness of an evolving universe, always in the process of 'becoming,' and at the same time, a unique expression and member of the Earth community.

The *Via Positiva*: 'Thou shalt fall in love at least three times a day'

The first of Matthew Fox's four paths, the *Via Positiva*, entails re-awakening awe, wonder, astonishment and delight. It has to do with reverence, with 'is-ness,' with 'becoming again as little children.'

"Forfeit your sense of awe, and the universe becomes a market place for you."[2]

Is this not exactly what has happened? Could we have ravaged and polluted the planet as we have done if we truly held it and the life it supports in awe? Yet once we have realized the extent of our 'autism,' once we have acknowledged how dulled we have allowed our senses to become, it is a small step to begin to see again through the eyes of wonder.

The poet Walt Whitman never lost his sense of the magic and wonder of life; there is nothing to stop us being the same.

Why, who makes much of a miracle?
As to me I know of nothing else but miracles,
Whether I walk the streets of Manhattan,
Or dart my sight over the roofs of houses toward the sky,
Or wade with naked feet along the beach just in the edge of the water,
Or stand under trees in the woods,
Or talk by day with any one I love, or sleep in the bed at night
with any one I love,
Or sit at table at dinner with the rest,
Or look at strangers opposite me riding in the car,
Or watch honey-bees busy around the hive of a summer forenoon,
Or animals feeding in the fields,
Or birds, or the wonderfulness of insects in the air,
Or the wonderfulness of the sundown, or of stars shining so quiet

and bright,
Or the exquisite delicate thin curve of the new moon in spring;
These with the rest, one and all, are to me miracles,
The whole referring, yet each distinct and in its place.

To me every hour of the light and dark is a miracle,
Every cubic inch of space is a miracle,
Every square yard of the surface of the earth is spread with the same,
Every foot of the interior swarms with the same.
To me the sea is a continual miracle,
The fishes that swim — the rocks — the motion of the waves — the
  ships with men in them,
What stranger miracles are there? [3]

Annie Dillard, who like Walt Whitman has refused to let go that sense of 'consciously being,' speaks of her own awakening, aged five, in her book *An American Childhood*. She says:

"Who could ever tire of this heart-stopping transition, of the breakthrough shift between seeing and knowing you see, between being and knowing you be?" [4]

Yet in our culture we often tire very quickly. Our potential to be amazed at 'being' is buried under words, numbers, measurements, explanations. 'Seeing differently' in this respect involves being consciously aware of the deadening effect of the attitude which teaches its young so early to 'take for granted' the moment by moment miracle of 'being.'

The *Via Positiva* invites us to live our lives open to wonder, to embrace again awe and reverence, to be consciously alive within the present moment...the eternal 'now.' To 'see and to know we see, to be and to know we be.'

The *Via Negativa*: Embracing the dark. Letting pain be pain.
*I said to my soul – be still
and let the dark come upon you
which shall be the darkness of God.* [5]

The second path is possibly the most radical in that it takes an alternative route towards understanding and embracing what is described as the 'paradox of good and evil.'

Starting from the wider awareness that the wholeness within which we have our being contains and reconciles all opposites, this path calls us to enter into the pain and the tragedy of existence. Instead of denying the pain and sorrow, we allow ourselves to feel and experience it; instead of conquering the darkness by will-power or stoicism, we acknowledge it, living with it and through it.

Embracing the dark, allowing pain to be pain and dark to be dark is not wallowing in misery and being martyrs, neither is it indulging in pessimism, nor is it trying to surmount pain by strength of will and denial.

Yet just as our culture distances our sensitivities from wonder and delight, so it does with respect to the dark and negative side of being; rather than face and acknowledge it, we seek to deny it.

Culturally our way of dealing with the darker side of existence follows the path that emerged in the eighteenth century during that period known as the 'Enlightenment,' when we set ourselves to control and defeat Nature. We, the human race, will surmount and defeat the pain and struggle of life. Virtually all our Western industrial, technological and materialistic society is a reflection of that attitude.

"Every added protection against the natural world contributes its bit to the steadily building illusion of independence from Nature, so that in time the greatest of illusions is erected: the omnipotence of 'man.'"[6]

As well as a devaluing of Nature without, we in the West have long devalued our own human nature. As Carl Jung points out:

"The predominantly rationalistic European finds much that is human alien to him, and he prides himself on this without realizing that his rationality is won at the expense of his vitality, and that the primitive part of his personality is consequently condemned to a more or less underground existence."[7]

This is a very clear reflection of our Western approach and its consequences; it is not the questioning human spirit that is in question here but its direction.

If our cultural assumption is that we can defeat and overcome suffering, and overrule the basic expressions of emotion within ourselves, then an admission of these realities is seen as failure. The result of this denial is the 'stiff upper lip' strength of will, the suppression of the natural expression of grief, and so on. Further results of this denial of the dark side are the ecological disasters that we are causing in our attempts to 'fix the world.' These results are now coming back to haunt us.

Above all, the *Via Negativa* is about 'letting go.' Letting go our desire to control and manipulate, to be 'in charge.'

There is nothing easy about the *Via Negativa*. It is not a 'spiritual' formula for finding another way to avoid suffering. It is only possible to move beyond suffering by going through it. The *Via Negativa* offers a different kind of strength, a vulnerable strength that willingly acknowledges the suffering and embraces it.

As Matthew Fox says: 'When the heart is broken, compassion can begin to flow.'[8]

Paradoxically the *Via Negativa* and the *Via Positiva* are the Yin and the Yang, the necessary correlation of each other. The extent of our willingness to embrace and engage with the darkness is in direct proportion to our openness to awe, wonder and delight. Moreover, to the extent that we deny the reality that wholeness includes both dark and light, both pain and joy, to that extent we diminish and undermine our own spiritual growth.

Man was made for joy and woe
And when this we rightly know
Through the world we safely go.[9]

LET THE DARK BE DARK.

The old voices kept insisting
Make up your mind
Now.
Refuse to suffer,
Indecision is weak,
Not knowing is a dumb game.
But the new voice whispered . . .
Wait . . .
Stay in the darkness.
It will enclose you as velvet,
Embrace the pain,
For it is a necessity of new birth.
And do not reject 'not knowing'
For to stand humbly with
Uncertainty
Is both trust and wisdom.
The answer will come in its own time...
Not yours.

There is, however, a darker side, which requires all our wisdom and courage to recognize. It springs directly out of the great venture of the universe—moving as it has towards consciousness—for contained within that lies the human gift of choice. Thus our human desire to avoid the dark and pain has also given rise to the pursuit of power over others. This has resulted in the devaluation and abuse of human by human. Here then is a subversion of the true *Via Negativa* and we need to recognize and acknowledge it.

We also need to acknowledge all the hidden potentials within ourselves, both 'dark' and 'bright,' all the unlived parts of self that Carl Jung described as the Shadow. For only by accepting all of what we are can we ever become whole.

The *Via Creativa:* Expressing our own true selves.

"You must give birth to your images. They are the future waiting to be born...Fear not the strangeness you feel. The future must enter into you long before it happens. [10]

The universe has unfolded to this point. It has poured into you the creative powers necessary for its further development. The journey of the Cosmos depends upon those creatures and elements existing now, you among them. For the unfolding of the universe your creativity is as essential as the creativity inherent in the fireball."[11]

The third path calls us to connect again with that creative power which already dwells within us, yet, as with so much else that was once spontaneous, our culture has numbed us to its voice by imposing a narrow definition of what is and what is not 'creative.' Most people, by the time they reach the adult world have lost touch with, as well as confidence in, their inner creative energy.

Yet this is a terrible denial of the reality of who we are; each one a unique expression of this sacred energy that unfolds itself in never ending abundance.

Trusting that creativity in each of us does not mean we should all become painters, musicians or poets, but what it does mean is that we shall learn again to trust our deepest feelings. It will mean giving birth to ideas and imagination, play and surprise, boldness and intuition.

Yes, as Rilke says, the future must enter into us before it happens, and that future will be formed by how these dreams and visions within us are either listened to and honored, or ignored.

Suppressing the natural creative energy within a person will result in it returning, thwarted, in a more destructive guise.

"Do you create, or do you destroy?" Dag Hammarskjold once asked. We cannot be neutral.

The greatest and most important thing we can do with our lives is to be who we truly are. But unless we pay attention to allowing this creative energy that is within us to express itself, then it will never be seen. There is no duplication; we are, each one of us, 'one-offs.' As every leaf and every blade of grass is unrepeatable, so are we.

The quotation used by Nelson Mandela in his inaugural speech is addressed to every member of the human race.

"Our deepest fear is not that we are inadequate.
Our deepest fear is that we are powerful beyond measure.
It is our light, not our darkness, that most frightens us." [12]

The *Via Transformativa*: Embracing Compassion, Justice and Wisdom.

"Nothing has changed, except the way I see things—and so everything has changed."
(Author unknown.)

The fourth path, named the *Via Transformativa*, brings the insights of compassion, justice and wisdom to bear upon our interpretation of the previous three paths, most particularly upon that of the *Via Creativa*. Do we create or do we destroy? Our creativity will need the compassionate direction of wisdom and justice, for we are not puppets. We are a species with self-awareness, a species that knows it knows, a species with the power to choose.

Our conditioning is deep however, and we slip back into old patterns of seeing so easily. Yet each small illumination, each seemingly slight shift in perception is a step along the way of our Cosmic unfolding.

I want in this final path to name five subtle transformations in perception that will mark our journey as the new vision of who we are dawns upon us.

From consumer to partaker.

As the new story penetrates our consciousness we see ourselves no longer as consumers but as partakers. A consumer devours without thought or consideration, as we currently devour and consume the precious life-sustaining systems of our planet. A partaker starts from a different viewpoint. A partaker shares, aware of mutual interdependence, a partaker takes only what is fair and just.

From observer to participant.

We are not detached observers in an inanimate world, which is the predominantly held view in our current western attitude towards life on this planet. However much we may prefer to be detached, we are not. The awareness of our total dependence upon our planet and our interconnectedness, will transform us from detached observers to participants. A participant, as with a partaker, comes from within, not without, as a member of the Earth community: active, responsible, compassionate, and involved.

From Tourists to Pilgrims.

"Put off thy shoes from off thy feet, for the place whereon thou standest is holy ground."
(Exodus 3:5)

A pilgrim is one who recognizes and seeks the sacred. The vision here is that of GreenSpirit, which views the whole of creation as sacred and thus worthy of reverence and awe. Within the attitude of the pilgrim seeking and recognizing the sacred there comes an enrichment, an enhancement of both parties. (Try it and see!) The tourist, on the other hand, is concerned with superficialities, a detached visitor to the planet, unconcerned with deeper meanings.

From Masters to Co-Creators, and from Doers to Listeners.

Both of these shifts acknowledge the reality that we, as humans, are not 'in control.' Yet our role—as the conscious self-awareness of the evolving Earth-community—is far from a passive one; it calls us to embrace our cosmic destiny as active participants in the great unfolding. No longer an embattled species in an alien world, we see ourselves as responsible co-creators, using all our wisdom and compassion to work with, and not against, Nature.

We now face our greatest challenge: how do we exercise that gift of self-conscious awareness that is ours?

"It is we who are alive today who have the responsibility of guiding this species on. It is we who have to find ways to release ourselves to the full significance of the present time."[13]

The reader can easily recognize that each one of these four paths points to nothing more nor less than 'a different way of seeing.' Nothing has changed except that we now know where we truly belong. We know that we are inextricably a part of a cosmic evolution, which here and now on a small planet on the edge of the Milky Way has blossomed into consciousness. We are that blossoming. We are the universe aware of itself.

We may choose to consider the dawn of consciousness as 'pure chance' or as 'pre-ordained'; the responsibility upon the human as the beneficiary of that awareness remains the same.

"What is the human?" asks Brian Swimme. "The human is a space, an opening, where the universe celebrates its existence."[14]

Each path weaves in and out of the others, each enhances and supports the others. Primarily, as stated at the start of this chapter, they are 'enablers' enabling us to see differently, thus becoming conscious participants in the unfolding of the great Cosmic Symphony in which every note counts.

"Because you are aware of the limits of life, you are compelled to bring forth what is within you; this is the only time you have to show yourself. You can't hold back or hide in a cave... the drama of the Cosmic story won't allow it. The supreme insistence of life is that you enter the adventure of creating yourself." [15]

Notes

1   Hillman, J (Ed.) *Re-visioning Psychology* (Harper Row, 1992)
2   Fox, M. *Creation Spirituality* (HarperSanFrancisco, 1991) p.19
3.   Whitman, W. *Leaves of Grass* (Project Gutenberg)
4.   Dillard, A. 'From *An American Childhood* ' in *The Annie Dillard Reader* (Harper Perennial, 1994) p. 140
5.   Eliot, T.S. 'East Coker,' in *Collected Poems, 1909-1962* (Faber & Faber, 1974)
6.   Turner, F *Beyond Geography: the Western Spirit Against the*

Wilderness (Rutgers University Press, 1992)
7. Jung, C.G. *Memories, Dreams Reflections* (Vintage Books, 1965) p.245
8. Fox, M. *The Four Paths of Creation Spirituality* (St. James's Church, 1987)
9. Blake, W. 'Auguries of Innocence' in Stevenson, W.H. (Ed.)*Blake: the Complete Poems*, (Longmans, 1989) p. 589
10. Rilke, R.M. *Letters to a Young Poet*, trans. Burnham, J.M. (Ingram, 2000) Letter 3
11. Swimme, B. *The Universe is a Green Dragon* (Bear & Co., 1984) p. 29
12. Williamson, M. *A Return to Love* (Harper Collins, 1992)
13. Russell, P. *A White Hole in Time* (HarperSanFrancisco, 1992) p. 224
14. Swimme, B. *op. cit.* p. 146
15. Swimme, B. *op. cit.* p. 117

The material in this chapter was adapted from Grace Blindell's popular booklet *What is Creation Spirituality?* published by The Association for Creation Spirituality in 2001.

The poem 'Let the Dark Be Dark' is by the Author.

11. Transformation

June Raymond

"Nature's path to God is direct, eternal and objective, without external chance."

So wrote Edith Sodergran. She understood that creation is our teacher and that in it is a truth that can act as a reliable guide to our own spiritual journey. Studying creation from its beginning, from the birth of the stars to the movement of life on our own planet, we find that evolution is punctuated by times of breakdown and destruction which become the gateway to new levels of complexity and awareness. This observation underlies the thought of both Teilhard de Chardin and his disciple Thomas Berry and it is at the heart of all major spiritualities and religions. It is reflected in the life-death-life pattern of the pre-patriarchal, goddess religions, as it is in the Christian Easter mystery.

In popular Western culture, however, it has become rather an unreal theory, probably because modern life has distanced us so effectively from Nature and her rhythms that they are no longer part of our lived experience.

Electricity means that we do not know sunrise as a daily miracle or winter as a closing down of life and beyond this we are protected from the fact of death itself as no earlier peoples have ever been.

A word we commonly give to this process of breakdown and rebirth when it occurs in our own lives is 'transformation.' But wherever we find it, modern humanity tends to run away from it in fear. In the poem, 'The Love song of J Alfred Prufrock,' Eliot expresses this powerfully as he explores his hero's inability to "ask the overwhelming question" and the terror that leads him to spend his life on trivia, "to measure out (his) life with coffee spoons," rather than face fundamental questions about himself and the meaning of his existence. Such questions will inevitably lead to a death, in his case involving particularly his own self esteem.

Today a collective 'overwhelming question', which we are barely beginning to ask, involves the future of our planet itself. It is an issue which seems to stare us in the face and yet for many people, especially those in high places, it is taboo. Possibly only those who have at some point in their lives dared to ask such questions or who have lived through experiences that seemed to destroy all that they held most dear and survived, can look at the questions at the heart of GreenSpirit and live with confidence in their hearts rather than terror. For it is on the edge of chaos that creative things happen.

Living the life-death-life process is radical and demanding, a hard birth and one that involves trust. It is about learning the power of powerlessness.

The process of transformation is the enemy of any sort of religion that imposes sameness. It is an inevitable part of growth and implies a spirituality of a personal journey and evolution.

When old patterns are no longer useful or simply don't work any more, systems break down and are replaced by new ones. The process is not one of a gradual transition as of for example a leaf unfolding. It is more akin to the transformation of a cater-pillar into a butterfly. The larva goes on eating and getting bigger until one day further development in its present form is no longer a possibility. Then instead of gradually changing into its adult form it spins a cocoon and waits suspended from a leaf while a process over which it has no control occurs. The form of the cater-pillar breaks down completely so that inside the chrysalis there is something like a soup, and it is out of this soup that a completely new life form evolves.

So in our journeys we can come to times when answers or patterns of behavior that worked in the past don't work any more and to a greater or lesser degree we enter some form of dark night in which we feel no longer in control. To pursue the analogy of the caterpillar a bit further, the ego is dying, and a more evolved and spiritual level of our journey is unfolding. The Self, the divine center from which we come, becomes more conscious and our kinship with Spirit in all life and indeed in all creation becomes less a matter of theory and more our lived experience.

This essay was first published in the Winter 2001 issue of the GreenSpirit Journal.

12. Something is Amiss in the World of Religion

Matthew Fox

Religion is in crisis the world over.

Islam has a problem, Christianity has a problem, Hinduism has a problem, Buddhism has a problem, the indigenous people have their problems, and of course the solution to religion's problems has always been spirituality, because that is the heart and the essence of any religion when it is being true to itself. Jesus came along at a time when his religion was in trouble. As Buddha came along at a time when Hinduism was in trouble, Martin Luther King came along in a time when Christianity in America was in trouble and Gandhi came along in a time when Hinduism was in trouble, etcetera.

So we're living in a time when the religious consciousness of humanity has to wake up, has to be reinvented, reborn, simplified and the name for simplification of religion has been spirituality. We have to carry spirituality much more lightly into the twenty first century. We don't have to carry 2,000 years of religious history on our backs in the West. In fact we can't afford to. There is not enough time left for our species. We have to simplify, simplify, simplify, not just our economic lives but our religious lives.

Thomas Berry names for us the context, the context for all human efforts including spirituality, and that context is the cosmology itself. It is creation itself. In 14,000,000,000 years of history, our species had been blessed long before we arrived because the universe made decisions time and time again on our behalf, without which we would not have arrived. This Earth would not have happened. The fine-tuning of oxygen that was so necessary for our delicate lungs would not have occurred. Many,

many, many decisions since the first millisecond of the fireball have been on our behalf. Einstein was asked years ago "What's the most important question you can ask in life?" and his answer was "Is the universe a friendly place or not?" The universe is not without terror, but that is the whole point. Beauty and terror go together. We do not live in a pretty universe. We live in a beautiful universe and that implies terror.

So by placing our history in the context of the history of the universe and of course the history of Earth, Thomas Berry has reset the stage for all our religions to wake up, to simplify themselves, to clean up their acts and for each individual among us, to find our center.

We are made for the universe itself. Our souls are cosmic in size but when we live in a culture that through the industrial and the modern age has set up corporations, fast food, plastic, malls, as somehow the archetypal temples for our souls, what really happens is that our souls shrink. We become smaller than we really are and far smaller than our ancestors were because they related to the universe.

We now live in an era where Father Sky can be responded to once again and what we're learning about Father Sky today is phenomenal, thanks to the Hubble telescope and other explorations. During the modern age we were told that the universe was essentially a machine. The sky was a junkyard for machine parts and it was dead and inert out there and I think in that context we shrank our souls. Especially men, because we had no place to invest in our greatness. I think violence and war achieved such huge proportions in human history because we were no longer connected to the universe. Our psyches had no cosmic bride, no cosmic husband to relate to.

All that is shifting today of course and Thomas Berry is one of the pioneers to point this out to us. He says:

"A constant awareness of the spatial context of life gives to human beings a deep security, but to move from the abiding spatial context of personal identity to a sense of identity with an emergent universe is a transition that has, even now, not been accomplished in any comprehensive manner within any of the world's spiritual traditions." [1]

Every spiritual tradition needs now to reawaken itself to its own cosmic dimensions and this will mean a cleaning up of our religious heritages for sure. And a simplifying.

It is there in the heart. As the Native American teacher Black Elk puts it: "True peace begins in the heart with the heart's relationship to the universe."

If we do not have a heart relationship to the universe, we shall never be at peace. We shall never be peace makers, because we are not living in peace. We are living in pieces, anthropocentric pieces of shopping and competing and beating up on one another with our superiority complexes, whether of race or gender, nationalism, economics or speciesism.

We must reset our entire cosmology, our entire spirituality in the context of cosmology and from a theological point of view of course, this is simply declaring, re-declaring, re-understanding, that the great temple of God is the temple of the universe. Every other temple, mosque, church, cathedral, whatever is merely a microcosmic expression of the great temple of the universe. The temple of the universe as Berry insists is not just spatial. It is historic. It is moving. It is moving along. It is expanding. It is growing and dying and being reborn. All those mysteries are part of the history that we are on board for because we *are* the drama. We are part of the theatre that the temple of the universe is about and the temple is not a noun. The temple is a verb.

A second gift of spirituality that Thomas Berry helps name for us is that the moral choices we make are about the local place in the cosmos that we call Earth, our planet. As Berry says, "Ecology is functional cosmology." So ecology is about what's going on in our neighborhood, and our neighborhood is the Earth. The Earth is part of the big cosmic going on but it is here that we will challenge all our professions to be morally based again. You are not a lawyer, you are not an educator, you are not a priest, you are not a healer, a doctor, a nurse for your own ego. You are committing yourself to serve with the skills, with the history, with the ancestry of your profession. We are all here to be healers in some way and ecology is functional cosmology. This means we must redo all of our professions, all of our work in the context of the sacredness of the universe, the sacredness of this Earth and the sacredness of the generations to come. For it is the ones not yet born who are the real judges of our morality today.

And morality is about choice. It is about the choices we make to choose the path of right behavior, the path of sustainability. I would propose that sustainability is a twenty first century word for justice. Because justice is all about balance, justice is all about harmony. Justice is about finding the equilibrium within society, within human societies connecting to other societies, to other species and within one's own self and one's own local relationships. So justice cuts through all relationships.

Friendship presumes justice. Meister Eckhart said in the fourteenth century that there is no love between master and slave. There can only be love, he said, where there is equality or where there is a struggle for equality. That is friendship. And Thomas Aquinas, who was mentor to both Thomas Berry and to Meister Eckhart, said that "All beings of the universe are questing for friendship. All beings love one another." When we get back to this understanding of ourselves as beings, not just as male, female, gay, straight, professional, unprofessional, employed, unemployed, English, British, Hindu, Buddhist, Muslim, what have you...we go deeper, deeper, deeper to the level of being. That is where morality itself is going to wash us anew with the energy and the inspiration to make a difference.

So what Berry has done then by saying that "Ecology is

functional cosmology" is to reset our moral base and again this is very indigenous because indigenous people, for example the Native Americans, the Celtic people of the European lands and the native peoples of Africa, are not given to purely speculative thinking, as we are. For them, all thinking leads to behavior. Behavior is what morality is about. How are we behaving or misbehaving? How does what we think about the universe and about the Earth and about our bodies, translate into our everyday behavior? In a recent survey, 27 percent of respondents said they were not interested in environment. Maybe if the researchers had not used the word 'environment' but had asked "Are you interested in food?" they would have gotten 100 percent 'yes' answers. 'Environment' sounds like an abstraction but the truth is the food comes from the environment. Most of us try to have it about three times a day. It is a pretty intimate relationship, what we choose to eat and don't eat and why and why not.

A third gift from Thomas Berry about spirituality is a statement he has made more than once, which is that we should put the Bible on the shelf for 20 years. Now this is a radical statement for someone who comes out of a Christian tradition, or it seems to be. But he is pointing out several things here. First of all, that religion goes to war over the silliest things, like holy books that in fact contradict themselves and always have to be interpreted by every generation because they are full of metaphors and no metaphor can be interpreted literally. One thing I have learned late in life is that everything important in life is a metaphor. Which is another way of saying that literalism is never important.

Think about it. Love is a metaphor, spirit is a metaphor, God is a metaphor, sex is a metaphor, death is a metaphor. If you cannot think metaphorically you are not even here yet. To try and turn the Bible into a literal canon of laws is an insult to everyone who contributed to that amazing document and also it is an insult to your own intelligence and to the God that created you with intelligence. "Put the Bible on the shelf for 20 years" he says. What is Thomas Berry telling us?

His mentor Thomas Aquinas said: "Revelation comes in two volumes: the Bible and Nature." What Thomas Berry is telling us is that the revelation of Nature has been shelved for hundreds of years in the West. We put Nature on a shelf and we go to war over the Bible. For example how many seminaries of any denomination in the West have mystical scientists on their faculty? In my program that I ran for 29 years, I hired mystical scientists. They are much more interesting than Biblical theologians. They are not all wrapped up in languages and words. They are looking out at the cosmos, they are looking at creation, they are looking at the temple. The *real* temple, not the human-built temple. They are looking at the sacredness of being.

So that is just one obvious test. I say not only should we put the Bible on the shelf for 20 years. We should shut down every seminary in the world for at least six months and re-invent seminary education so it starts from the revelation of Nature because the revelation of Nature is 14,000,000,000 years older than the Bible. And what kind of an insult is it to say that the Bible, which is a book about 2,500 years old, is the only source of revelation?

In England, the Anglican Church has been burning itself down over the so-called issue of homosexuality. Yet the homosexuality issue is an issue of science. The Bible is no more qualified to tell us about the morality of homosexuality than it is to tell us about whether the Earth goes around the sun or the sun goes around the Earth, and I thought we wrestled with these issues 400 years ago. Pope John Paul II, 25 years ago when he lifted the 400-year condemnation of Galileo, was very proud of himself. We all held our breath for that one, didn't we, for 400 years? And when he did that, the Pope said "Well there's a lesson here that religion has something to learn from science." Well he is right about that but he has not learned the lesson because he,

135

like his successor, has contributed to the ongoing bashing of gays. A bishop in Africa, leading the crusade to destroy the Anglican Church in the name of homophobia, said "Well homosexuality is unnatural." Has he consulted a scientist about that? Because scientists do explore the nature of things and so far they have counted 464 other species with homosexual populations, including dolphins, dogs, cats, many birds...and it goes on and on and on.

So it is not unnatural, it is natural. It is a minority, but homosexuality is natural for that minority. What would be unnatural would be condemning that minority into heterosexual marriages when they're not geared to that. So this is a scientific question, this very question that is burning down about half of the western religions at this time in history. Are we going to consult science or are we going to hide in our man-made books?

Another contribution from Thomas Berry is his emphasis on creativity. This we now know is a law of the universe. From its beginning 14,000,000,000 years ago, this universe has been birthing, birthing, birthing and birthing. It is profoundly immersed in creativity. How different this is from Newton's view that the universe was a machine, the process of creation essentially done and we were here to fit in and be obedient. Didn't that set us up for the militarism of the twentieth century, that obedience was a way to fit into the universe? It was a mistake.

What the universe sets us up for is creativity. As Meister Eckhart said in the fourteenth century "What does God do all day long? God lies in a maternity bed giving birth." It's a bias in the heart of the universe, this bias towards creativity. Thomas Berry, in his book *The Great Work*, connects creativity to wildness. He says:

"Wildness we might consider as a route of the authentic spontaneities of any being. It is that wellspring of creativity whence come the instinctive activities that enable all living beings to obtain their food, to find shelter, to bring forth their young, to sing and dance and fly through the air and swim through the depths of the sea. This is the same inner tendency that evokes the insight of the poet, the skill of the artist and the power of the shaman." [2]

Notice how we marry so beautifully what the whales are doing, what the flowers and the trees are doing and what the poets and the shamans and we are doing. It all comes from one wellspring of creativity, our shared wildness. A spirituality that does not lead us to the fountains of wildness and the sources of our creativity is not a spirituality. It is a control chip. It is part of the problem and in no way part of the solution. Because I believe that all human solutions to the corner into which we have painted ourselves today, of ecological degradation and so forth, are going to come from our creativity. Creativity is the strongest thing our species has going for it.

It is also the most dangerous thing our species has going for it. With our creativity, we can build gas ovens and we have. We can build nuclear bombs and we have. We can build nuclear submarines and we have, or we can tear down rainforests in a day that have taken Nature 10,000 years to give birth to and will never be repeated, will never be replanted. We do that with our creativity and we also can reinvent the way we live on the planet, with different forms of energy, different forms of transportation, with simpler lifestyles and so forth. All that is about our creativity.

None of our religions have all the answers and even if we gathered the wisdom of all, that's not enough today. We have to bring in the wisdom of science and I would say yes, the wisdom of technology and even then we have to give birth to new forms of worship, to new forms of celebration, to new forms of forgiveness. And yes, of grieving. I was very inspired in terms of my work with the cosmic mass to do that kind of thing, to create new forms of worship and I have seen people's hearts turn very fast. You see that's what healthy liturgy, healthy ritual does. It is the shortcut to bringing the universe in and you do it with aesthetics, with beauty, with joy, with wonder.

The great work that Thomas Berry calls us to is to put our spirituality into action. That spirituality without action is not spirituality. Love without action is not love. Love without affecting our behavior is not effective.

If human history survives and our species survives into the twenty second century, believe that history will record that among us a certain prophet rose in the latter part of the twentieth century, imbued with the spirit of Teilhard de Chardin, the intellect of Aquinas, the Eros of Hildegard, the humility of Francis, the science of Einstein and the courage and imagination of Jesus. His name was Thomas Berry. We will remember him by carrying on his vision, by building institutions and movements and infiltrating all of our professions from education to politics, to business to worship, with his many and sustainable visions and, surely, spirituality.

Notes

1. Berry, T. *The Great Work* (Random House, 2000) p.190
2. *ibid.* p.51

This chapter is an edited and abridged version of a talk given at the 'Earth is Community' event held in London in September, 2007, to honor the life and work of Thomas Berry.

.

13. Spirit in East and West

Jean Hardy

The author of the previous chapter, Matthew Fox, in one of his early books *Western Spirituality*, celebrates the roots and sources of all organized religion:

> "...all spirituality is about roots. For all spirituality is about living a non-superficial and therefore a deep, rooted, or radical life. Roots are collective and therefore not merely personal..." [1]

This was part of his discovery in Paris, in his years spent there 1968-70, working for a doctorate at the Institut Catholique de Paris on the relationship between prayer, mysticism, and social justice. He was already a Dominican priest, and in his late twenties.

His choice of teacher was key to the whole of the rest of his life. Pere M.D. Chenu, was then in his seventies and a medieval scholar, a wise and profound thinker. Matthew signed up for a seminar on 'Spirituality in the Twelfth Century' (in Europe, of course). Chenu taught that there are two traditions in Christianity which are, and have been from its very early days: 'Fall/Redemption' which looks for the redemption of a fallen humanity and, alternatively, 'Creation-centered spirituality' which rejoices in the Earth and human beings within it.

Fox writes in his book *Confessions* that in learning of the existence of this second alternative choice, "...scales fell from my eyes: I was bumped from my horse!" [2] He found a resonance between the liberation protests then in full swing at the Sorbonne and elsewhere in the Western world in 1968, and his subsequent study of the creation doctrines that a much earlier Christian church had taught at various times in its long history. He learned that the Catholic church had once accepted that a human could be seen as a microcosm of divine Nature; in the twelfth century, this was exemplified in the glorious Cathedral at Chartres. A contemporary nun, Hildegard of Bingen in Germany, who died in 1179, celebrated, both in writing and music, her concept of the human being, rejoicing in a divine world, finding her soul through relationship with God in the universe, recognizing this connection was subjective.

St Francis of Assisi was born just after Hildegard's death, in Italy, in 1181, and was strongly influenced by Celtic Christianity. Francis' relationship with Brother Sun, Brother Wind, Sister Poverty, was remarkable in his acknowledgement of the human dependency on—and love of—the rest of creation.

Discoveries of the changing nature of the early Christian church led to the work that Matthew Fox undertook in reading many European mystics over the next years, particularly Meister Eckhart, Thomas Aquinas, Catherine of Siena and many women in the Catholic and Celtic traditions, making their experience available to others in his readable books. He writes that those three years in Paris were the foundation for the work of the next 24 years of his life.

In his first Appendix in *Original Blessing*[3], called 'Toward a family tree of creation-centered spirituality,' Matthew quotes large sections of The Hebrew Bible, especially the Wisdom literature and the Psalms, as the foundation of creation awareness. He specifies and highlights the wisdom aspects of the New Testament. He values profoundly the teachings of Jesus Christ himself, and his "prophetic and compassionate ministry," which gloried in the natural world: "Consider the lilies of the field...Solomon in all his glory was not arrayed like one of these." All the men named at the beginning of Matthew's list, from St Irenaeus, Bishop of Lyons (c130-220), and St Ephraim (306-373), to St Benedict (480-550), contributed Eastern influences, presumably mainly from the Byzantine Church at that time.

Western Christianity became a formal part of the Roman Empire from its adoption by the Emperor Constantine (306-337 C.E.) at the Council of Nicea in 325. It has ever since then been in position of power, an imperial religion, in states and kingdoms and throughout the institutionalization of the Church itself. Later, in Ireland, a softer, gentler, much less patriarchal and more Earth-centered Christianity developed. This Celtic stream was, however, symbolically defeated at the Synod of Whitby in England in 664 C.E., partly over the question of defining the date of Easter, a key dogma, and the Western church in Europe became more and more forcibly and universally defined by Rome through the Holy Roman Empire.

Doctrines of the Church were decided and judged by big, international convocations in the Early Church. The key decision about the nature of humankind was made in the Council of Carthage in 418, in a dispute between St Augustine, who had no doubt of the reality of original sin which he believed to be inborn, and therefore of the 'fallenness' of the human race and its need for redemption, as against Pelagius and his followers who believed that:

"Since each soul is, as he believes, created by God, it cannot come into the world soiled by original sin transmitted from Adam"[4]

Pelagius' view was outlawed in unambiguous terms at Carthage and Ephesus. The Augustinian understanding has prevailed in the Church, by and large, for the rest of its history, and to this day.

The doctrine of Original Sin was not accepted by the Byzantine Church, which was more optimistic in its view of human nature, though it was accepted that divine Grace is needed for the ordinary human being to live without sin.

These then are the issues that Chenu discussed in Paris in the late 1960s,[5] and which were the spark which led to Matthew Fox's work tracing a more 'Pelagian' view through his research, his books and the formulation of Creation Spirituality. In most conventional Christian churches, however, we are still 'miserable sinners...with no health in us.'

At the Institute for Creation-Centered Spirituality, set up by Matthew Fox and others in 1977 in Mundelein College in Chicago, a powerful strand in the teaching was to draw on quite alternative and distinct views of human nature found in cultures other than Christian. Indigenous religions and spirituality, and the Eastern religions of Hinduism, Taoism, Confucianism and Buddhism carry no sense of original sin, in contrast to most of the Christian churches, both Catholic and Protestant.

Thomas Berry was among the staff at the Center after it moved to California in 1983, and brought not only "his prophetic voice of outrage at the killing of the planet" and his elegant writing which was made manifest in his joint book *The Universe Story*, produced with another staff member, cosmologist Brian Swimme, published in 1992[6], but also his profound knowledge of the religions of the Orient. His book, *Religions of India* was published in 1994, and represents a long lifetime's work.

Berry has high respect for the quality of Asian spiritual understanding:

"These spiritual traditions of Asia are so highly developed that they frequently attain a level that corresponds more with the higher mystical traditions of the West than with its ordinary levels of religious and moral life" [7]

They are about existential questions (expressed in male terms).

"They intend to make man truly man by carrying him beyond himself to a participation in divine existence, for only there is man truly what he should be, only there are the sorrows of life totally healed, only there is the full vision of truth."[8]

Joseph Campbell puts it very succinctly:

"The whole point of Oriental wisdom and mythic themes is that we are not in exile—but that the god is within you."[9]

The symbols used may be different for the vast impersonal forces, creation and destruction, that rule the universe— Brahman, Tao, Ma'at—but the forces they represent are the same, they are of Nature, of the cosmos, and they are the forces that operate within us all and all living creatures. The energies of creation and destruction are directly within all living beings, including humans, and those forces make the whole universe work; the opposites are not on different sides, but are all part of the same natural process. There is no original sin, though of course there are moral, spiritual and ethical questions pervading all life, and much suffering pervades the living world, frequently caused by people.

Where Christ in Christianity is seen as a unique being, and is the mediator to the Father, in Eastern religions there is no inter-mediary; you have the deepest universal spirit within you if you can only realize it. It is you.

Western thinkers, mystics, have come to be freed from what Campbell calls "our shut-in lives" by this liberating though quite disturbing Eastern vision of reality. And we can now see that the insight has long been present, if not usually recognized for what it is, in the West. There is a liberating spiritual element in the Romantic poets of the nineteenth century who were in touch with eastern thought through Coleridge: in the American Transcendentalists: early Quakerism: and above all in the Christian mystics, many of whom have been rejected by the Church.

It is quite impossible to do more than mention something of the vast literature of the East, which started to be translated into Western languages in the nineteenth century. The major Hindu text is the Bhagavad-Gita, which is part of the Vedic tradition, and is concerned with how a person can act effectively and morally in the world yet remain tranquil, following the leadings of the divine within and growing into the larger soul. The teachings of the Buddha are concerned with the nature of suffering in the world, and how to live without adding to it, either for yourself or others. The richness, depth and variety of oriental spiritual thought is limitless, across many cultures over time. There are of course many accretions to this fundamental point—concerning gender and caste issues in particular—but that is also true of Christianity.

Eastern and Western spiritual understanding is at last meeting in creation-centered spirituality, and in many forms throughout the world, and is evolving toward a new vision of reality and action for humans at this time. Will it be in time to change our actions?

"The same stream of life that runs through my veins night and day runs through the world and dances in rhythmic measures.

It is the same life that shoots in joy through the dust of the earth in numberless blades of grass and breaks into tumultuous waves of leaves and flowers.

It is the same life that is rocked in the ocean-cradle of birth and of death, in ebb and in flow"

– Gitanjali. Rabindranath Tagore.

Notes
1. Fox, M. *Western Spirituality* (Bear & Company, 1981) p.1
2. — *Confessions* (HarperSanFrancisco, 1996) pp.69/70
3. — *Original Blessing* (Bear & Company, 1983)
4. Kelly, J.N.D. *Early Christian Doctrines* (A&C Black, 1983)

p.358

5. Chenu, M.D. *Nature , Man and Society in the Twelfth Century* (University of Toronto Press, 1997)

6. Swimme, B. and Berry, T. *The Universe Story* (Harper, 1992)

7. Berry, T. *Religions of India* (Columbia University Press, 1996) page 1 of Introduction to the First Edition

8. *ibid*. p.6

9. Campbell, J. *Myths of Light* (New World Library, 2003) p.2

14. On Christ

June Raymond

People often ask me why I remain a Christian despite all the negative and limiting things about the system.

The following is a very personal response to this question, not an attempt to suggest that what is right for me will necessarily be everyone's path.

It is also a reflection on some of the issues about who we are and what is our place within the cosmic order. Sometimes we have seen humanity as the best and sometimes as the worst thing in creation and sometimes as totally irrelevant! I am writing from the view point of the Little Prince who says that "only the heart sees truly," not for any sentimental reasons but because it seems to me that any other approach ends by going round and round in circles until it becomes an abstraction rather than a description of reality. The circumstances of the destruction of our planet are too urgent to be dealt with in any superficial way.

Above all, as I work with people I find that in the end the heart must be healed if there is to be any lasting improvement to physical or psychological health.

At the heart of the cosmos is the dynamic of love, but it is a polarity of joy and pain, presence and absence. Every star, atom, stone, plant, all mountains and oceans, insects and tigers, carry this dynamic at every moment. Stars blaze into being and eventually die just as the transitory beauty and delicacy of a flower inevitably fades. Daylight is followed by darkness and the life of summer is replaced by the cold of winter. The animal kingdom in particular often experiences death in what seems to us the cruelest ways. Everything in Nature lives in balance with this dynamic and none protest.

In the human heart love is most consciously itself. The English mystic, Julian of Norwich, says that while God's presence is in all creation, in us "is his homeliest home." So it is that we experience the pain of the absence of love, its other face, in a way that is unique. Often it is too much for us to bear and in an effort to deal with the intensity of our pain we stifle love that is the cause of it. So we humans, capable of the fullest experience creation can know of the joy, the keenness of cosmic love, deny it and unaware, we suppress life itself. This is no mere abstraction for hymn writers and theologians. At the practical level, the resulting disorder is manifest first in our emotional health and then in our bodies. As the life force is partially blocked and can no longer flow freely, disease and dysfunction eventually set in. And because we are not separate from but intrinsic to the rest of creation, the life force of everything on our planet is affected: atoms, stones, plants, mountains, oceans, insects and tigers.

Where we have the courage and skill to unwrap our pain; disease or anger, terror or despair, at its core we find the pain of the absence of love, a pain so real that in comparison, all other suffering seems to us acceptable.

In my own case when I look for the Ariadne's thread that will lead me back through the labyrinth of denial and confusion I find Christ on the Cross. This is where I see the meaning we have all been searching for, the core within my own heart, the heart of humanity and of Creation itself that is able to contain the wholeness of the joy and the pain of love together. Here is the pain of love rejected in a heart that is able to hold the suffering without denying love.

For the last two millennia the Western world has honored this truth and sustained its power. When I listen to Bach's St Matthew's Passion or look at the paintings of Giotto I catch glimpses of our collective intuition and know that what they are witness to is far deeper than philosophy or science.

And so to return to my original question: why I remain a Christian while disapproving of so much that organized religion stands for. It obviously is not because I love the institution. On the whole I don't, but the best of it as well as its shadow is part of me and in this strange mystery of Christ I find my deepest being and a way back to the truths that transform and offer meaning and hope. I know we all share in these things wherever we come from and would never value less those people whose perspectives about them are different.

Nevertheless I am glad of this particular faith, I don't take it for granted and am profoundly grateful for all I have received through it.

This essay was first published in the Winter 2002 issue of the GreenSpirit Journal.

15. Green Buddhism

Joyce Edmond-Smith

Whilst there is general consensus concerning the magnitude of the challenge facing humanity, there is as yet little recognition that it is essentially a spiritual crisis and requires much more than practical and technocratic changes or political posturing.

For those trying to grapple with how to respond to the situation, the Dharma (that is, the guidance and teachings given some two and a half thousand years ago by Shakyamuni Buddha) offers an explanation as to why we have reached the present social and ecological catastrophe and a way forward to enable humanity to realize its true place and relationship with the planet.

It is important to see that the ecological crisis that threatens all life, and perhaps the planet itself, is part and parcel of the social, economic and political structures humans have created. It is about how we live and what we are. Human beings have separated themselves, as individuals, as groups, and as a species from the 'other', but Buddhism teaches that everything is part of everything else. This is not just a question of 'linking' with Nature, caring for Nature or 'going back to Nature.' It is that we *are* Nature and Nature (everything) is us. This is what the Buddhist teacher Thich Nhat Hanh calls 'interbeing.'[1] It is traditionally expressed in the metaphor of the jeweled net of Indra, where at every intersection there is a clear jewel and where the jewels all reflect each other's images, appearing in each other's reflection ad infinitum. "In one is all in many is one." There is no sense here that Nature is 'at the service' of humanity, nor that humanity dominates Nature; on the contrary, by harming and destroying other sentient beings and their environment, we are harming and destroying ourselves.

Buddhist ethical teachings uphold this with the precept of non-injury and the *Metta Sutta* [2] which enjoins the practice of loving kindness towards all beings "...be they timid, bold, long, short, big or small, visible or invisible, near or far." Hence the Haiku :

Fireflies
Entering my house
Don't despise them [3]

But if we are interdependent with everything, what is the implication for our sense of 'self'? The Dharma teaches that our sense of self as 'individuals' different and 'other' to everyone and everything—a feeling which is mirrored at group and global level as well as with regard to the whole of Nature—is a delusion. As a delusion it is insecure, so to bolster our sense of self and to allay our deep anxiety we spend vast amounts of energy and resources on activities to make our 'self' feel good. At worst the duality between ourselves and other human beings leads to wars and aggression and that between ourselves and the biosphere leads us to act as if it is there essentially for us to use and abuse at will. This is of course not to say that Buddhism teaches that we don't exist, but rather that our sense of self is more a psychological and social construct than an unchanging reality (which indeed is echoed by much recent psychological research).

This delusion leads to the alienation which is at the heart of the teachings on suffering. Buddha taught that there is suffering and that there is a way out of suffering. Suffering is caused by the three Fires: Greed, Aggression, and Delusion. These are the fires that we can see raging away and destroying our world. To escape our anxiety at our separation we crave things 'outside': money, success, power, goods. Our attempt to secure them can lead to hatred, to conflict and, with the creation of our political/socio-economic systems, these fires have become profoundly embedded and amplified in our modern society, bringing us to the edge of ecological catastrophe. Such as the idea of 'economic growth.' When will there be enough growth? Growth is open-ended; the carrying capacity of the planet is not.

So what does Buddhism offer as a remedy? First, one is enjoined to act. One of the great archetypal figures at the heart of Mahayana Buddhist practice is the Bodhisattva, who is the embodiment of the two prime Buddhist virtues of Compassion and Wisdom and who hears and responds to the pain of the world. Hence one of the Buddhist vows: "Beings are numberless. We vow to free them all." Or as Thich Nhat Hanh says "Once there is seeing there must be action." That action needs to be buttressed by an ever-growing awareness of our oneness, our lack of separateness. It is the inner work of 'practice' or meditation which can lead us to such awareness.

"To Study the Way is to study the self.
To study the self is to forget the self.
To forget the self is to be enlightened by all things.
To be enlightened by all things is to remove the barriers between oneself and other." [4]

Or as Kenneth Kraft says:

"An abiding faith in the fundamental interconnectedness of all existence provides many individuals' activities with the energy and focus that enables them to stay the course."[5]

But action without the grounding of meditative practice can lead to burn-out or to increasing anger and frustration, which can only add to the fires. As The Network of Engaged Buddhists[6] sees it, it is essential to combine the cultivation of inner peace and awareness with social compassion in a mutually supportive and enriching practice.

So what does this all mean for the situation we find ourselves in where crises, fed by the three fires, seem to be piling up: conflict, financial breakdown, food and water shortages, species loss and that overwhelming danger that overlays and feeds everything else, the heating up of our planet to a point where all life is threatened. It is clear that humanity has lost its way and that only a profound personal and collective transformation can bring about the change we need. As the Dalai Lama has said:

"In recognition of human frailty and weakness, the qualities of (moral scruples, compassion, and humility) are only accessible through forceful individual development in a conducive social milieu, so that a more human world will come into being as an ultimate goal...a dynamic revolution is deemed crucial for instigating a political culture founded on moral ethics." [7]

This is what Ken Jones, a Zen teacher, calls "A Radical Culture of Awakening" [8] and Joanna Macey [9] calls "The Great Turning." The move to such a change in consciousness or spiritual awakening would be one and the same with the move to a more harmonious society. Engaged Buddhism aims to encourage such a transformation, where not only our behavior and lifestyles change, but so does our relationship with the world around us of which we are a part, and where wisdom and compassion are the motivating forces. This would require a personal examination as well as complete questioning of presently accepted assumptions about globalization, economic development, needs and wants. A world where humans live in harmony with the biosphere is possible and each and every one of us can be involved in bringing about such a transformation. And, indeed, there are signs everywhere that it is already on the way: The Transition Town movement, the ideas and planning for a Steady State Society [10], the in-depth questioning of the place of greed in our society brought about by the collapse of financial institutions, as well as the many groups working to stop climate change, and the hundreds of groups and organizations involved in a wide range of movements towards a better world. But this will not go far enough without the inner work which Buddhism and other bodies which include spiritual training have to offer. We are all Bodhisattvas now.

Notes

1. Thich Nhat Hanh *The Heart of the Buddha's Teaching* (Random House, 1998) p.225
2. The Metta Sutta is part of the Suttinapata which contains some of the oldest Buddhist texts, in Kaza, S. and Kraft, K. (Eds) *Dharma Rain: Sources of Buddhist Environmentalism.* (Shambhala, 2000) p.29
3. Dogen , in Batchelor, M and Brown, K (Eds) *Buddhism and Ecology* (Cassell,1992) page14
4. Dogen, Shobogenzo, in Cook, F.H. *Sounds of Valley Streams: Enlightenment in Dogen's Zen* (SUNY, 1989) p.66
5. Kraft , K. 'The Greening of Buddhist Practice', in *Cross Currents : Journal of the Association for Religion and Intellectual Life* 44 (2)
6. Indra's Net , Journal of the Network of Engaged Buddhists www.engagedbuddhists.org.uk
7. The Dalai Lama, *Collected Statements, Interviews and Articles,* 1982, in Jones, K. *The New Social Face of Buddhism* (Wisdom Publications, 2003)
8. Jones, K. *op. cit.*
9. Macy, J and Brown, M.Y. *Coming Back to Life,* (New Society Publishers 2008)
10. New Economics Foundation, 'A Green New Deal' www.neweconomics.org

16. Green Judaism: Alaskan Salmon Taught me Bible

Rabbi Jamie Korngold

I once lived in a small tent, on a gravel bar, on the outskirts of a rainy Alaskan fishing town called Cordova. The town was so small that there were two roads, a handful of stop signs, and no traffic lights.

The main road started at the docks, where fisherman hauled supplies back and forth between town and their boats. From there the road headed up Main Street, past the post-office, grocery store, general store and café, and then headed out of town, past my gravel bar and finally a mile or so out to the canneries, where I worked. There the road curved back into the sea, where incessant waves washed onto the gravel.

Each morning at 4:30 a.m., my alarm jarred me from a deep sleep. The rain, which had lulled me to sleep at night, usually still played a tapping rhythm on the tent fly in the morning. I unzipped my sleeping bag quickly, like tearing off a Band-Aid so it won't hurt, and scrambled out into the tent vestibule where I kept my grimy work clothing. I liked to pretend this separation kept my tent somewhat clean.

I pulled on long underwear, wool pants, a shirt, and a fleece jacket, rain gear, boots, and finally my homemade knit hat, and stepped out into another Alaskan morning. I walked half a mile along the coast to the salmon processing plant, where I worked 18 hours a day gutting fish on the 'slime-line.' The factory was loud, despite my double set of earplugs, cold, despite my wool layers and raingear, and smelly. Oh, did it stink! The work was repetitive and tiresome, but the money was good.

Toward the middle of August, when the rains began in earnest, our makeshift campground began to flood. My neighbors and I put our tents up on wooden pallets, first one high, and then two high. One morning I awoke to strange thrashing sounds. I looked outside and saw that the gravel bar had practically become a lake, and the salmon were trying to swim across it. But the water was so low that the salmon couldn't actually swim, so they just sort of thrashed up against the gravel, indignantly pushing their way through the rocks, and many were suffocating in the low water.

A local explained that the river used to flow fast and free through what was now our campground. However, when the area had been mined for gravel, a few years ago, the river had been redirected a quarter mile to the east, and the salmon, which had spawned in that river for centuries, had not gotten the memo that the river had been moved. When it is time for salmon to lay eggs, they swim up river, back home, and even if the river that used to be home is no longer there, they still try to 'go home,' so to speak.

When I lived in Alaska, it was easy to see first-hand the inter-connectedness of human beings and Nature. Every day I saw the impact of our choices on the land and sea around us, and I became acutely aware of the power and resilience of Nature, but also of its vulnerability.

Now that I live in the lower 48 however, it is much more difficult to get the connection between driving or cranking the air-conditioning and the food shortage riots on the other side of the globe. Paying close to $100 to fill my gas tank or cooling my house hurts my wallet, but it's just not the same as having confused salmon swim through your living room.

Some days, I think the rise in gas prices is the best thing to happen to America in a long time. As my husband rides off to the office on his bike, and the kids 'carpool' to gymnastics in a bike trailer, I realize the higher gas prices have pushed us to conserve as we should have years ago.

I worry that legislation will lower the prices again and we will revert to our irresponsible consumption. We must remember that conservation is not just a financial issue but also a moral one.

As a rabbi, my moral compass is religion. What does the Bible teach me is my role in regards to Nature?

One of the first things God does in the Bible, directly after placing Adam in the Garden of Eden, is to lay out Adam's job description: "And the Lord God took the man, and put him into the Garden of Eden to till it and tend it." (Genesis 2.15)

The crux of the Bible's ecological arguments is the humility expressed in this verse, "to till it and tend it." The Earth is not ours; we are simply caretakers of God's creation, the Earth.

There are many other scriptural passages that build on this, to which I turn for inspiration and instruction. Perhaps the most prescient is a breath-taking passage in the Jewish scriptural text, Midrash Ecclesiastes Rabbah, written around 800 C.E., which says:

"When God created the first human beings, God led them around the garden of Eden and said: 'Look at my works! See how beautiful they are, how excellent! For your sake I created them all. See to it that you do not spoil and destroy My world; for if you do, there will be no one else to repair it.'"

I am amazed that these prescient words were written so many years ago, and that even then there was concern that we might spoil and destroy the Earth. This additional text makes it clear that although God made the Earth for us, God did not intend for us to use it recklessly. It is God's Earth, not ours. "Take good care of it," God commands. What a clear call to action! Fortunately, today, many religious leaders have come to understand this message and many churches and synagogues are now leaders in the environmental movement.

For me, an equally strong call to action, and perhaps an even stronger argument for taking care of the Earth, comes from something more immediate than the text. Some of my colleagues wonder what could be stronger than the words of the Bible, but for me it is the feeling I have when I am outdoors, riding my bike past a green pasture filled with blue chicory flowers as far as my eye can see, or sitting on the red rock high above town and watching a hawk ride the thermals round and round.

As the Adventure Rabbi, I am extremely blessed to have created a rabbinate that allows me to combine and share my twin passions of Judaism and Nature. Accompanied by my community, I celebrate Shabbat on skis and on hiking trails, Passover surrounded by the red rock of Moab Utah, and Rosh Hashanah in the high mountains of Colorado. You see for me, Nature is spiritually potent, a place of indescribable connection, ripe with spiritual awakenings. Wilderness is a place where I learn more about myself, my community and my God. When I combine it with Judaism, the potential for transformative experiences abounds.

My Jewish outdoor experiences educate me in the same way the salmon in Alaska did. They both teach me that we must take care of the planet, for as we destroy the Earth (either through action or lack thereof) we destroy our opportunity for spirit, and we destroy ourselves.

In the words of the Psalmist:

"How many things You have made, O Lord; You have made them all with wisdom; the earth is full of Your creations....May the glory of the Lord endure forever." (Psalms 104:24&31)

May we have the wisdom, the tenacity, and the fortitude to help God's garden endure.

17. The Ecology of Heart: A Sufi Journey

Neil Douglas-Klotz

Love flies without limits.
Cuts through all veils.
Rejects the life you knew without looking back.
Gives up on feet entirely—much too slow!
Sees right through appearances.
Ignores obsession and addiction.
My soul remembers its source:
I was in the potter's hands while
he mixed clay and water—
a new home for me, I think.
The kiln is hot. I'm trying to escape!
Willing, unwilling—what does it matter?
No longer resisting, I get kneaded and molded,
just like every other lump of clay.
–Mevlana Jelaluddin Rumi [1]

"Die before death."
–traditional Sufi saying

My journey into the Sufi path began like this:

In June 1976, a little after 2 a.m., I found myself speeding through a moonless night in the middle of the Great Salt Desert in Utah. Working as a freelance ecology journalist in my mid-twenties, I was traveling from Denver to San Francisco. I had hitched a ride, and, along with a chance companion, was picked up by a small Toyota truck driven by a man in his thirties with short-cropped black hair, wearing a frayed Army surplus jacket.

A few hours into the ride, the driver revealed that he had been in and out of several mental institutions and was driving to San

Francisco to "claim his girl". The maniacal expression around his eyes, which we had thought to be driver's fatigue, began to take on other, more ominous meanings. Unknown to us riders at the time, under the camper van in back of the truck was a huge boulder that the driver later told us he was taking to California to "carve." With all of that hidden weight unsecured in the back, any quick change of direction at speed would put the truck into a roll. But we didn't know that until a few hours later.

I could spin the story out a bit longer, but at 2 a.m., in the middle of a dark, two-lane highway, we began to pitch back and forth in reaction to a small, but sudden steering change. I felt fright, confusion and anger at the strange way the truck was acting. I still didn't know about the boulder in the back, and it didn't make sense. As an alternative journalist, I had spent most of my too-brief adult life trying to make sense out of things. We were out of control, and there was no more time for making sense. As the truck rolled over, just before I blacked out, the fast-action life review many people talk about happened.

I grew up in a multi-cultural family near Chicago. My grandparents on both sides were refugees from Europe with German, Jewish, Russian and Polish blood in their veins. I was raised by parents who were both devout and free-thinking. They brought into my early life the impulse to worship and praise, as well as to question everything that constricted and opposed the injunction "love your neighbor as yourself." My father was one of the first chiropractors in Illinois, and he and my mother were students of the health education of Edgar Cayce, an American psychic. They raised me with a respect for the body and the wonders of Nature, as well as a disdain for the superficial innovations of humanity that polluted both body and Nature.

Hearing German, Yiddish and Polish in our home from childhood, having been raised on the stories and miracles of Jesus, and taught the practical truth of Rachel Carson's book *Silent Spring*, I formed an interest in language, spirituality, the body and ecological justice early in life.

After graduation from college in 1973, I pursued a career as a journalist in the fields of social justice, environmentalism and consumer protection for several years before turning to the following questions: Why do people change? What causes me to change? Is there a more powerful level of motivating change than that of ideas?

In the Great Salt Desert, when I regained consciousness, I was upside down, smelling petrol, spitting out sand and blood. Everyone was somehow still alive. Not only alive, the three of us pulled ourselves out of the truck, flipped it back over, and continued down the highway. For the next 24 hours I felt that my entire body or self had been torn apart and put back together, but all the pieces didn't fit. During the frantic rest of the trip, I was looking at a new, more frightening world.

I finally arrived at the apartment of a college friend in San Francisco, with no money, only a receipt for something called a 'Sufi Camp' in the woods of northern California, which was my original reason for coming West this time. The camp was supposed to teach walking, movement and dance to change one's consciousness. As a frustrated student of yoga, I thought it might make a good, lighter story, something to take my mind off my usual work.

I had been in a crisis about my work as a journalist ever since reading a poll in which Americans were asked a) whether they saw any feasible solution for the disposal of nuclear waste and b) whether, if there were no solution, they would be willing to give up some of the comforts that this form of energy brought. Seventy percent of those polled voted "no" to both questions. I concluded from this that people did not make decisions in life based on factual evidence or rational logic. Perhaps this should have been obvious to me, but I saw myself part of a generation of idealistic, crusading, independent journalists. Over the past 30 years, the centralization of the media in the hands of a few large corporations make such a way of spending one's time sound fanciful today.

One week later, at the Sufi Camp, I was standing in a circle holding hands in a group of people breathing in silence as the music to a Dance of Universal Peace died away. I was joyously, freely, fully me for an instant, a giant "Yes!" to the near-extinction of a week before. The Sufi path, I was told, accepted that there was truth behind all of the religions (including Nature religion). The main problem was not arguing about the details, but how to make the wisdom a reality in life. The great stresses that had blown me apart had somehow also allowed for a new putting-back-together to begin. For a moment at the end of one particular dance, I was both fully present and fully absent and the sense of 'I' was completely transformed. This realization did not last, but it pointed me in the direction of trying to make the experience a reality in my life. It took the better part of the next five years of work and practice to realize what had happened to me, and there were many peaks and valleys.

I had left Denver wondering how to change, how to get out of the rut I was in as a journalist. In an instant, the question itself had altered: if change is always going on, just as it does in Nature, how can I allow its effects to go on through me in the most beneficial way possible?

The Western Sufi Ahmed Murad Chishti (Murshid Samuel L. Lewis, d. 1971) once said, "The reason we don't solve problems is that the answers interfere with our concepts." We tend to look with and through our conscious mind, rather than going into the shadow side of our subconscious where the answers may lie.

In general, Sufi stories, poetry and spiritual practice aim to help us 'unlearn,' that is, to go beyond the emotional boundaries and mental concepts that enclose the sense of who we think we are. As we go beyond these boundaries, we find ourselves in the province of what one might call 'wild mind.' We discover an inner landscape that is both richer and less controlled than the safety of fixed ideas and rules. Gregory Bateson (1974) called this type of approach the 'ecology of mind,' recognizing that consciousness operates much more like an eco-system than anything else, and that 'mind' is embedded in an ecological reality, within and without.

Seven hundred years earlier, the Persian Sufi Mevlana Jelaluddin Rumi said something similar:

The inner being of a human being
is a jungle. Sometimes wolves dominate,
sometimes wild hogs. Be wary when you breathe!
At one moment gentle, generous qualities,
like Joseph's pass from one nature to another.
The next moment vicious qualities
move in hidden ways.
A bear begins to dance.
A goat kneels![2]

As we recover a sense of the wild within, we may also come into a new relationship with Nature outside us. Each being in the natural world is beautiful and of value in itself; each is a unique face of the inexpressible, Only Being, the divine Beloved.

Specific aspects of Sufi spiritual practice work with the part of our psyche called the 'animal soul' and even the 'plant soul.' The arrogance of considering only humanity worthy of an interior life is renounced. One begins to realize that no adequate life of any kind—'spiritual' or 'practical'—is possible without considering the whole of our nature, that which we fear as well as that which we enjoy.

In this sense, the types of Sufi poetry story and spiritual practice I relate in my books represent an early ecopsychology. This is no doubt one of the reasons why Sufi stories in particular appeal to the modern, Western mind. We have lived for hundreds of years in a cosmology that divides humanity from Nature and the sacred. One of the main insights of ecopsychology says that much of what we call a personal psychological problem finds its roots in a deep collective denial and despair about what is going on in our natural environment.

Only when the universe breaks through to shock us — through the death of someone close, through falling in love, through intense joy or through a confrontation with some experience we cannot categorize — do we waken from sleep. We "die before death" and have the opportunity to feel within us the greening of our heart and mind.

Notes

1. Douglas-Klotz, Neil. (2005). *The Sufi Book of Life: Ninety-nine Pathways of the Heart for the Modern Dervish*. New York: Penguin Putnam, p.37

2. Barks, C. *Delicious Laughter: Rambunctious Teaching Stories from the Mathnawi of Jelaluddin Rumi* (Maypop Books, 1990) p.113

18. On Devotion and Duty: A Pagan View

Emma Restall Orr

In 'alternative' circles, amongst those who consider themselves to be the ones who are truly thinking, the beliefs and practices of religion are often considered to be naive, unhelpful and even dangerous. Religion is effectively a dirty word. It implies faith in an intangible construct beyond experience or reason, those who believe only expressing a flaw of human weakness.

In my teenage years, my rebellion embraced such rejection of convention and its religious traditions, for clearly they were failing, my world crawling as it was through recession and nuclear fear. Furthermore, when age brought me to the brink of adulthood and I began to ponder my own identity, in common with many of my generation, being critical of religion was a part of the process of crafting an independent individuality. Nevertheless, and again not unusually, at much the same time, an inherent need to find a truly fundamental meaning and value to life drew me to dive into what was called spirituality. Somehow I could accept this word as one that didn't crush my sense of self, nor repress my right to find a personal vision of sanctity and truth. I still believed I was special, as was—I heroically asserted— each and every individual who was walking their own path.

Yet as life has moved through me, and yearly I recognize how very little I will ever know, as my fertility slips away and I reflect upon my middle age, and gently I accept that humankind really has little changed over many millennia, I find myself willing to acknowledge that I am in truth a deeply religious person.

What I am not is monotheistic. My religious perspective is one of the many broadly embraced by the term 'Pagan.' Rooted in the Latin *pagus*, a rural village, the word speaks of an important key within human attitudes: while the urban dweller (*cives*) relies upon civilized society for law and order, the *paganus* is dependent upon Nature, and so looks to Nature as his source of authority. So do Pagans still seek out and study Nature's patterns, her lore, in order to find an essential peace and well-being. One might say, then, that an environmental awareness is foundational to natural Paganism.

Of course, some Pagans transfer their allegiance from a Christian father deity to a belief in an ever-loving goddess expressed as Mother Nature. For most Pagans, however, such an attitude is deemed sentimental; Nature is rapacious, merciless, and to imagine she cares for humanity is to anthropomorphize her in a way that can only severely limit our comprehension of her. To most, there is no overseer, no conscious creator (or creatrix) propelled by a force of tender caring. Indeed, the wisdom of Nature comes not from some deity judging just who does and does not deserve what; the wisdom is in the balance that is Nature's exquisitely sharp knife-edge of tenability.

As an animist, I would say that wisdom is here not simply a poetic term, however. While traditional animism may acknowledge wind, river and mountain as inspirited, the modern animist cannot declare a line distinguishing that which is innately vital and that which is not alive; in the river, stream, pool or drop of shining water, as in the molecule, atom or subatomic particle, the animist accepts the vibrant forces of life to be inherent. It is these, the smallest building blocks of Nature, that inspire the flow of ongoing creativity. That I call it wisdom expresses my perception that Nature exists as a beautifully woven fabric of interactions, each one enriched by the wealth of possibly infinite experience. Yet each one's existence lingers too on that delicate edge of tenability.

This animistic perspective can be (and is, by some) under-stood with validity as spirituality or even a spiritual philosophy, but I am not content to say so for myself. For, though we may define religion as a set of shared beliefs that allows for coherent community, it is the word's association with deity that makes it fundamental to my point of view. My Paganism is not just animistic, but also polytheistic: the gods and my interaction with them are crucial to my life, for they are the currents of existence that underlie my every breath, and guide my every step.

Of the countless deities that populate the multiverse, many of those whom I revere might simply be perceived as forces of Nature. They hold an authority over me merely because, without adequate respect for their nature, my life or well-being would be comprehensively at risk: of the many I could name here, a handful are darkness, thunder, mist, lust, growth and decay. There is seldom any value in self-negating through subservience to such gods, nor is it sensible to attempt to control them. Our task is to learn all we can about their being, in order that we might live with them in richly beneficial and tenable relationship.

Yet, just as we human beings are not separate from but an integral part of that fabric of Nature, neither are we isolated in time. For hundreds of thousands of years, through the process of learning how to survive and thrive, our ancestors have been forging relationships with those same gods. Here then are further gods: mythic heroes, at one time perhaps ancestors themselves, raised to the status of deity. To the Pagan, these are the gods who guide us in those fundamental, critical and yet mysterious relationships that—socially and personally—we need to have with Nature. Here are the gods of myth and folklore, who wake us to be respectful, to be cautious, courageous, generous, loyal and grateful, that we may live in ways that would make our grandmothers, our grandfathers, proud.

Such a sense of connectedness is fundamental to natural Paganism. Where a religious perspective inspires us to explore the currents and patterns of Nature, we are inspired, also, to explore how those move through human nature, pushing and pulling us, flooding and parching us, provoking our selfishness and our breadth of empathy. In the experience of being wakefully human, part of the great river of ancestry, we hear the stories of our grandmothers, and in doing so we experience our innate connection to them; for every crisis of hunger, trauma, heartache and heartbreak, every betrayal and achievement, is a story that has been lived before. So do we find Nature's wisdom once more, for even here, authority comes not from some human declaration, but through the commitment of relationships, honed over generations, each walking its path along the knife-edge of tenability as though it were a broad and sun-blessed road.

This is the heart of my religion. For these gods of Nature, and the gods who teach us of Nature, inspire a non-selfish love that is absolute devotion—to a landscape, a tribe, a people—a devotion that makes us willing to die, to lose our 'selves' completely.

The understanding of, the visceral experience of, and the expression of this devotion is a central part of the natural Pagan's religious practice: it is the forging of honorable and sustainable relationship with the gods. We do it not just for ourselves, but, just as we reach to learn from our grandmothers, to offer a sound legacy to our grandchildren, and *their* grandchildren.

Yet we are still human. Though a sincere and devotional love may keep us wakefully unselfish, it can take a lifetime to achieve such a relationship that is not isolated but integrated, inspiring honorable interaction within the fabric of Nature as a whole. In reality, day to day, whatever our intention, we stumble, prioritizing, benefiting this to the detriment of that. Sometimes still selfishly we choose what we want.

We need a source of discipline. And here I use a word that many find as archaic and uncomfortable as religion: duty. I love the word. Rooted in the Latin *debere*, it reminds me of just what I owe and to whom. For if I am using only the keen blade of my wit and reason to decide how to behave, in truth I know I am capable of justifying the validity of almost any course of action; reason is not enough to counter the strength of wanting. Through duty, however, I cannot hide from the truth of all that has made me who I am: the environment and my ancestors. These are the powers of Nature within whom I perceive authority. What do I owe them, every day, moment by moment, for all they have given me?

I bow to the ancient gods, of rain and sunshine, of love, thunder, darkness and hunger, I bow to those ancient heroes of my people who now shimmer with divinity, listening to the ageless stories of my grandmothers as they walked the knife-edge finding peaceful, sustainable, tenable existence. That heart-fire of devotion glows within me. And when its heat burns low, I breathe in and set my feet to the road, remembering my duty, remembering.

So may it be.

Part III: Greening Our Culture

"Humans are capable of a unique trick, creating realities by first imagining them, by experiencing them in their minds. ...As soon as we sense the possibility of a more desirable world, we begin behaving differently, as though that world is starting to come into existence, as though, in our mind's eye, we are already there. The dream becomes an invisible force which pulls us forward. By this process it begins to come true. The act of imagining somehow makes it real... And what is possible in art becomes thinkable in life".

– Brian Eno

About Part III

19. The Vital Shift

Marian Van Eyk McCain

As Grace Blindell remarked in the first chapter, it must have been tremendously discombobulating, back in the sixteenth and seventeenth centuries, if you had spent your whole life believing what you were taught about the sun going round the Earth, to be told "Oops, sorry, we got it wrong; actually it is the *Earth* that moves." Especially since your eyes corroborated the old story. But in time, people came to acknowledge and understand the new story and adjusted their beliefs and attitudes accordingly.

Sadly, although it was eventually accepted that the Earth revolves around the sun, many millions of people believed—and unfortunately still do—that everything on Earth revolves around human beings. If you are human, that seems as obvious as the sun's 'journey' across the sky. Yet it is just as much an illusion

All the key institutions of our Western society are constructed on that erroneous, anthropocentric illusion. Yet anthropocentrism—the belief that everything revolves around humans and that the planet is just a big pile (a shrinking pile, now) of 'resources' for our use —has put the human race on 'death row.'

What the universe story has taught us, and what is becoming clearer from all the writings in this book up to this point, is that if we are to earn a reprieve, the foundation on which we have built our culture needs an urgent retrofit. We need to shift, urgently, from that outdated and dangerous anthropocentric perception to an ecocentric one if we are to have any hope of moving to a sane, sensible and sustainable way of life on this planet. Our survival, and that of many other species, depends on that all-important shift.

So the next question is: what will our institutions be like when we have retrofitted them with green foundations? If we put our green spirituality into practice and place the needs of Gaia — rather than our own narrow, human needs — at the center of everything, what are the implications for medicine, for education, for law, for economics, for the way things get grown, designed and built?

In the next part of the book, we turn to experts in all of these fields to hear their answers to that question.

20. Greening Health: Full Spectrum Wellness

John Travis and Meryn Callander

Part 1. John's Story: From Medicine to Wellness

My father had a big garden that he cultivated using natural methods such as composting. He was also a country doctor. By the age of five, I had decided to follow in his footsteps. But while taking my medical degree, I got discouraged by what modern medicine had become, compared to his practice.

Giving drugs to cover over symptoms didn't seem like a solution to me, so I looked at other approaches. During my internship, I was exposed to Benson's studies on lowering blood pressure via meditation, which amazed me. Soon after, I was introduced to 'natural' foods, and alternative lifestyles by a fellow intern. It was 1970, the hippie movement was in full flower, and my life opened up to a whole different way of being.

I was midway through a five-year training in preventive medicine when I realized that it was mostly just about early detection of disease, not true prevention at all.

It was then that I encountered *High-Level Wellness* by Halbert Dunn, MD, on the clearance table of the medical bookstore. The word 'wellness' was new to me, nevertheless, I spent two dollars on what was to be the best investment of my life.

This small, out-of-print book, published 11 years earlier, opened me to a whole new universe. Dunn's multidimensional view of health incorporated body, mind, emotions, and spirit. It was radical for that time and remains so even today. Seldom do health programs, conventional or alternative, pay more than lip service to the non-physical dimensions of emotions, mind, or spirit. Dunn provided the key to alleviate my frustration with the medical system's terminal focus on the physical body, disease, and drugs. His model offered the promise of true disease prevention and even more: his term 'high-level wellness.'

The first Earth Day had happened only two years before, *Silent Spring* was becoming well known, and by now I was living in an intentional community on 100 acres with an organic garden, yoga and meditation classes, and a strong focus on sustainable lifestyles.

I had also, through psychotherapy for my own marital problems, discovered that I had *feelings*, and had begun to explore the psychological dimension of wellness. That's when I began to realize that *the currency of wellness is connection*, beginning at birth. Although I was not to grasp this fully until later, I now believe it is the frequently failed connection with the mother—and subsequently all other relationships—actually *encouraged* by modern parenting practices, that leads to later addiction, depression and violence against each other and the environment we live in. (If we don't feel connected to the world, we don't see a need to take care of it.)

Although I thought the word 'wellness' was too weird-sounding ever to catch on, when I opened my little office in Mill Valley, California in 1975, I named it the Wellness Resource Center. When we found ourselves constantly spelling out 'w-e-l-l-n-e-s-s' to callers I began to regret this decision, but thanks to a colleague, Don Ardell, who wrote and spoke about wellness to hospitals and planning agencies, the word *did* catch on in the next few years, helped, too, by the *Wellness Workbook* that I co-authored with Regina Sara Ryan. In it we defined wellness as:

- A choice: a decision you make to move toward optimal health.
- A way of life: a lifestyle you design to achieve your highest potential for wellbeing.
- A process: a developing awareness that there is no endpoint, but that health and happiness are possible in each moment, here and now.

- A balanced channeling of energy: energy received from the environment, transformed within you, and returned to affect the world around you.
- The integration of body, mind, and spirit: the appreciation that everything you do, and think, and feel, and believe has an impact on your state of health and the health of the world.
- The loving acceptance of yourself.

Three key concepts in the book are:

1. The Illness-Wellness Continuum
Wellness is a process, never a static state.

Most of us think of wellness in terms of illness; we assume that the absence of illness indicates wellness. There are actually many degrees of wellness, just as there are many degrees of illness.

Treatment can bring you up to a 'neutral point' on the continuum, where the symptoms of disease have been alleviated. The wellness paradigm, which can be utilized at any point, helps you move further along the continuum toward higher levels of wellness.

Even though people often lack physical symptoms, they may still be bored, depressed, tense, anxious, or simply unhappy with their lives. Such emotional states often set the stage for physical and mental disease. Even cancer can be brought on by excessive stress that weakens the immune system. Negative emotional states can also lead to abuse of the body through smoking, excess of alcohol, and overeating, all of which may be seen as attempts to substitute for other more basic human needs such as acknowledgment and respect, a stimulating and supportive environment, and a sense of purpose and meaning.

Wellness is not a static state. High-level wellness involves giving good care to your physical self, using your mind constructively, expressing your emotions effectively, being creatively involved with those around you, and being concerned about your physical, psychological, and spiritual environments. In fact, it is not so much where you are on the continuum that is important, but *which direction you are facing*. High-level wellness does not preclude periods of illness and weakness, nor does it attempt to deny that death is a natural part of life. Contradictory as it sounds, even dying can be done from a place of wellness.

2. The Iceberg Model of Health and Disease

Illness and health are only the tip of an iceberg. To understand their causes, you must look below the surface.

Your current state of health, be it one of disease or vitality, is just like the tip of the iceberg. This is the apparent portion: the part that shows. If you don't like what you see, you can attempt to change it, do things to it, chisel away at an unwanted condition. But, whenever you knock some off, more of the same comes up to take its place.

To understand all that creates and supports your current state of health, you have to look underwater. The first level you encounter is the lifestyle/behavioral level: what you eat, how you use and exercise your body, how you relax and let go of stress, and how you safeguard yourself from the hazards around you.

Many of us follow lifestyles that we know are destructive, both to our own wellbeing and to that of our planet. Yet, we may feel powerless to change them. To understand why, we must look still deeper, to the cultural/psychological/motivational level. Here we find what moves us to lead the lifestyle we've chosen. We learn how powerfully our cultural norms influence us, sometimes in insidious ways, like convincing us that excessive thinness is attractive. We can learn, also, how our childhood experiences may have created defense mechanisms that in adulthood have become obstacles to intimacy.

Exploring below the cultural/psychological/motivational level, we encounter the spiritual/being/meaning realm. This includes the mystical and mysterious, plus everything in the unconscious mind, your reason for being, the real meaning of your life, or your place in the universe. The way in which you address these questions, and the answers you choose, underlie and permeate all of the layers above. Ultimately, this realm determines whether the tip of the iceberg, representing your state of health, is one of disease or wellness.

3. The Wellness Energy System

We are all energy transformers, connected with the whole universe. All our life processes, including illness, depend on how we manage energy.

We take in energy from all the sources around us, organize it, transform it, and return it to the environment around us. The efficient flow of energy is essential to wellness; disease is the result of any interference with this flow. This is true of energy usage in all life processes, from breathing to dying.

When the flow is balanced and smooth, you feel good. When there is interference at any point—the input, the output, or in between—you can feel empty, confused, pressured, or blocked. Illness is often the result.

***

As a result of the *Wellness Workbook*, I was soon traveling far and wide giving talks and workshops, especially to other helping professionals. Gradually, the world 'wellness' seeped into the language. But unfortunately, when the medical system co-opted the word, they gutted it of the mental, emotional, and spiritual components and continued to focus mostly on treatment, rather than the self-awareness, education, and growth that are central to the paradigm of wellness.

Meanwhile, seeing ever more clearly how unsustainable our modern culture had become I found myself tiring of life in the fast lane and longing for a simpler, self-sufficient life on a remote island.

That was when I met Meryn.

Meryn now takes up the story ...

Part 2. Meryn's Story: Making the Connections

I read about John and the Wellness Resource Center in Don Ardell's book *High Level Wellness*. A social worker with delinquent youth in Australia, I felt I was doing little more than applying Band-Aids. What I read about wellness excited me. How could I apply this to my work with these kids? A period of extended leave culminated in my participating in a program at the Center in California—and meeting John. He had just closed the Center and was ready for a major life change, and so began a relationship which was to lead to marriage.

In late 1980 we moved to the mountains of Costa Rica where we bought a 100-acre farm within a long-established intentional community of North American Quakers and attempted to live off the land. We became involved in what later became known as the Green movement, along with a lifestyle of voluntary simplicity, based on a book that had just been published by the same name. Becoming self-sufficient was more difficult than we expected, but we learned a lot and loved the lifestyle in Monteverde. We continued to make periodic visits to the United States, traveling about in a Volkswagen bus doing workshops for both helping professionals and the general public on various aspects of wellness.

We moved back to the States in the mid-1980s. Here, my immersion in feminist spirituality fueled my awareness that the wellness of an individual cannot be addressed in any meaningful way unless viewed within the context of the prevailing consciousness of our world. Many wellness concepts were not sustainable in the face of basic tenets of Western culture, particularly the belief that we are separate from each other, the Earth, and divinity. Healing our broken connection with our own inner being, each other, our Mother Earth and spirit seemed paramount. It seemed pointless to try to save a rainforest or stop a nuclear waste dump inside a mountain if the next generation came along and tried to do the same thing all over again. The realization that the prevailing culture is at the root of self-, other- and planet-destructing behaviors launched John and me into the next era of our wellness work, which we called 'CultureMaking.'

The *Wellness Associates Network for Helping Professionals* was launched in 1987. The Network was dedicated to developing an awareness of the impact of the prevailing cultural norms on personal and planetary wellness: affirming the immanent worth of self and other: fostering the norms of partnership and connection to replace those of domination and competition: and honoring the larger journey of life, individually and collectively, on planet Earth. We became more and more involved in political actions to try to reverse the destruction of the planet.

Then we discovered Jean Liedloff's *Continuum Concept*. This book radically impacted our understanding of the roots of wellness — and again, the power of the prevailing culture.

Liedloff had lived with the people of the Yequana and Sanema tribes in the rainforests of Venezuela off and on for several years. She found them to be the happiest people she had ever encountered. The children of these tribes never fought, were never punished, and obeyed their elders happily and instantly. The very young were seldom out of the arms of others, and were never left to cry; their discomforts were quickly soothed or alleviated. They were breastfed on demand, and continued to suckle for up to five years. In time, she concluded that we 'in civilization' are laboring under some serious misconceptions about human nature, and that the way we treat babies and children is a primary cause of the alienation, neurosis, and unhappiness that is so widespread in our culture.

Liedloff's experiences left me with a burning need to question not only the prevailing assumptions about the nature of humankind, but also 'popular' notions on how to nurture an infant or child. I determined to look beyond popular practices to find seeds for harvesting a new consciousness in the child we were soon to conceive, and in myself—if indeed Liedloff's observations were to be proved correct.

I found an abundance of research, both scientific and cross-cultural, supporting a clear association between early childcare practices and later personality development, health and wellbeing. The bond with the mother is primary, and is the foundation upon which all future bonds—with the family, then community, Earth and spirit—are predicated.

Relationships within the family shape the relationships that a child will manifest throughout his life, be they loving, cooperative and communicative, or selfish, violent, and isolating. This of course means that most of the aberrant behaviors we see around us are *not* innate to human nature, but are artifacts, symptomatic of a misperception—culturally perpetuated—of the needs of infants and children, and the nature of humankind.

Birthing and early child 'care' practices collude in destroying the natural connection between mother and child: separating the two at birth: denying the breast: abandoning infants into cribs, carriers, and a 'room all their own': anticipating discordant behavior. Add to these practices the fact that we live in a culture that denies the child's early awareness that matter is imbued with spirit, that the Earth is our home and we are a part of everything in it, and there is little wonder that we experience alienation and violent behaviors as the 'normal' condition of 'civilized' peoples. If we retained, as many native peoples do, the infant/child's awareness of our connectedness with all of life, we would not be able to do what we are doing to the planet and to each other.

Breaking this cycle of enculturated disconnection begins with recognizing the sensitivity and intelligence of the preborn and infant/child, who thrives on loving connections with others.

Cries or other attention-seeking behaviors are expressions of valid needs, *not* attempts to 'manipulate.' Innate needs include near constant physical contact (in-arms and in slings), breast-feeding on demand, and shared sleeping arrangements. Meeting these needs is not 'spoiling', but rather the best way to ensure optimal development. Connection-based parenting trusts that children *want* to cooperate and learn, respects their developing personalities, their unique interests and learning styles, and includes them in daily life and activities. Adopting even one of these practices will deeply impact a child's wellbeing.

We do not like to think that what we have done, or are doing, to our children is harming them, nor that what our parents did to us harmed us, yet we are all products of our time and culture. Neither guilt nor blame will serve us.

Clearly, there are difficulties in translating this knowledge into our daily lives. The difficulties range from a social and economic fabric that directly opposes continuum practices to the wounding that we each carry from our own childhood: the sense of estrangement that runs so deeply in each of us as to seem to be reality itself.

It becomes increasingly apparent that wellness is not about 'quick fixes.' Many will argue that we are powerless in the face of an economic and social structure and collective psyche that does not support such radical perspectives and proposals. However, if we are concerned for the future of our children and this planet, not to mention the liberation of our own minds, bodies, and spirits, we have no choice but to do our very best.

In 1993 John and I conceived our daughter, Siena. Convinced of the validity of connection parenting principles, in 1999 we co-founded, along with 11 other experts in various disciplines, the Alliance for Transforming the Lives of Children (aTLC). aTLC produced both a Proclamation and Blueprint of evidence-based actions that foster optimal human development.

In essence, our journey in wellness has taken us into an ever-deepening understanding that indeed the currency of wellness *is* connection, initially with the mother, and then with family, community, Earth, spirit. So nowadays, we speak of this whole-systems approach as 'full-spectrum wellness.'

Part 3. Full-Spectrum Wellness: a Multi-Dimensional Approach to Health and Wellbeing.

Full-spectrum wellness is about the connections between our state of wellbeing and:

- our body, emotions, mind, and spirit,
- our earliest life experiences and later health and personality development,
- our family, friends, and community, personal and work-life,
- our environment, from our internal mind-chatter, to our home space, our neighborhood, and the entire planet.

Full-spectrum wellness covers our entire lifespan. Full-spectrum wellness recognizes that the crucial connections established and nurtured (or not) during pregnancy, birth, and infancy shape the rest of a person's life, culminating in our transition at death. In addition to the linear spectrum of our lifespan, full-spectrum wellness addresses the wide range of energies that connect adults with their inner world, and the world around them, from their micro-environment to the whole planet.

Full-spectrum wellness recognizes that personal wellbeing is interdependent with the wellbeing of the planet. Today, findings from quantum physics validate what the mystics, our ancestors, and indigenous cultures have always known: *we live in an inter-dependent, interconnected world* and our every thought, feeling, and action, reverberates throughout the web of life.

As we begin to live more fully within our bodies and to recognize our connection to each other and to the Earth, cooper-ation and compassion replace the prevailing norms of competition and domination. Releasing old, fragmented, competitive ways of thinking, we recognize we are a global community. Rather than acting from duty or obligation, we act out of our wholeness and integrity as 'cells' of this larger body and grow beyond the Western ideal of individual rights and freedoms to a larger context of interdependence and compassionate connection.

As we become more aware of the impact of our thoughts and feelings on those around us, there is no place for blame and guilt. Blaming others, we avoid responsibility; feeling guilty, we blame ourselves and deny our power. Either way, we cast ourselves in the role of victim. By contrast, when we hold ourselves accountable, without blame or guilt, we simply recognize what is and acknowledge the role that we have played. This awakens our ability to respond creatively and propels us towards right action.

As we recognize the pain of the Earth and her creatures as *our* pain, and their beauty as *our* beauty, compassion floods our being. This, combined with skilful action, affords the means for restoring wellness to our world. Yet there is no endpoint where we can congratulate ourselves for having 'made it.' The ending of one era heralds the beginning of a new. Evolution is an ongoing process. Wellness is the journey, not the destination....

21. The Crisis in Education

Matthew Fox

The Dalai Lama says that education is in crisis the world over and I find that very comforting. That it is not just an Oakland problem or a California problem or an American problem or even a Western problem that education is in crisis. It is a human situation. Of course education is in crisis because our species is in crisis. Everything has to change.

Thomas Berry has a phrase: 'academic barbarism.' It is a very strong phrase. He was fired by a Jesuit university because they said what he was teaching was not Christian enough. Well the truth is that what he was teaching was exactly the teaching of the cosmic Christ. That the Christ is present in every being in the universe, just as the Buddha nature is. You see the omnipresence of the sacredness of our relationship to all things but that University, even though peopled by many Jesuits, had lost—as had all of western Christianity— the tradition of the cosmic Christ for about three or four hundred years because they lost the cosmos. How are you going to stay on the cosmic Christ if you don't have a cosmos?

Berry says most of the destruction on the planet is happening at the hands of people with PhDs. That's why it is barbarism. Barbarism is strong. Barbarism attacks. Barbarism is violent and it has weapons. A PhD can be a weapon. If you have only educated the left side of your brain, you are a dangerous person. Your culture is a dangerous culture and your education is extremely dangerous.

For 29 years I have been trying to reinvent education with

adults and the key to it, I have learned, is bringing in the creativity, bringing in what we call 'artist meditation,' bringing the body back to education and balancing the right hemisphere of the brain with the left hemisphere. Getting that dialectic going again so that when we give degrees it is not just for the left brain. It includes the right brain, the heart and all the chakras.

Now I've chosen to work with young people. I've linked up with a rapper and film maker — Professor Pitt we call him — and together we are working with inner city kids. Pitt grew up in the ghetto of Milwaukee and he learned Kung Fu when he was ten. Kung Fu saved his life, literally, and then he went on and learned tai chi, qigong and other spiritual forms of bodily prayer and he said he had been looking for years for someone with content. Then he found me and he said, "You're the guy." So we are linking up and we are now helping to reinvent education from the inner city out, from the bottom up. You can go online and find out more about this and about my latest book on education which is about the AWE. Project That stands for Ancestral Wisdom Education but also for awe: bringing awe back. That's what awakens the right brain — awe. When you awaken awe, you awaken reverence and you awaken gratitude. With that, then we would be releasing people on the Earth who are not violent, who are not selling their souls to chemical corporations or to people who tear down rainforests.

Connecting, reconnecting, conscience and education. Conscience and consciousness. It is possible.

Seventy-six percent of black boys in the US do not graduate from high school. Now you tell me, does that mean that these boys are stupid or does it mean that the adults running education are stupid and that we don't provide the variety of forms of education that are appropriate for a diverse species like ours? All studies in America show that the most creative kids in America are inner city kids and they are the ones most likely to be dying — literally dying — from bad education, because in the ghetto when you don't have education, incarceration follows.

I have written an essay entitled: 'Education Versus Incarceration'; to me these kids are the canary in the mine. It is just what the Dalai Lama says: if we can't change education, our species is doomed.

Except for fish, we are the only ones who go to school and we have to ask, is school part of the problem? You bet it is! Of course it is! But adults run schools so adults have to wake up. This is where your spirituality hits the road in reinventing our professions. I call school the funnel through which we pass so many of our professionals. They all go to school. That is what they have in common. That is what makes us dangerous. We have to change that funnel and it can be done. What I have learned from 29 years of working with adults is that tremendous things can happen in a week or two.

One fellow came in our program a few years ago. He had been teaching engineering at a great university in America for 29 years. He came in burned out by education and burned out by engineering, ready to quit both. In two weeks he came to me and said "I found my soul." He went back to his school and he started Engineers without Borders where they are sending engineers to Haiti, to the Amazon, to Africa to help people create solar generated irrigation systems and all the miracles that engineers can do when they have their hearts on board. He has had a conference every year. In 2006, 900 people came to his conference from 92 countries, many of them with inventions, simple inventions of purifying water and all the basic things that two-thirds of the world is without today. All this happened because he underwent a two week shift in education. So don't tell me we can't change education. You are not going to change it by going to the school boards and going through all the politics of it. No! You are going to change it by creating other forms of school and then people are going to realize hey, there's another way to do this.

185

This chapter is an edited and abridged version of a talk given at the 'Earth is Community' event held in London in September, 2007, to honor the life and work of Thomas Berry.

22. Touching The Earth

Ruth Meyers

"Above all, we need human beings who love the world."
— Gary Snyder[1]

When the Buddha became enlightened after a week of visiting his demons and sitting quietly with his strong reactions to those demons, the first simple but hugely symbolic gesture he made was to touch the ground as if to steady, root and embed himself on the planet. Thus he acknowledged his identification with the Earth and his participation and oneness with the raw clay of life. No longer alienated or entangled and tormented by his mind's meanderings, he presented to us, in this simple act, his authentic nature, his ground of being. Connection to the Earth is as basic a need as the air we breathe, the food we eat and the clothes we wear.

Without that feeling of participation in life, we are too easily led astray and may need to rescue ourselves at some crisis/opportunity point in our lives.

How is this need honored in our educational system? The relationship we have with our planet and the psychic health of us humans are interdependent and must support each other. If the planet's health reflects our health and vice versa, we need to start the healing process with some urgency. Our primary schools, in particular, have a golden opportunity to do so in a way that will impact on children for the rest of their lives. Reaching children early in this way offers them a way out of the estrangement and entanglement that lack of real contact with the Earth can so easily lead to. I reel at the absurdity of compartmentalized subjects floating around like untethered balloons and the madness of trying to squeeze these subjects into smaller and smaller time spans while balloons with new subject labels continue to appear on the horizon. All children need is a meaningful and contactful relationship with their world. If, as David Orr, Professor of Education at Oberlin College, Ohio, proclaims that "All education is environmental education,"[2] where do we start? How can we earth those balloons and invite those disparate subjects to join forces and come down to Earth, their rightful home?

How can children become ecologically literate and learn to cherish and love the world if they are never taken for a walk in the woods or even given a lump of clay to play with? Very many three year olds today are terrified of insects and spiders. From whom did they learn to be fearful, rather than curious? When we instill such a fear of the wild in our young children, their natural willingness to encounter their world contracts and withdraws. Rachel Carson wrote a book called *The Sense of Wonder*. She wrote that if she was to be the good fairy at the birth of a child she would bestow each child with a sense of wonder...

"...so indestructible that it would last throughout life, as an unfailing antidote against the boredom and disenchantments of later years, the sterile preoccupations with things that are artificial, the alienation from the sources of our strength."[3]

What responsibility do we take for seeing our own fears clearly so that we are not colluding in the closing down of a gift that the new child has innately? We can be that good fairy by allowing that natural interest to flourish and affirming the young child's reaching out to the environment. With their uncluttered and sharp vision they may show us things we've never seen before! Fear and its accompanying thoughts inhibit the dialectic that is a necessary component of relationship and kinship. A responsive and easy way of being on the planet is stolen from children if the adults around them are unable to participate in their enthusiasm and recoil at the sight of a tiny creature. All the senses need to be willingly engaged in relationship with the Earth and its creatures if environmental education is to be fruitful and meaningful for the developing child. Environmental education, like life, is essentially expansive and physical; it must break through those classroom walls. To re-establish our child's rightful home on this living, breathing, shifting body of the Earth, we adults too, need to get our hands and knees mucky and reconnect alongside them. "Nature," says Bill Plotkin, "has much to teach us in her vast classroom. You can acquire an entire education merely by observing carefully."[4]

By excluding Deep Ecology from the school curriculum, we deprive our children of community. Mother Nature is devalued as we struggle to tame and sanitize her wildness. In this way, we tell our children that the planet is a resource for our thoughtless manipulation and that it is perfectly acceptable to strive to acquire cars, cell phones, violent computer games or that 'street cred' you get from a pair of name-brand trainers made by cheap labor in a foreign sweatshop. Profit, at all costs, is the driving force. The 'hungry ghosts' of consumerism just get hungrier and hungrier; in fact, they are insatiable because money and profits, unlike Mother Nature, have no built-in, innate, moral limits, no self-regulating restraint. The Ancient Greeks understood the Earth as a mother and called her Gaia. It has now been scientifically recognized and acknowledged that Gaia acts as an intelligent, evolving, sustainable, self-regulatory and living being. Gaia's laws and systems of maintaining her health and wellbeing have an organic morality that has grown from the miracle of interdependence and connectedness. We ignore the wisdom of Gaia at our peril. As humans, we are blessed with the awareness and consciousness to see how Gaia's equilibrium has been shaken; we alone among beings have the capacity and therefore the responsibility to heal the damage we have inflicted. Our bodies are subject to the exact same laws of nature as Gaia, our Mother, and reflect that exquisite ability to withstand disease. Even under toxic attack, our bodies have huge reserves of rehabilitation if we could but trust that return journey home. What is rehabilitation but a refusal to disown those wounded, disparate parts of ourselves that have become refugees in our own psyches? To rehabilitate is to redress that balance. What does it mean to inhabit a home large enough to accommodate and welcome all the dislodged fragments? Preparing fresh lodgings for long forgotten wanderers is the process of atonement. This process of atonement (or 'at-one-ment') has to be evident in the schools and in our child-rearing attitudes. What more valuable gift can we give our children?

The accelerated pace of growth of the new technologies leaves us children of the sepia-tinted fifties reeling and suffering from acute culture shock. The youngsters very readily grasp these technologies and enthusiastically embrace new learning tools such as the interactive white board and ITC programs that are available to 'aid' every disembodied subject under the sun. There is no going back. But the more we move away from intimate contact and full-bodied (and full-blooded) knowledge of the environment towards distanced, simulated, virtual reality, easy access accumulation of data and images, the more we are removed from our Earthly roots at a time when reconnection, recollection and remembering are urgent and vital to save ourselves and this ailing and dysfunctional planet. How can we have moved from millennia of interrelation and interdependence on the planet to dependence and loss of relation in such a tiny time span? If a teacher is vexed because her interactive white-board or computer has broken down and 'computer rage' takes over when her prop is out of action, what could be a more vivid display of dependency and impotence than that? Where are her teacher's skills then? Total reliance on technology leaves us feeling impoverished and rather absurd.

Over the millennia, the intimacy of knowing the homely and local names of plants such as the 'jack-go-to bed-at-noon,' 'the heartsease,' or the 'eyebright,' together with the ability to differentiate plant types for their healing and culinary proprieties kept us with our feet reverently on the ground. We may have physically moved on from sustainable rural communities where close knowledge of the land was essential for survival but we have not moved on from that spiritual need for belonging and relation. What legacy has the loss of kinship left? We have evolved alongside the natural world; we are that clay. We delude ourselves if we imagine we can 'go it alone.' Only in our demonic imaginations have we outgrown our need for Gaia's benign presence and only in our fantasies do we really have power over her; only in such a 'hell realm' do we believe we can function without her. This illusion of 'power over' Nature is reflected in our loss of kinship with our children and our culture's loss of kinship with the Earth. As David Orr points out, we have created a monster in our educational system. "The planet," he says, "does not need more 'successful people.' But it does desperately need more peacemakers, healers, restorers, storytellers and lovers..." [5]

Notes

1. Snyder, G. 'Writers and the War against Nature' in *Resurgence* 239 p.12
2. Orr, D. *Ecological Literacy* (SUNY Press, 1992)
3. Carson, R. *The Sense of Wonder* (Harper Collins, 1998) p.54
4. Plotkin, B. *Nature and the Human Soul* (New World Library, 2007)
5. Orr, D. *Op. cit.*

23. Greening the Law

Cormac Cullinan

"The universe is a communion of subjects, not a collection of objects."

This observation by Thomas Berry is fundamental. For a lawyer this changes everything because almost all contemporary legal systems are based on the opposite premise.

In most legal systems the only subjects are human beings and those strange creatures we call 'juristic persons.' Juristic persons such as companies are created through what lawyers call a 'legal fiction' which means that even though we know they aren't really people, we choose to *pretend* that they are.

In the eyes of the law everything else, every other aspect of creation, is an object and consequently can't have rights. In the same way as defining some humans as objects (in other words, as slaves) made it lawful to abuse and exploit them, by defining Nature as a collection of objects or 'natural resources' the law legitimizes and facilitates the exploitation of Earth by humans. So it is not very difficult to see that any legal system that defines human beings and corporations as subjects and everything else on the planet as objects, will result in humans exploiting the rest of the Earth community.

In the field of human rights we now accept that each human being has certain fundamental human rights which cannot be taken away even if that person lives under an oppressive regime which legislates to deny those rights (for example by authorizing torture), and the courts uphold that law. We believe that each of us has these fundamental human rights by virtue of the fact that we exist as a human being. So if that is true for humans, it must be true for all the other members of this vast community with whom we have co-evolved in intimacy. They must also have fundamental rights by virtue of their existence.

If other members of the Earth community also have fundamental rights, what are those fundamental rights? Thomas Berry says that at the heart of it is the right to exist, which we all share. Secondly, we must each have a right to a place to be, to habitat. Thirdly, we must have the right to play our part within the continually unfolding story of this great community of life. After these fundamental rights, the rights of different members of the community may differ. As Thomas points out, the rights of a river would be of no use to an insect and *vice versa*.

The important thing is that the source of these rights is the universe itself or if you like, Earth. All members of the Earth community are entitled, as of right, to the basic conditions which allow them to live and flourish and to play their roles in this great community of life and these rights arise from Earth rather than from human laws. In other words there is a source of law that lies outside of the human realm. The laws from this source are currently not to be found in the law schools or legal institutions of the world.

When I first came across Thomas Berry's ideas about the origin of rights, I had a sense of *déjà vu* because as a white South African male I was born into the oppressor class within a society based on domination. When I was growing up in South Africa, apartheid was the political system and it was premised on the argument that one particular sector of the society, the white people, was inherently superior to the rest of the society. Accordingly it was appropriate to have a system of laws which allowed that group to dominate and exploit the rest of that society.

Eventually white South Africans found that they couldn't be free to be fully human, to be generous, to have connected relationships, or to experience a sense of belonging and self-worth while other South Africans were not free. The freedom of the oppressor class was inherently tied up with the freedom of the whole community and the only way for white people to be free was to give up domination and to recognize that everyone had human rights. The apartheid government tried to say "Oh we'll just be a little bit nicer to black people but we'll stay in charge. We just won't oppress them quite as badly." It didn't work. True freedom cannot be attained like that. The only way to achieve democracy and freedom is by going the whole hog and saying "We are a community and a community can only be healthy if it is based on the recognition that we are mutually interdependent and that everyone has certain fundamental basic rights that must be respected." Healing South African society could only be achieved by rejecting apartheid as a heresy and throwing out the political system and the laws that institution-alized it.

If the universe is a communion of subjects, the relationships or 'communion' between the subjects is fundamental because it constitutes that community. Natural communities are charac-terized by webs of intimate, symbiotic relationships, including food chains. We call our most intimate and intense relationships 'loving relationships' so in this sense we could say that much of Nature is a manifestation of incredible love. However, by and large legal systems promote exploitative rather than intimate, loving relationships between humans and the other members of the community that makes up Earth. Consequently it should not surprise us that the contemporary world is characterized primarily by destructive, alienated relationships between humans and the rest of Nature rather than intimate, mutually beneficial relationships.

Once we shift perspective from seeing humans as masters of a universe of inanimate objects to understanding that we are simply participants in a communion among many diverse members of a beautiful and complex community, it also changes how we respond to conflict. Instead of trying to resolve disputes like lawyers—meaning by reference to particular rules and who is right or wrong—we can respond like lovers who negotiate a solution based on a common desire to maintain the quality of an intimate relationship. In other words, in our relationships with the natural world we need to act more like lovers than lawyers.

More to the point (at least for lawyers) is how do we move to a situation where lawyers can be lovers? Lawyers who understand that human society is part of the wider Earth community will need to know more about the fundamental laws and principles that govern the Earth community as a whole if they are to give useful advice on how to regulate human conduct. In many cultures that have an intimate relationship with Nature, shamans are responsible for keeping an eye on the relationship between their human community and the rest of the natural world. Shamans are required to have expertise in both the laws of Nature and in human laws so that they can identify when humans are violating fundamental natural principles and make sure that corrective action is taken whenever necessary to maintain the dynamic balance between the two. Strange as it may sound, I think that the lawyers of today are going to have re-invent themselves and expand their expertise so that they can play a role in contemporary societies that is equivalent to that played by shamans in tribal societies.

We also need what I have called 'Wild Law.' Wildness is that thread, that magical skein of creativity that runs through the human heart and connects human nature with Nature itself. It is the thread that runs far back through wild time into the wild spaces from which we come, and which is our heritage. It is that creative thread which is our genetic inheritance as well as our cultural inheritance, and which binds us into this community of life. It is the source of our creativity. We have to devise legal systems that recognize and foster that connection, not systems that are based on domination and on enforcing conformity. We need systems that rejoice in the fact that the universe is diverse and don't try to stamp out that diversity.

The most important thing is to align human laws with

Nature's laws, which is what I've called the 'Great Jurisprudence.' There is a system of order in the universe and we must align our laws with it. Human laws must work *with* the laws of Nature and not against them. There is no alternative to complying with the laws of Nature and the laws of the universe. If one consistently breaks the laws of the community, eventually one will be excluded from the community. Climate change suggests that that process may already have started.

It is plain to see that Earth is now in transition. Many of the natural systems within which we exist are stressed and are changing fast. The question is not whether or not we can prevent the change but rather what is the nature of that change going to be? Are we going to continue with the industrial mode of civilization until the existing natural system of order breaks down and re-orders itself to exclude humans from the community of life? Alternatively are we going to accept the reality that the role of humans is not to be masters of the universe but rather to use our immense creativity and powers for the benefit of the Earth community as a whole? What I am talking about is not speculative and hypothetical. It is about getting down to Earth, being real, looking the situation in the face and saying "However difficult it is, we must and will make the changes to our societies that are necessary to enable us to fit in with the greater community of which we are part."

I would like to end by sharing a poem which my partner Mary Ann Cullinan brought to my attention and suggested I use to communicate an ancient perspective of what it is like to be part of the community that is Earth. The poem is called 'Claim to the Country' and is made of up of the words of San or Bushmen people, recorded while they were imprisoned at the Breakwater Prison in Cape Town, and only recently republished from archives. None of the members of that tribe survive today. To me, these words of an extinct people convey very poignantly and beautifully what industrialized cultures have lost. We have not only lost the diversity and wisdom of uncounted cultures but also the sense of what it is to be an integral member of the Earth community.

CLAIM TO THE COUNTRY
An anthem*

I am the land: of the early times
I am the time: of the blackest night
I am the sound: of the distant rain
I am the spring: that never dries
I am the scent: of the sho-/oa root
I am a star: in the water pit
I am /xue: who is all things
    I am the dying Moon. Who but I
    Walks the sky at dusk?

I am the dream: whose house is little
I am the legs: of !khwa
I am the Sun: tossed in the sky
I am the sound: of the falling star
I am the clouds: unequaled in beauty
I am the honey: of the eland
I am the Moon: who comforts the orphaned child
I am the fire's child. Who but I
Dispels the darkness?

I have been the whisper of every desire
I have been the healer of every sickness
I have been the hope of every hunger
I have been the fear of every night
I have been the rumour of every danger

I am the snake: on the grave

I am the fly: who listens and tells
I am the tick: on the sheep's back
I am the shadow: of the lion
I am a baboon: whose death lives on your brow
I am the back-apron: of a mouse's skin
I am the animal: before there were animals
    I am the son of the wind. Who but I
    Changes from man to a bird?

I am the wings: of a dreaming Mantis
I am the song: of the beast of prey
I am the tobacco-pouch: stolen by a dog
I am a stripe: on the springbuck's side
I am the horn: on the antelope's head
I am the dancing rattle: of springbuck ears
I am the spoor: of the eland
    I am the waterhole. Who but I
Passes from father to son?

I have been the arrow for every bow
I have been the stone for every stick
I have been the shelter from every he-rain
I have been the fire for every camp
I have been the fat of every feast

I am a dancer in the moonlight
I am the lash of the European
I am the lord of the desert lands
I am the breath of the spoiled lung
I am the tear in the firelight
I am the hope of my engagement
I am the song of the broken string
    I am the gun. Who but I
    Takes care of an old man in the middle of the cold?

I am the names: that are no longer known
I am the prisoner: at the Breakwater
I am the book: in which my story is written
I am the hunter: calling for rain
I am the owl-spirit: of my pupil Wilhelm
I am the teacher: of my language /xam
I am the healer: of sickness
  I am a magician. Who but I
  Throws stories to the wind?

I have been the wind of every soul
I have been the strings of every thought
I have been the murmur of every wind
I have been the end of every hope
I have been the place of every memory.

* After Robert Graves's restoration of the *Song of Amergin*

From *The Archive of Wilhelm Bleek and Lucy Lloyd, Claim to the Country—An Anthem*, by Pippa Skotnes, 2007 Jacana Press, Johannesburg, reproduced here with permission. (Editor's note: the unusual characters in the 'Anthem' represent verbal 'clicks', a typical feature of many African tribal languages.)

This chapter is an edited and abridged version of a talk given at the 'Earth is Community' event held in London in September, 2007, to honor the life and work of Thomas Berry.

Greening Economics

24. The Post-Corporate World

David Korten

Over the nearly 600 years since the onset of the Commercial Revolution, we have as a species learned a great deal about the making of money and we have created powerful institutions and technologies dedicated to its accumulation. But in our quest for money, we forgot how to live.

Now, in the third millennium, we find our planet beset by growing climatic instability, disappearing species, collapsing fisheries, shrinking forests, and eroding soils, while the institutions of family, community, and the nation-state disintegrate around us and the gap between rich and poor becomes more unconscionable by the day.

Our obsession with money has led us to create an economic system that values life only for its contribution to making money. With the survival of civilization and perhaps even our species now at risk, we have begun to awaken to the fact that our living planet is the source of all real wealth and the foundation of our own existence. We must now look to living systems as our teacher, for our survival depends on discovering new ways of living—and making our living—that embody life's wisdom.

Living Economies

Since the dawn of the scientific revolution, we have been so busy subduing Nature that we have given little thought to the possibility that living systems might embody wisdom essential to our own lives.

All living systems, from individual cells to biological communities, are complex self-organizing economies in which many individual entities cooperate to sustain themselves and the life of the whole—as when plants produce food and oxygen needed by animals, which in turn produce fertilizers and carbon dioxide that feed plant life. As Willis Harman and Elisabet Sahtouris write in *Biology Revisioned*, "Trees shelter birds and insects, bees pollinate flowers, mammals package seeds in fertilizer and distribute them, fungi and plants exchange materials, sapotrophs, whether microbes or vultures, recycle, birds warn of predators..." The species that survive and prosper are those that find a niche in which they meet their own needs in ways that simultaneously serve others.

Life, then, consists of countless individuals self-organized into 'holarchies'—nested sets of cells, multi-celled organisms, and multi-species communities or ecosystems with ever greater complexity and capacity. Each individual functions both as a whole and a part of a greater whole.

Take our own bodies as an example. Each of us is a composite of more than 30 trillion individual living cells. Yet even these cells constitute less than half of our dry weight. The remainder consists of microorganisms, such as the enteric bacteria and yeasts of our gut that manufacture vitamins and help metabolize our food. These symbiotic creatures are as necessary to our survival and healthful function as our own cells. Each cell and microorganism in our body is an individual, self-directing entity, yet by joining together they are able as well to function as a single being with abilities far beyond those of its parts.

Throughout its life span, each organism constantly renews its physical structures through cell death and replacement. Ninety-eight percent of the atoms in our bodies are replaced each year. Yet the identity, function, and coherence of the body and its individual organs are self-maintained—suggesting that each cell, organ, and body possesses some degree of inner knowledge and awareness of both self and the larger whole of which it is a part.

Life's Lessons

Life creates economies for living. We, in contrast, have created an economy for making money at life's expense. What if we were to retool our economy according to the principles of a living economy? What might be its major features? From our observations of living systems, we may distill a number of principles helpful both in understanding why our existing economy is destroying life and how we might redesign it to serve life. Living systems are, for example:

• **Self-Organizing and Cooperative**: Though we once assumed that cells are centrally controlled by their DNA and the body by the brain through the nervous system, science is discovering that the body's control processes are actually highly decentralized and involve a substantial element of self-regulation at the cellular level.

The regulatory processes of biological communities are even more radically self-organizing, with no functional equivalent of a centralized planning or control system.

Yet living economies do have mechanisms to control or eliminate rogue elements that do not serve the whole. For example, our immune system is comprised of cells that specialize in identifying and immobilizing or destroying harmful cells and viruses that pose a threat to the whole. In a cancer, when a genetic malfunction causes cells to forget they are a part of the larger whole of the body and unleashes the pursuit of their unlimited growth, the healthy cells attempt to destroy the defective cells by cutting off their blood supply.

This has potential implications for how we think about our human economies. The global corporation, which is programmed by its internal structures to respond to the incessant demand of financial markets to seek its own unlimited growth, behaves much like a cancerous tumor. Furthermore, the economy internal to a corporation is centrally planned and directed by top management, not to serve the whole of the society on which its existence depends, but rather to maximize the capture and flow of money to its top managers and shareholders. These characteristics—growth at the expense of the whole and centralized planning—represent serious violations of the principle of cooperative self-organization in the service of life. Given that the economies internal to the largest corporations are larger than the economies of most American states, this is cause for serious concern.

Many large corporations do organize their operations around smaller operating units and worker teams. But because the rights and powers of ownership flow downward from absentee shareholders whose only interests in the firm are financial, the corporation's singular goal remains profit, and any authority delegated to subordinate units can be withdrawn at any time.

A good first step in creating self-organizing economies that honor the freedom and responsibility of the individual in economic as well as in political life would be to sell off those decentralized units to their stakeholders: people such as workers, customers, suppliers, and community members. Doing so would make managers accountable to those who have a living interest in the firm and the health of the community and natural setting in which it is located.

• **Localized and Adapted to Place**: Each bio-community creates its home on a particular place on Earth. Its members organize themselves into numerous, multi-species sub-communities where, through a process of progressive experimentation and adaptation, they learn to optimize the capture, sharing, use, and storage of the resources available. As each living community adapts itself to the most intricate details of its particular physical locale, it, in turn, modifies the physical landscape, creating soil and holding it in place, holding and releasing water, creating micro-climates, creating the conditions for the further evolution of the ecosystem.

The global human economy likewise could comprise a holarchy of self-reliant, place-based economies each of which adapts to the conditions of its physical place by becoming proficient at the collection and conservation of energy and the recycling of materials. Each could be organized to offer all who reside within its borders a means of livelihood consistent with their full and free development.

Our existing global economy, by contrast, is dominated by financial markets and corporations programmed to reorient the purpose of local economies from meeting local needs to meeting the financial interests of distant institutions. They do this by imposing cultural and genetic monocultures and by extracting as much wealth as possible while contributing as little as possible in return. As corporate control over markets, technology, land and other resources becomes more pervasive, people and communities become less able to adapt their local economies to local needs and conditions.

Humanity has a long history of achieving sustainable, long-term relationship to place. A small farmer who knows the land and its characteristics learns to adapt her crops and methods to local micro environments to get high yields without chemicals, energy subsidies, and wastage. So too an economy comprising many decision makers can adapt efficiently to the opportunities of a locality, and to the needs and preferences of each of its members, in a way that is impossible when critical decisions are made by distant corporate managers.

Furthermore, the need to manage the business firm in service to more than purely financial values becomes self-evident to decision makers who must live with the social and environmental consequences of their decisions. They are unlikely to sacrifice schools, the environment, product safety, suppliers, employment security, wages, worker health, and other aspects of a healthy community for short-term, shareholder gain when they are the workers, customers, suppliers and community members as well as the owners.

• **Bounded by Managed, Permeable Borders**: To sustain itself, life must be open to exchange with its environment. Yet to maintain its internal coherence, it must be able to manage these exchanges. It thus depends on boundaries that are both managed and permeable: neither totally open nor totally closed. If the cell had no wall, its matter and energy would mix with the matter and energy of its environment and it would die. Multi-celled organisms must have a skin or other protective covering. Bio-communities are bounded by oceans, mountains, and climatic zones. Even our planet isolates itself from the rest of the universe; its gravitational field holds in place an atmosphere and ozone layer that control the exchange of radiation with the larger universe.

Human economies similarly require permeable—but managed—borders at each level of organization, from the household and community to the region and nation, that allow them to maintain the integrity, coherence, and resource efficiency of their internal processes and to protect themselves from predators.

Political and economic borders define a community of shared interests, identity, and trust: what we call 'social capital,' which is a form of embodied energy that makes a community far more than a collection of individuals and physical structures. Without borders, this energy dissipates, much as the cell's energy dissipates if its cell wall is removed. On the other hand, impermeable boundaries result in stagnation and a loss of opportunity for the exchange of useful information, knowledge, and culture essential to continuing innovation. As with all living beings, living economies need permeable and managed boundaries.

The institutions of money have been using international trade and investment agreements to remove the political borders

205

essential to maintaining the economic integrity of communities and nations. This process leaves economic resources exposed to predatory extraction, leading to a breakdown of the trust and cooperation essential to any community.

The real agenda of those promoting these trade agreements is not to eliminate borders, but rather to redraw them so as to establish that what once belonged to the community to be shared among its members now belongs to private corporations for the benefit of their managers and shareholders. Thus, in the name of property rights, corporations draw heavily defended borders around their lands, factories, offices, shopping centers, broadcast facilities, publications, technologies, and intellectual property. With the protection of private guards and lawyers backed by the public's police and military forces, they thus ensure that all uses of these assets benefit their private corporate interest and they silence voices of protest.

● **Frugal and Sharing**: Biological communities are highly efficient in energy capture and recycling, living exemplars of the motto, "Waste not, want not." Energy and materials are continuously recycled for use and reuse within and between cells, organisms, and species with a minimum of loss, as the wastes of one become the resources of another. Frugality and sharing are the secret of life's rich abundance, a product of its ability to capture, use, store, and share available material and energy with extraordinary efficiency.

Human economies can be similarly organized to contribute to life's abundance through the conservation, frugal use, equitable sharing, and continuous recycling of available energy, information, and material resources to the end of meeting the needs of all that lives within their borders.

Our existing global economy creates islands of power and privilege in a large sea of poverty. The fortunate hoard and squander resources on frivolous consumption, while others are denied a basic means of living. Furthermore, those who control the creation and allocation of money use this power to generate speculative profits. These profits increase the claims of the speculators to the wealth created through the labor and creative effort of others—while contributing nothing in return to the wealth creation process.

In our present economy unemployment, hoarding, and speculation are endemic, resulting in a grossly inefficient use of life's resources. In Nature, unemployment and hoarding beyond one's own need are rare, and there is no equivalent to financial speculation.

• **Diverse and Creative**: Life exhibits an extraordinary drive to learn, innovate, and freely share knowledge toward the realization of new potentials. The result is a rich diversity of species and cultures that give the bio-community resilience in times of crisis and provide the building blocks for future innovation.

History provides ample evidence that the same drive is inherent in humans as well. Our most brilliant scientists, innovators, and teachers have been those driven not by the promise of financial rewards, but by an inner compulsion to learn, to know, and to share their knowledge.

In our present global economy, corporate controlled mass media create monocultures of the mind that portray greed and exclusion as the dominant human characteristics. Intellectual property rights are used to preclude the free sharing of information, technology, and culture essential to creative innovation in the community interest.

We live at a time when our very survival depends on rapid innovation toward the creation of living economies and societies. Such innovation depends on vigorous, community-level experimentation supported by the creative energies of individuals everywhere. It is far more likely to come from diverse, self-directed, democratic communities that control their economic resources and freely share information and technology than from communities whose material and knowledge resources are controlled by distant corporate bureaucracies intent on appropriating wealth to enrich their shareholders.

From Global Capitalism to Mindful Markets

In my book, *The Post-Corporate World: Life After Capitalism*, I call economies with these life-affirming characteristics 'mindful market economies,' because they combine mindful ethical cultures with self-organizing economic relationships that bear a remarkable resemblance to the market economy described more than 200 years ago by British moral philosopher Adam Smith in *The Wealth of Nations*. Smith wrote about place-based economies comprising small, locally owned enterprises that function within a community-supported ethical culture to engage people in producing for the needs of the community and its members. The economy Smith envisioned is nearly the mirror opposite of our existing global economy, which is best described by the term 'capitalism.'

The term 'capitalism' was coined by European philosophers of the mid-1800s to describe an economic regime in which the benefits of productive assets are monopolized by the few to the exclusion of the many who through their labor make those assets productive.

The relationship of capitalism to a market economy is that of a cancer to a healthy body. Much as the cancer kills its host—and itself—by expropriating and consuming the host's energy, the institutions of capitalism are expropriating and consuming the living energies of people, communities, and the planet. And like a cancer, the institutions of capitalism lack the foresight to anticipate and avoid the inevitable deathly outcome.

We have a collective cancer, and our survival depends on depriving it of its power by restructuring our economic rules and institutions to end absentee ownership, rights without account-ability, corporate welfare, and financial speculation. Specific measures to these ends are elaborated in *The Post-Corporate World*.

At the same time, we can direct the energy we reclaim from the institutions of capitalism toward the institutions of the mindful market. These institutions exist today, quite likely in your community. They include values-based family, community, and worker-owned businesses, consumer cooperatives, community banks and credit unions, organic farmers, independent health food shops, print shops specializing in recycled papers and soy-based inks, farmers' markets, local restaurants featuring local organic produce, local water and power utilities, holistic health practitioners, fair traded coffee shops, and organic wineries.

Mindful businesses are being matched by the mindful consumption choices fostered by the rapidly growing voluntary simplicity movement. Tens of thousands of socially responsible investors are making mindful investment choices.

These and countless other positive initiatives are creating the outlines for self-organizing, life-sustaining economies that are:

- radically democratic
- rooted in place
- made up of human-scale firms, owned by and accountable to people with a stake in their function and impacts
- frugal with energy and resources, allocating them efficiently to meet needs, recycling the 'wastes'
- culturally, socially, and economically diverse, supportive of innovation and the free sharing of knowledge
- mindful of responsibility to self and community
- bounded by permeable borders, that allow democratic self-regulation.

In such an economy, enterprises would be owned by community members who work in them, depend on their products, and supply their inputs, with each entitled to a fair return for their labor and their investment.

Community economies would be self-organized by community members according to their self-determined priorities and mutually agreed rules. They would have their own speculation-proof currencies to facilitate local exchange.

The Earth and its resources would be managed as the common property of posterity, a sacred trust whose principal is to be maintained as its product is equitably shared.

The design of production-consumption processes would give high priority to working in balance with the natural productive processes of the ecosystem, using local renewable material and energy resources, and generating zero waste. Each community economy would have its distinctive features and culture reflecting its history, the circumstances of its place, and the preferences of its members. All would engage in mutually beneficial trade with their neighbors on their own terms, while freely sharing useful information and technology.

If enough of us decide we value life more than money, we have the means and the right to create an economy that nurtures life and restores money to its proper role as life's servant.

Moreover, the actions involved are familiar and give expression to principles that underlie millions of years of evolution, along with more recent human values of democracy, community, and freedom. Curing a cancer is rarely easy, but once we become clear that the task centers on reclaiming our life energies to live fully and well, this cure might actually be fun.

This chapter by David Korten is adapted from an article originally published in YES! magazine (see http://www.yes magazine.org/article.asp?ID=780), and is based on his book *The Post-Corporate World: Life After Capitalism*, co-published by

Kumarian Press and Berrett-Koehler Publishers. The author gratefully acknowledges Dr. Mae-Wan Ho and Elisabet Sahtouris for their insights into living systems on which it draws.

25. Permaculture: Bringing Wisdom Down to Earth

Maddy Harland

Permaculture is primarily a thinking tool for designing low carbon, highly productive systems but its influence can be very pervasive! What starts as a journey towards living a more ecologically balanced lifestyle can go far deeper, transforming even our worldview and radically altering behavior. That is the inspirational nature of permaculture. It is a means of connecting each of us more deeply to Nature's patterns and wisdom and of practically applying that understanding in our daily lives.

The discipline of permaculture design is based on observing what makes natural systems endure, establishing simple yet effective principles, and using them to mirror Nature in whatever we choose to design. This can be gardens, farms, buildings, woodlands, communities, businesses, even towns and cities. Permaculture is essentially about creating beneficial relationships between individual elements and making sure energy is captured in—rather than lost from—a system. Its application is only as limited as our imaginations.

Permaculture Ethics

Before we learn the principles and how to apply them, there is the bedrock in permaculture, its three ethics: Earth Care, People Care and Fair Shares. These are its motivation, its heart. They are not exclusive to permaculture and were derived from the commonalities of many worldviews and beliefs. They are therefore shared ethics, indeed shared by most of the world. What permaculture does is make them explicit within a design process that aims to take them out of the realms of philosophy and practically root them in everybody's lives, transforming thinking into doing. It is their combined presence in a design that has a radical capacity for ecological and social transformation.

Earth Care

Imagine the originators of permaculture, Bill Mollison and David Holmgren, looking at the Australian landscape in the 1970s and seeing the devastating effects of a temperate European agriculture on the fragile soils of an ancient Antipodean landscape. Like the dust bowls of Oklahoma in the 1930s, an alien agriculture has the capacity to turn a delicately balanced ecology into desert. Their initial response was to design a permanent agriculture with tree crops and other perennials inhabiting all the niches from the canopy to the ground cover and below. The soil is left untilled to establish its own robust micro-ecology. Key to this is that the land must be biodiverse and stable for future generations.

This ethic of Earth Care was the basis of permaculture design but it was bound to grow and pervade all aspects of permaculture. How can we have an organic agriculture or horticulture and manage our landscapes to sustain themselves over generations on one hand and then consume goods from industries managed in ecologically damaging ways on the other? It is pointless designing an organic garden and then buying a gas guzzling vehicle or building a house from concrete and steel when we can use local materials with less embodied energy. The original vision of care for all living and non living things has grown to embrace a deep and comprehensive understanding of Earth Care that involves our many decisions, from the clothes we wear and the goods we buy to the materials we use for DIY projects. Though we can't all build our own houses or grow all of our own food, we can make choices about what and how we consume and conserve. Key to this is the understanding that up to one third of our ecological footprint is taken up by the food we buy and so even a small amount grown in a city allotment or container garden can make a difference. Permaculture is all about making a difference.

People Care
Embedded in permaculture is the concept of Permanent Culture. How can we develop a permaculture if our people are expendable, uncared for, excluded? There can be no elites here, no plutocracies or oligarchies. All members of the community must be taken into account. People Care asks that our basic needs for food, shelter, education, employment and healthy social relationships are met. Nor can genuine People Care be exclusive in a tribal sense. This is a global ethic of Fair Trade and intelligent support amongst all people both at home and abroad.

At the core of People Care is an understanding of the power of community. We can change our lives as individuals and make incremental differences and we can do even more in community. The permaculture designers who helped initiate Cuba's post-oil, urban agriculture are a good example.[1] They mobilized a whole country to become self-reliant. Ecovillages and cohousing communities that can significantly reduce their ecological footprint by sharing resources are other good examples. In smaller ways, in our cities, towns and villages, we can all benefit from deepening community links. I may not have all the skills to grow all my food or eco-renovate my house, for example, but by developing good networks I can expand my capacity to live more sustainably and become more self-reliant. This is a decentralized, democratic vision of social transformation where grassroots initiatives like the Transition Towns movement can begin to plan for low carbon 'energy descent' on a community level.[2] There is no time to wait for central government to act (or react).

Fair Shares
The last ethic synthesizes the first two ethics. It acknowledges that we only have one Earth and we have to share it with all

living things and future generations. There is no point in designing a sustainable family unit, community or nation whilst others languish without clean water, clean air, food, shelter, meaningful employment, and social contact. Since the industrialized North uses the resources of at least three Earths and much of the global South languishes in poverty, Fair Shares is an acknowledgement of that terrible imbalance and a call to limit consumption, especially of natural resources, in the North. Permaculture fundamentally rejects the industrial growth model of the global North at the core of its ethics and aspires to design fairer, more equitable systems that take into account the limits of the planet's resources and the needs of all living beings.

Permaculture Principles

Whilst these permaculture ethics are more like moral values or codes of behavior, the principles of permaculture provide a set of universally applicable guidelines that can be used in designing sustainable systems. These principles are inherent in any permaculture design, in any climate, and at any scale. They have been derived from the thoughtful observation of Nature, and from earlier work by ecologists, landscape designers and environmental science.

David Holmgren recently redefined these principles in his seminal book *Permaculture: Principles and Pathways Beyond Sustainability*.[3] Every principle comes with a 'proverb' and is followed by my explanation.

Observe and interact. "Beauty is in the eye of the beholder."
For me this element of stillness and observation forms the key of permaculture design. In a world of instant makeovers, of 'fast' everything, having the capacity to observe the seasons, watch the changing microclimates on a patch of land, understand how the patterns of wind, weather and slope affect the frost pockets and plant growth is an opportunity to begin to learn the deeper

aspects of Earth care. It also makes us more capable of making wise decisions about how we design or eco-renovate our houses and plan our gardens and farms.

Catch and store energy. "Make hay while the sun shines."
Intimately connected to observation is the art of capturing energy in a design so that we minimize the need to seek resources from the outside. In a garden this is about avoiding planting tender seedlings in frost pockets in spring or maximizing solar gain by siting a greenhouse/conservatory on the south side of a building so that we can both extend the season and heat a house with passive solar gain. We are attempting to capture water, sunlight, heat, soil, biomass and fertility whenever we can, to become more self-resilient.

Obtain a yield. "You can't work on an empty stomach."
Food can account for as much as one third of our ecological footprint so it makes sense to grow as much as we can, even if it is only tasty sprouted grains on the windowsill in an apartment. So a permaculture garden is by default an edible landscape with good floral companions to attract beneficial insects and a building is a potential heat store and structure for solar panels. But the concept of 'yields' is not merely about renewable energy or vegetables; a yield can be about social capital. For us at *Permaculture Magazine*, seeing people changing their lives for the better, building community links and reducing their carbon after reading our books or magazines is the ultimate positive yield for a publisher.

Use and value renewable resources and services. " Let nature take its course."
Whenever possible, permaculture seeks to use resources that can be renewed. This naturally applies to energy, soil conservation, and the planting of perennials food crops as well as annuals and

seed saving. It is also a principle that encompasses People Care. Compassion for all things is key to this principle.

Produce no waste. "Waste not, want not. A stitch in time saves nine." In the UK, we throw away the equivalent of 24 bags of sugar per household per week: 14.1 kilograms. That's 29,000,000 tonnes (55 percent of which is household waste) for a year. I have a favorite saying that the landfill of today will be the 'mine' of tomorrow. At *Permaculture Magazine* we have no waste collection and our business is designed on permaculture principles. We reuse first and then recycle all possible materials—paper, cardboard, textiles, glass—and compost all organic materials, from kitchen waste to shredded paper. The subsequent compost feeds our edible container garden outside our office and provides a medium for growing plants for other projects at the Sustainability Centre. Zero waste also means saving money.

Design from patterns to details. "Can't see the wood for the trees." When my husband Tim and I designed our house and garden, we read up on permaculture design, forest gardening, renewable energy, eco-architecture and eco-renovation as much as we could. We spent a year observing the land before we started planting, in order to figure out how best to make our house a happy, energy efficient place to live in. We observed the seasons, the climatic variations, the weather, the soil patterns, slope and our own human activities on the site as a family. We also considered the 'edge' between house and garden and how we might make this both aesthetic and productive in terms of food crops and energy harvesting.

In other words, we started off looking at the bigger picture— the pattern of what sustainable living might be—with examples from other places, and then we refined our exploration into the detail appropriate for our particular site. We didn't make a 'shopping list' of individual items or projects and try and mesh them together in a hotchpotch of what might be regarded or described as 'green.'

Integrate rather than segregate. "Many hands make light work."
We have a cultural tendency to separate vegetable gardens from flower gardens and use hard edges to design our spaces, but companion gardeners will know that the more integrated the orchard is with the wildflower meadow or the vegetables are with flowers frequented by beneficial insects, the less the pests will prevail. The same is true for people. Cultural diversity brings a robust and fertile culture. Rigid monocultures of politics and religion, for example, bring sterility, even social and political repression.

Use small and slow solutions. "The bigger they are, the harder they fall."
Our society currently depends on vast inputs of fossil fuels whilst our biosphere is overloaded by their outputs. The more accessible and fixable our technology and chains of supply are, the more robust the system. This principle speaks of hand tools, of appropriate technology that can easily be fixed, and of relocalisation. Currently we have a three day 'just in time' supply chain of supermarkets. If the fuel supply is interrupted, the supermarket shelves will empty at an alarming rate. Better to build resilience into our systems by relocalising our essential needs as much as possible and having technological alternatives that we can fix.

Use and value diversity. "Don't put all your eggs in one basket."
Biodiversity makes healthy ecosystems. Diversity in terms of crops, energy sources, and employment, make for greater sustainability. Valuing diversity amongst people makes for a more peaceful, equitable society. Conflict and wars are the biggest slayers of sustainable development.

Use edges and value the marginal. "Don't think you are on the right track just because it is a well-beaten path."

Examples of edge in Nature are:

- where canopy meets clearing in the woodland, inviting in air and sunshine and a profusion of flowers
- where sea and river meet land in the fertile interface of estuaries, full of invertebrates, fish and bird life
- where the banks of streams meet the water's edge and fertility is built with deposited mud and sand in flood time, giving life to a riot of plant life
- where plains and water meet, flooding and capturing alluvial soil.

Edge in Nature is all about increasing diversity by the increase of interrelationship between the elements: earth, air, fire (sun), water. This phenomenon increases the opportunity for life in all of its marvelous fertility of forms.

In human society, edge is where we have cultural diversity. It is the place where free thinkers and so-called 'alternative' people thrive, new ideas are allowed to develop and ageless wisdom is given its rightful respect. Edge is suppressed in non-democratic states and countries that demand allegiance to one religion.

Creatively use and respond to change. "Vision is not seeing things as they are but as they will be."
In Nature, there is a process of succession. Bare soil is colonized by weeds that are in turn superseded by brambles. Then pioneers follow like silver birch, alder and gorse which stabilize the soil. The latter two even fix nitrogen to create an environment that can host slow growing temperate climate species like oak, beech and yew. But Nature is dynamic and succession can be inter-rupted by browsing animals, storms that fell trees and create clearings, or a changing climate that is less hospitable for certain

climax giants like oak and beech. The challenge of a permaculture designer is to understand how all these factors interact with each other in a landscape or on a particular plot of land, and design accordingly. It is no good restoring coppice without fencing out deer. And it is no good planting trees if they will shade out the solar panel in a decade's time.

Equally well, we need to appreciate how climate change will affect our agriculture with higher summer temperatures, greater volumes of rain in winter and springtime and more violent storms with higher wind speeds. In England, for example, hotter summers may allow more vineyards on the gentle southern slopes of the chalk downland. They may also make English oaks less viable in the south. What then do we plant and how do we design in resilience to our settlements? One example is to plant more shelterbelts for farmland as well as housing estates and forgo building on floodplains.

This principle goes deeper than that, however. It invites us to imagine a future world, a world without cheap oil, and a world that necessarily radically reduces its carbon load in the atmosphere. By doing this, we take the first steps towards creating it. We stand on the bedrock of permaculture ethics—Earth Care, People Care and Fair Shares—and are empowered by a set of principles that can inform our planning and actions.

Human beings can either be the destroyers or the self-elected stewards of our planet. We have the capacity to put our ethics into action, to 'walk our talk.' With permaculture design, we create the potential for a powerful, beneficial relationship with the Earth. We can become stewards for our world whilst still maintaining an openness and humility to accept Nature as perhaps our most powerful and wisest of teachers. What a culture we could build if these two perspectives were the bedrock of our civilization!

I believe that as we awaken as human beings and our awareness grows, we turn away from designing our own private

Eden and engage more fully with the rest of humanity and the biosphere. We cannot build ecological arks on a failing planet. We are part of an interdependent ecological system. There can be no 'them' and 'us' in ecology. Permaculture is about low carbon, eco-friendly, even abundant living. It is also an ethically based design system for people who want not only to transform their lives and the lives of the people around them, but also to play their part in bringing an ecologically balanced, equitable and kinder world into existence. That is our challenge.

Notes

1. www.communitysolution.org/cuba.html
2. www.transitiontowns.org/Totnes/
3. Holmgren, D. *Permaculture: Principles and Pathways Beyond Sustainability* (Holmgren Design Services, 2002)

26. Complexity, Form and Design

Jean Bee

Introduction; form, flow and uncertainty

Our current dominant worldview, which underpins most mainstream schools of thought in economics, architecture, management, education and development, still centers on the idea that the world is objective, measurable, predictable and controllable, despite almost overwhelming evidence to the contrary. Has this always been the case? Early philosophers in both the East and West held a much more sophisticated view of the world as changing and flowing, but yet with a degree of order and patterning that arose intrinsically, from within.

This image is captured in the following fragment, part of the very few remaining writings of Heraclitus.[1]

"Upon those that step into the same rivers different and different waters flow...They scatter and...gather...come together...and flow away...approach and depart."

The Hindu Upanishads and the Dao de Jing present a similar sense of temporary patterning emerging, without the need for extrinsic design or planning. And the Dalai Lama, speaking at a conference in April 2008, captured this beautifully when he said:

"There is no self-defining discrete reality to cause or effect. Forms or feelings are devoid of inherent existence; it is only on the basis of aggregation of subtle elements that forms exist; forms can only be understood in relational terms to their constitutive elements."

Plato refused to believe that form or patterning could arise without external design and introduced the idea of a Creator who, building on perfect forms, created a world which emulated and aspired to these perfect forms. Uncertainty and fluctuations were seen as irritating limitations and something to be overcome; they were not seen to serve any useful purpose.

This theme of perfection and order then paved the way for the seizing of Newton's mechanics as the dominant world view, where order, prediction and control are regarded as attainable and desirable and variation is viewed both as a nuisance and largely irrelevant.

It was Darwin who recognized that uncertainty was indeed *necessary* for change to happen. Whilst the realization that animals and plants evolve had been recognized for nearly 100 years before Darwin's expedition on the Beagle, Darwin's contribution was to suggest that variation was the part of the key to how this happened.

The need for variation in order for evolution and change to happen was a Big Idea that subsequently captured the imagination of philosophers, psychologists, sociologists—and eventually even hard scientists.

The Pragmatist philosopher Charles Peirce was one of the first to recognize the wider implications of evolution as a worldview. In 1891, he wrote:

"Now the only possible way of accounting for the laws of nature and the uniformity in general is to suppose them results of evolution. This supposes them not to be absolute, not to be obeyed precisely. It makes an element of indeterminacy, spontaneity, or absolute chance in nature." [2]

James, also part of the Pragmatic school, explains in his lecture, 'The Dilemmas of Determinism,' given in 1884:

"Of two alternative futures which we conceive, both may now

be really possible; and the one become impossible only at the very moment when the other excludes it by becoming real itself... To that view, actualities seem to float in a wider sea of possibilities out of which they are chosen; and, **somewhere**, indeterminism says, such possibilities exist, and form a part of truth." [3]

The pre-Socratics noticed that the world *was* uncertain but nevertheless had form; Darwin recognized that variation and uncertainty was in fact *central* to the emergence of new form; it was Prigogine[4] who took the next step. He started to explore *how* uncertainty led to emergence and evolution, and how the future is *in principle* unknowable. This was the start of the so-called new science of Complexity.

Complexity
Complexity theory[5] has arisen, over more than half a century, out of the work of many scientists and social scientists who seek to investigate the implications of embracing the world as messy, interconnected, open to influences and change, able to learn— indeed more like the river Heraclitus envisaged. Essentially, this work tells us that:

- Things interrelate, affect each other in a messy, complex, systemic fashion
- Variation and diversity are *necessary* for creativity, change, evolution, emergence
- Things build on the past, but not with clear one-to-one correspondences and cause-effect relationships
- There is more than one possible future; the future cannot be reliably predicted from the past
- At key moments or tipping points, radically new features and characteristics can emerge
- Top-down design and control will certainly have an effect, but

may lead to unintended outcomes

- Systems which are diverse, richly connected and open to their environments can evolve a sort of form, or patterning, and this may be more harmoniously in tune with its surroundings that one imposed from above.

This emerging worldview, which seems more in tune with our personal experience of life, creates a powerful new image for all sorts of institutional thinking, including spiritual traditions. It is itself paradoxical and uncertain in that we are less clear how to act, how to intervene. Does it mean there should be no design, no leadership, no control? Is emergent structure always helpful and generative? Might we not just sink into chaos and disorder? Indeed, are our current problems the result of too much control or not enough? It raises issues of ethics, of the politics of partici-pation, of power and domination.

There are no easy answers. But imagining that the world is predictable and controllable when it is not is not helpful either; our current economic, social and environmental crises are, perhaps, ample evidence of that.

Architecture

The architect Christopher Alexander has grappled with what the ideas of complexity theory mean for design of buildings and communities. As he comments:

"The huge difficulties in architecture are reflected in the ugliness and soul-destroying chaos of the cities and environ-ments we were building during the twentieth century—and in the mixed feelings of dismay caused by these develop-ments…in nearly every thinking person." [6]

These sentiments are echoed by Jane Jacobs, who, in the landmark book *The Death and Life of Great American Cities*, challenged the dominant establishment of modernist professional planning and asserting the wisdom of empirical observation and community intuition. [7]

Alexander poses a series of linked questions that must be addressed in relation to architecture. These are paraphrased below:

1. There are issues of *value* that cannot be separated from the main task of serving functional needs. Thus aesthetics lies at the core of architecture.
2. There is the issue of *context*: a building grows out of, and must complement, the place where it appears. Thus there is a concept of *healing* or making whole and building into a context.
3. There is the issue of *design and creation:* processes capable of creating unity.
4. There is the issue of human feeling; buildings must connect to human feeling.
5. There are the issues of *ecological and sustainable and biological connection to the land.*
6. There is the vital issue of social agreement regarding decisions that affect the human—and wider—environment.
7. There is the issue of the emerging *beauty of shape*, as the goal and outcome.

Alexander's list captures beautifully the paradox inherent in complex, systemic thinking. How do we design yet do it in a participative fashion? How do we balance use, context, sustainability and aesthetics? How do we take notice of what people *feel*? How do we incorporate qualitative questions with quantitative design principles?

"We design outdoor wooden play systems - for schools and families. If we work with a school, we get the pupils to draw what they would like; sometimes we work with 30 drawings. We can pick out common features, understand what matters to them. Obviously it is up to us to make it all work, do the technical bits—but they can come up with ideas that we would never have thought of. Also, when they have been involved in the design, they are proud of it and don't want to vandalise it or rubbish it."

– Mark Hughes, Designer, Bigwoodplay

Brian Goodwin, who was very interested in Alexander's work, invited him to become involved in designing possible new structures for Schumacher College in Devon. The process would take account of the nature of the land, the nature of existing buildings and the intended use of the proposed new buildings. Goodwin explains that this involved a week studying the qualities of the land and: "...brought us into a relationship of sensitivity to place." He goes on to say:

"What we experienced was a design process that offered the possibility of a deeply authentic and participatory involvement of those engaged in it, giving us some insight into Alexander's principles of design based on the properties of living form with its wholeness, coherence and capacity to heal." [8]

Where does this take us?
Christopher Alexander asks us, when designing buildings or developing communities, to slow down, to take account of the particularity of place and context and history and feel, to consider the views of the people who will use the building; he asks us to try things out, at least conceptually, and see how they feel, not just forge ahead with a standard model. This is not to deny the limitations of cost or the value of expertise, nor does it necessarily imply consensus.

This approach embraces the ideas implicit in complexity thinking. Viewing the world as complex tells us that every situation is a bit different, that good ideas can emerge through joint inquiries, that aesthetics, use, sustainability and economics can be addressed concurrently, with much to gain in so doing and little to lose.

I am reminded of visiting my demented aunt in her nursing home. The home had individual rooms down long corridors. The rooms were beautiful, complete with personal showers, TVs and expensive carpets. All this was of little use to demented patients, who spent most of their time in the inadequate, crowded, small sitting room. There was also no contact with the outdoors. What would it have taken to modify the basic design with the needs of the patients in mind? It is hard to imagine it would have cost more. And as the 'green' geriatrician William Thomas has shown with his Eden Alternative programs for elder care in the US, designing such care around the perceived needs of patients— especially their need for contact with Nature—can significantly lower running costs as well, since increased patient and staff wellbeing dramatically lowers staff turnover and absenteeism.[9]

What seems so pernicious about the dominant worldview is that it is predicated on the idea that there **is** an optimal solution, a right answer, a best way. Alan Greenspan[10] points this out. In a recent article, he said: "...our economic models, as complex as they have become, are still too simple to capture the full array of governing variables that drive economic reality." He goes on to suggest that economic thinking fails to grasp the fact that consumers do not make what economists regard as rational choices. Perhaps the more worrying issue is that economists ever *did* imagine people made rational, consistent and predictable choices.

Our world is increasingly complex. This does not imply we should not take action, but that we should regard actions as experiments and be prepared to learn, modify our approaches, listen to feedback and, quite often, just be prepared to pay more attention to what is there, what is plain to see. This is not to say that an evolutionary approach, applied naively, necessarily leads to a positive outcome; the story of evolution is as much about what did not work and was destroyed as it is about what sustained. Consider the dinosaurs! How can we do our best to create a future which is harmonious, just, rich and sustainable? Complexity thinking shows that it *is* important what we put into the mix, by way of intentions, values, 'right action' in a Buddhist sense. In that way we do our best, in the knowledge that the future cannot be controlled and designed, to enhance the emergence of a positive future; the intention to provide 'good' ingredients for this co-created future is what elevates this approach to the sacred, as Kaufmann describes in his book, *Reinventing the Sacred.* [11] William James captured the essence of this approach when he said:

"I am done with great things and big plans, great institutions and big success and I am for those tiny invisible, loving human forces that work from individual to individual, creeping through the crannies of the world like so many soft rootlets, or like the capillary oozing of water, yet which, if given time, will rend the hardest monuments of pride." [12]

The task of 'greening' and re-sacralizing our culture's institutions begins with a stepping back from our previous assumption of narcissistic assurance, hubris, dominance and control. It begins with a movement towards humility, towards admitting our ignorance, honoring mystery, learning from Nature, careful observation, trusting the process, and asking, in the broadest sense, *what is needed* rather than imposing our will. Alexander's approach illustrates this process beautifully. And Heraclitus, Darwin and Complexity suggest that this is the way the universe indeed works.

Our willingness to take this step and to learn from Nature rather than try to control it is what can make *all* our institutions whole and by doing so can begin to heal the sickness we've imposed on Gaia. Green spirituality in action can allow the universe itself to flow through us into the creation of new forms. Through an ongoing process of relationship—with materials, with place, with all the stakeholders, both human and other-than-human—we can play a positive part in design, creation and evolution, help to sustain the diversity of life that makes Gaia thrive; and hopefully bequeath our role in all this to our great-great-grandchildren.

Notes

1. Kirk, G.S.et al. *The Pre-Socratic Philosophers* (Cambridge University Press, 1957) p. 195
2. Peirce, C. *Philosophical Writings of Peirce* (Dover Publications Inc., 1955) p.318
3. James, W. *Selected Writings* (Everyman Paperback Classics, 1995) p.275
4. Prigogine, I. *Etude thermodynamique des phenomenones irreversibles:* (Desoer, Belgium 1947),
5. Boulton, J. and Allen, P. 'Complexity and Strategy,' in Ambrosini,V. Jenkins, M. and Nardine Collier, N.(Eds) *Advanced Strategic Management: A Multi-perspective Approach* (Palgrave Macmillan, 2007)
6. Alexander, C. *New Concepts in Complexity Theory arising from studies in the field of architecture* (www.natureoforder.com /library-of-articles.htm)
7. Jacobs, J. *The Death and Life of Great American Cities* (Random House and Vintage Books, 1961)
8. Goodwin, B. *Nature's Due* (Floris Books, 2007) p.173
9. Thomas, William H. *What Are Old People For? How Elders Will Save the World* (VanderWyk & Burnham, 2007)
10. Greenspan, A. 'We will never have a perfect model of risk'

FT.com March 18 2008 p. 1

11. Kaufman, S. *Reinventing the Sacred* (Basic Books, 2008)

12. James, H. (Ed) *The Letters of William James* vol. 2 (Little Brown, 1926) p. 90

Part IV: Walking Our Talk

We must not, in trying to think about how we can make a big difference, ignore the small daily differences we can make which, over time, add up to big differences that we often cannot foresee.

– Marian Wright Edelman

About Part IV

27. Walking the GreenSpirit way

Marian Van Eyk McCain

'Walking our talk' means that every single facet of our lives needs to be examined to see whether there are discrepancies between the beliefs and ideals we express and the way our lives are actually lived, day by day, decision by decision. Because that is where the transformational power resides. Not in heaven, but in the millions of decisions made, day after day, by millions of ordinary people

I once attended a Deep Ecology conference where the food was all served on disposable, polystyrene plates and the drinks were poured into disposable, polystyrene cups. There we all were, talking about how deeply we cared for the Earth and drinking our tea out of cups made from petrochemicals, disposable items that would pollute the ground for hundreds of years to come. That is what I mean by discrepancy. The organizers, I must add, were as dismayed as the participants. They had not thought to check this detail ahead of time. As that famous frog said, it is not always easy, being green.

Neither is greening one's personal lifestyle something that can be accomplished overnight. But in the same way that John Travis, in his chapter on health, spoke of high level wellness, we can think of 'high level greenness' as a *direction* rather than a goal.

And the good thing is that in this venture, none of us is alone.

In the year 2000, Paul Ray and Sherry Anderson coined the term 'Cultural Creatives' to describe all the people they had found who were working for causes like social justice and sustainability and who were hungering for the sort of changes in their personal lives that would bring them less stress, better health, lower consumption, a deeper spirituality and more respect for the Earth.[1]

Ray and Anderson, whose research was extensive, discovered that this group of people was much, much larger than anyone had realized. They estimated that at the time they published their results it numbered around 50 million in North America and 80-90 million in the European Union. And those numbers will have increased substantially by now, especially with all the publicity about climate change and peak oil.

Since you are reading this book, you are almost certainly one of this group. You and I and all the other millions of Cultural Creatives are part of what Thomas Berry calls 'The Great Work:' the work of pulling our human civilization, and the rest of life on our planet, back from the brink of ecological disaster.

Thomas Berry found an excellent rule of thumb to help him walk his talk and make those important, moment by moment decisions: a rule that could quickly distinguish good from bad, desirable from undesirable, sustainable from unsustainable. When he was a child, there was a meadow behind his house, full of flowers and birds. He loved that meadow. One of his most vivid memories, he said, was of being 11 years old, standing at the fence, looking across the stream into the meadow and thinking how beautiful it was. So the health of that meadow became a measuring stick that he would use for the rest of his life. He realized that everything, in the larger world, impacts in some way on that meadow. Intensive farming practices will cause bird species to decline so that there will be fewer birds in his meadow, the water quality in the stream will be affected by runoff. Pollution and global warming will create flood and drought that will irrevocably alter his meadow. Anything and everything can be examined in the light of what its ultimate effect on the meadow, and others like it, might be. As he puts it, in his book *The Great Work*:

"Whatever preserves and enhances this meadow in the natural cycles of its transformation is good; whatever opposes this meadow or negates it is not good. My life orientation is that simple. It is also that pervasive. It applies in economics and political orientation as well as in education and religion."[2]

When our love of the Earth and our astonishment, our marveling, our wonder and reverence for the vastness and mystery of the universe become the focus of our spiritual lives, rather than some far off, dreamed-of heaven, then just as the Earth feeds our bodies, she also feeds our souls. That is when walking our talk soon becomes our natural way of walking. We can no longer think of walking any other way.

In this fourth and final section of the book we shall first hear the story of GreenSpirit, the UK organization which had its early roots in the Creation Spirituality of Matthew Fox, how it grew from there and what it offers its members today. This is followed by some thoughts on what it means to live the GreenSpirit way, bringing our lives into full alignment with our beliefs and making all our decisions on the basis of what is best for the Earth we love. In other words, to walk our talk.

Notes

1. Ray, P. and Anderson, S. *The Cultural Creatives: How 50 million people are changing the world.* (Three Rivers Press, 2000)
2. Berry, T. *The Great Work: Our way into the future* (Random House, 1999) p.13

28. GreenSpirit in the UK: The Early Years

Petra Griffiths

The Beginning

It was the first beat of the drum in what I later knew as the Greek greetings dance, *Enas Mythos*, that drew me in.

I was listening to the tapes of Matthew Fox's talks on the four paths of Creation Spirituality, held at St James's Piccadilly in May 1987, and the first thing I heard was *Enas Mythos*. I knew immediately that here was a form of spirituality that addressed our whole being through our body, and connected us with others and with the Earth and its cycles. The words that followed described the most expansive and holistic vision I had yet come across and I was surprised to find such a life-affirming philosophy within the Christian tradition, which I had always associated with self denial.

Under the headline "Rector to Launch Religion of Joy," Walter Schwarz, religious correspondent at *The Guardian*, reported on the impact of Matthew Fox's talks, and on Donald Reeves' desire, as Rector of St James's, to provide a platform for the insights of Creation Spirituality to be taken forward within the UK. *The Guardian* article immediately made a lot of people aware of the new movement.

The early days were quite chaotic. Groups were formed, mainly in London initially. Donald Reeves wanted to honor the idea that Creation Spirituality would not be a church-based phenomenon, since the spiritual leaders of the future were to be artists, social catalysts, *animateurs*, rather than priests. But in practice, a central administrative focus was needed in order to keep people in touch (in those days before email), to organize the events that would bring people together to explore the new paradigm, and to enable coordination to happen.

So after a year in which the 'office' was taken around in a briefcase, and momentum was being lost, Donald agreed that a space be made available in the offices at St James's, which would act as an administrative hub, enable the core team to generate events, produce programs and newsletters aimed at the movement within the whole of the UK, and disseminate information about the local contacts and about groups which began to be formed in various parts of the country. Being based right in the center of the city, in a building that people often pass through or visit when in London to see what is going on, gave Creation Spirituality in its early years a higher profile than would be expected from the size of its membership of a few hundred. This was a very creative period, in which invaluable initiatives were taken by members of the network. Francis Miller formed Mountain Books in order to launch a UK edition of *Original Blessing*, giving the opportunity for a great deal of publicity around Matthew Fox's 1990 speaking tour in locations around the country. Alan Shepherd formed a mail order book service, thus solving access problems to important published items, and making very helpful donations towards the overhead costs of maintaining a center. The book *Visions of Creation* was published as a result of an initiative by Eileen Conn and James Stewart, taking up the themes of an educational course on the creation tradition held at St James's (see below). The founding of residential centers such as The Old Stable House in Suffolk and Fresh Horizons in Essex helped greatly in developing the opportunities for study and experience of Creation Spirituality .

Important Themes

The title of Matthew Fox's book, *Original Blessing*, captured the idea that motivated people so much: of humans being intrinsically whole and wholesome rather than 'fallen' and in need of redemption. Creation Spirituality was therefore an expression of cosmic sacramentalism and of panentheism (as described in the earlier chapter on '-isms'), which sees the whole of Creation as contained within the sacred, as well as God being within all things. The life, death and resurrection of Jesus Christ is understood within this paradigm as a revelation of a life lived in deep connection with the divine, which has the power to inspire others to live at the same depth. This is closer to the Eastern Orthodox theology of divinization than to the understanding of redemption that has prevailed within mainstream, Western Christianity.

The idea of people living with a sense of self esteem, and of conducting relationships on an 'I-thou' basis rather than objectifying others, meant treating with respect all other parts of the creation. This did not eliminate the sense of wrongdoing and injustice when human actions impact on other people or on Nature. Neither did it mean that there was no need for healing and reconciliation on an individual and a communal/social level. This way of understanding people did, however, move away from a constant and self absorbing feeling of shame, guilt and inadequacy.

The reintegration of the human faculties of imagination, intuition and creativity, which had often not been valued in previous religious paradigms, enabled many people with a creative and artistic bent to get in touch with spirituality again after a long period in the wilderness. The focus on embodiment, and the valuing of emotions, worked out through things like body prayer and ritual, as well as dance, massage, and exercises such as tai chi and qigong, helped to bring spirituality into the here and now and the everyday.

Birth of the Journal

The first journal we published was called *Interchange*. It had a simple format with line drawings. This journal enabled dialogue between the participants in the new movement, and meant that events including rituals and liturgies that took place could sometimes be captured on paper for those who had not benefited in person. *Interchange* later grew to become the GreenSpirit Journal, which remains a key means of connecting the contemporary movement within the UK and, increasingly, beyond.

Activities

A large number of activities had developed by the autumn of 1989. These ranged from Native American Medicine Wheel Teachings through explorations of Celtic spirituality to discussions of international politics and personal growth workshops.

By then, there were at least 20 regional contacts and a residential center in Suffolk where the weekend program gave opportunities for people to participate in more in depth workshops, and to go for individual, spiritual support and reflection.

The position of Creation Spirituality at St James's was very dependent on the vision held by its incumbent, Donald Reeves, and there were some problems when he had a period of illness. The Reverend Mary Robins, who did a great deal to help develop the new tradition, experienced some criticism from people who were not signed up to this new vision. Yet during that period St James's hosted one of its most inspiring events ever: a live enactment of the 'Missa Gaia' with Paul Winter and Consort during the 11 a.m. parish Eucharist.

Educational work

The core activity of this new movement in those first few years was its educational programs. Initially much of this took place at St James's Church, and it incorporated many home grown visionary teachers whose work resonated with the Creation Spirituality approach, such as Jonathon Porritt, Anita Roddick, Rupert Sheldrake, Chris Clarke, Sarah Parkin and Paul Ekins.

A number of high profile American speakers were also part of the programs, for example Fritjof Capra, Joanna Macey, Brian

Swimme, Neil Douglas Klotz, Jerry Mander and Charlene Spretnak. A successful link was also formed with Birkbeck College in the University of London that enabled people to do academic courses outside normal working hours, and introductory courses in Creation Spirituality were held in association with Birkbeck.

One of the themes most consistently explored in the first few years of our educational program was the roots of the Creation Spirituality tradition. These roots were examined through a series of talks on the work of theologians and mystics such as Thomas Aquinas, Julian of Norwich, Hildegard of Bingen, St Francis of Assisi, Thomas Traherne and John Scotus Eriugena, all of whom were part of the Christian tradition, but all of whom had a more holistic vision than the predominant dualistic theologies.

Talks like these, often by people with in-depth knowledge of the subject, brought alive the idea of a tradition going back to the early days of Christianity and surfacing regularly throughout the centuries, a tradition that had been so far underground as to come as a revelation.

Celtic tradition

Learning about the Celtic tradition of the British Isles was a new experience for many who had only come across forms of Christianity such as Roman, non-conformist or evangelical. An ongoing exploration of Celtic spirituality seemed more meaningful for many within the UK than focusing on Native American spirituality. The way in which traditions from the Pagan Celtic period were carried over into Celtic Christianity also illustrated the many links and common elements between spiritual traditions.

The Festival of the Celtic Spirit at St James's in July 1991 was one of the most striking series of events from this period. It involved visual and musical inputs as well as talks, workshops and a liturgy. David Iona's sculpture of the Welsh shaman/bard Taliesin was an important feature, placed in the back south corner of the Church. A concert and story-telling with the inspired Irish singer Noirin ni Riain and storyteller Peter Vallance drew a lot of interest. The well known writers on Celtic spirituality John and Caitlin Matthews took part in the Festival and remarked that it was the first time that Pagan and Christian aspects of the Celtic tradition were being celebrated together.

The New Universe Story

Educational work on the new universe story was based on the insights of Brian Swimme, Thomas Berry and others. Series such as one on the New Paradigm, included Chris Clarke speaking about the new science, Alex Wildwood on Deep Ecology, Madeleine O'Callaghan on the new story of the unfolding cosmos, and John Doyle on the new paradigm. Brian Swimme's 12 part video series *Canticle to the Cosmos* provided source material for group study.

Politics and Economics

More everyday topics such as politics and economics were also explored. One of the groups that met monthly for the first couple of years was the political and social transformation group, looking at the linkages between spirituality and campaigning and other collective action. Days such as the one on 'Politics with a Soul,' led by Jean Hardy, examined whether a new and more inclusive spiritual/political myth was emerging. Speakers such as Paul Ekins, of The Other Economic Summit, put forward 'A new Vision for the Economic Summit. Living in harmony with each other and the planet,' coinciding with a G7 summit in London. And the Green Spirituality Festival, in the autumn of 1992, following the Rio Earth Summit, introduced some leading green thinkers.

Individual healing

Many found the spirituality of the creation tradition healing in and of itself. Others benefited from workshops and groups that worked towards healing splits within the person, particularly scars formed by limited and wounding forms of religion. I recall moments when the old paradigm of a judgmental and separate 'father God in the sky' fell away, and was replaced with a sense of immanence, love, energy and blessing, touching individuals and connecting them with the whole of humanity. The focus on befriending the darkness and the wounded aspects of oneself prevented this from falling into a denial of the shadow. A more harmonious, less fractured sense of who human beings are, began to be a felt reality.

St James's today

This view of human identity has fed back into the conduct of services at St James's, where the Anglican prayer of humble access ("We are not worthy so much as to gather up the crumbs under thy Table…") is no longer said. Most Sundays the idea of original blessing rather than original sin features in the Fractions, where the bread is broken by the celebrant facing the four directions at the start of the Eucharist. Worshippers are reminded of the gift of the Earth and of the myriad ways in which people worship their gods. They are reminded, too, of those who have nothing, and of the wounded child in each of us who is in need of healing.

When babies are christened, the parents are invited to take part in a special event that is part of the Sunday morning parish Eucharist, where the whole congregation witnesses a blessing under the catalpa tree in the courtyard, and the connection with the whole of creation is explicitly made.

At St James's Piccadilly we no longer organize activities under a specific Creation Spirituality banner (apart from an annual creation-centered liturgy and our monthly Labyrinth walks), since so many of its themes have been taken on board within the church and the rector who followed Donald Reeves, Charles Hedley, had already developed a respect for the impact of Creation Spirituality during his time in a previous parish.

St James's own community is now working on practical issues like climate change, and has installed photovoltaic cells on the roof. An environmental audit is carried out every few years. Christian Ecology's LOAF principles are used for community lunches (local, organic, and animal-friendly food is encouraged). Activities like recycling are carried out regularly.

Becoming GreenSpirit

In 1995, The Association for Creation Spirituality was officially formed as a registered charity in the UK. The title 'GreenSpirit' was adopted as the working title of the charity at the AGM in 1997 after many years of discussion. Shortly after that, the administrative center of the organization was moved away from St James's Church and became the responsibility of a part-time, paid administrator, working from home.

The impact of the green spirituality movement in the UK

Both now and in the early years, UK members come from a wide range of backgrounds, not just from Christian roots. Creation Spirituality often has the effect of changing the relationship people have to the tradition they are in. A number of people have eventually moved out of their role in monastic orders or as priests as a result of its impact, but others have been able to find a place within the Christian community as a result of discovering that there is a breadth and depth to the tradition that they had not previously been aware of.

In 1996 Jonathan Porritt, in a lecture at the Royal Institution, commented that Creation Spirituality "...goes to the core of (the) attempt to persuade people to transform themselves as part and parcel of transforming the world."

GreenSpirit today continues to be part of this transformation, as the next chapter will show.

29. GreenSpirit Today

Marian Van Eyk McCain

"On a spectacular morning, I am sitting on a bench looking out at the ocean enjoying the perfection of nature. Looking into the cloudless blue sky, I remember that the air we breathe is part of the whole history of our planet. Maybe that breath I just inhaled was previously inhaled by one of my great-great-grandmothers as she crossed the country in a covered wagon, or maybe it was breathed by a buffalo as he grazed across the vast wild prairie. I can let my imagination take that one breath back to the beginning of creation.

I will think about that every time I take a drink of water! Maybe a dinosaur drank this first, or it was part of the rain that floated Noah's boat, or a whale spouted it into steam that became a cloud and snowed on a mountain, then became spring melt into a river, down to my faucet and is now in my morning coffee.

Today I will keep in mind that we are all living in a closed system and there are no new elements. I am praying for a conscious awareness of the need to care for our Mother Earth."

– Sharon McKinney

The 'Three Jewels' of Buddhism— the Buddha, the Dharma and the Sangha—have their counterparts in most religious and spiritual traditions and GreenSpirit is no exception. For tradi-tional Buddhists, of course, the historical figure of the Buddha himself forms the central point, while in other religions the central point is God, Goddess, Allah, Yahweh, the Trinity, Great Spirit...the list is long. For GreenSpirit, the central point is anywhere and everywhere. In other words, it is the wholeness—

of our planet, or the universe, of 'all-that-is'—which for us takes the place of the Buddha. And for many, another word for 'all-that-is' is 'God.' Which of course is why so many are able to remain true to our green beliefs and practice within one of the other spiritual traditions at the same time.

The Dharma, for us, is the teachings of all those wise people whose work has been quoted in this book, especially Thomas Berry, Brian Swimme, Matthew Fox and the teachers who inspired *them*, such as Teilhard de Chardin. And above and beyond that, our dharma is what we have learned—and continue to learn—from the Earth itself and from all the creatures with whom we share it. For as Sharon McKinney says in that quote, above, and as so many others have said throughout the preceding pages, those creatures are us and we are them. Separateness is an illusion.

The third of those Three Jewels is what I want to speak of now, as we near the end of this book on green spirituality. For although it is possible to walk a spiritual path alone, and many do, for many others the sangha is essential. This is the congregation. It is that group of like-minded others with whom we share ideas, experiences, ritual, and conversation about the spiritual aspects of our lives. These are the people we talk with, explore with, dance with, laugh and cry with and work with in ways we hope will help to birth a new, green, consciousness in the world. Which is why, in this chapter, you will hear the voices of people from our world-wide GreenSpirit community describing their personal experiences of communion, with each other and with the rest of Nature.

For me, one of the delights of belonging to GreenSpirit, as an organization here in the UK where I live, is the opportunity to attend gatherings. These may be regular events, such as:

• the Annual Gathering, held each September or October, with locations chosen for their ease of access and often for their special ambience

• the 'Wild Week,' where a group of members come together for a week in a beautiful and remote area to share daily life and activities, eat, swim, play, talk, sing together and share their stories

• the annual Walking Retreat, where members spend several days hiking together in some of Britain's beautiful countryside, staying in youth hostels

• local group meetings of many different kinds in various parts of the country.

"Caverns and clouds - caverns, wind and clouds - caverns, wind, rock and clouds - caverns, wind, rock, water and clouds. Wind for air, rock for earth, streams for water, lights in the caverns for fire, so 12 or so pilgrims enjoyed the peaks around Castleton. Climbing Mam Tor nearly blew us all away. Sharing the dining room with a crowd of young people, French and English, was another heartening experience. Tourist centre provided information, church on a rise in the centre, signs of old mills by the stream. Research on the tea rooms and pubs proved rewarding. Evenings were creative, art, music and poetry being produced, and the last night sharing of the spiritual aspects of relating to all creation, touching stories on the theme of human ignorance and arrogance, lessons for us all. We came away refreshed to encounter the human dominated world again."

– *Anne Adams*

Or they may be special events: talks by visiting speakers, workshops, conferences, seminars and meetings on specific topics such as climate change, ecopsychology or the relationship between science and spirituality. Almost all GreenSpirit events are open to members and non-members alike.

"It's a good sign when adults can blow bubbles! It was that kind of a conference. Never mind the squared off red brick buildings eyeing each other dispassionately, the clinking of dishes coming from the kitchen in our main meeting room; we all more or less fell in love with David Abram, an American sensualist from New Mexico, who removed his shoes during his engagement with us, wore a little earring in his right ear, used lots of hand gestures...

'The GreenSpirit approach to life is about awakening the erotic (Eros) spirit outward to the world, and finding nourishment by having an active relationship with everything... including conversations with bushes and rocks. How else to endure the sadness of this era unless we become 'nested' in the full web of being that is woven around us? Everything breathes,' he said. 'Everything has a pulse, a rhythm, a rate of participation, a kind of animism. Everything listens to, is aware of the other shapes of experience around it; they percolate through each other, and energies are aware of the other energies around them...'

And so he goes on, with great passion and expressiveness, urging us to build bridges that connect us to our origins. He builds his bridges with us, enabling us to cross over into the realm of the sensuous, a pulsating, dynamic, expansive world that pulls us together even as we share the spell of his wildness inside a building in the city of Leicester".

– *Karen Eberhardt Shelton*

Sometimes, these special events combine meeting and talking with performing some important restorative actions for the Earth. Such as this one in Wales:

"Twenty-six of us met on the Saturday morning, including three children, entranced by the way the village and ruins of Abbey-Cwm-Hir in Mid Wales were encircled by beautiful wooded hills. One of our number later commented: 'As we gathered we became a village within a village, actually outnumbering the local residents who were wonderfully welcoming.' We spent the afternoon in joyful circle dancing amidst the ruins. It felt like we were bringing back laughter and celebration to a sacred space which, centuries ago, was an important centre of Welsh community and spirituality.

Later, in the little village pub, we joined locals in banter and sporadic singing.

On the Sunday we moved some eight miles away to Pen-y-Garreg Woods to help with a regeneration project. Some planted chestnut trees bought with money raised at a GreenSpirit event in Portsmouth Cathedral, some cleared a patch to encourage the heather to grow and others went to clear the footpath that crosses the larger wood. It was also gratifying to see the natural changes at the 'GreenSpirit pond' that some of us had dug last year in the smaller wood.

All in all it was a weekend that fully lived up to the dreams of our energetic organizer, to whom heartfelt thanks. Thanks also to the villagers who fed us, sheltered us and so freely gave of their time. As one of us reflected: 'It is hard to believe that so much richness occurred in one weekend. Conservation, shared entertainment, shared meals, circle dancing, walking, companionship.'"

– Don Hills

Local groups in various parts of the country get together regularly to celebrate the solar festivals and to join together in discussion, meditation, ritual, walking, camping, circle dancing, being *in* Nature, and learning together about green spirituality through videos, books and discussions. There is a lot of creativity. Group activities have ranged from the artistic, such as writing or painting, to the practical, like talks on soulful gardening and responsible recycling. Or to the adventurous, like camping under the stars without tents.

"My intention for meeting locally is that we should have a place where we can express our relationship with the planet, sometimes in grieving (like during the foot and mouth epidemic) sometimes in celebration. I think people are so often busy and surrounded by concrete/electric lighting etc and need opportunities to rediscover their delight and their creativity. Local groups can be a place, a circle for sharing.
We have rituals to make the ordinary sacred."
– *Hilary Norton*

Some members and their friends and families also support London-based events like political marches and demonstrations, marching together under the green and white GreenSpirit banner.

Thanks to the Internet, even those whose daily lives do not bring them into much contact with those 'like-minded others' can now find those people online. There is a special joy in being able to link up, share ideas and form friendships with others all over the globe. GreenSpirit, which has its main base in the UK, but increasing numbers of members from elsewhere, has its own online social network specially for members. It also has an email group where a wide range of topics is discussed. In addition to these, there is another, rapidly-growing, online social network, open to all, that brings together individuals and communities from around the world who are or have been inspired by the Creation Spirituality of Matthew Fox and/or other strands in the GreenSpirit weave. (See the GreenSpirit website for all details and links.)

"My daily connections with people from around the world inform my spirituality of interconnectedness, telling me that the actions I take affect other people everywhere—from the food I eat, the products I buy to the way that I travel.

My concern for the environment on which we all depend for our very survival gives rise (in part) to my view of the Earth as a living being, pulsating with energy and continually bringing forth new life. I remind myself that I am embedded into the ecosystems of the planet. My learning from science has told me that the universe is continually unfolding; life on Earth is constantly changing, growing, dying and renewing. My spirituality is like a flowing river, forever changing. It both affects and is affected by the world around me."

– Ian Mowll

There is much collaboration between GreenSpirit and other like-minded organizations. Some members take the GreenSpirit message into public places like schools, hospitals and prisons. Newsletters are circulated around the world. The website, journal, networks, newsletters and other publications continue to celebrate creativity and green spirituality.

The GreenSpirit Book Service, which was mentioned in the previous chapter, has played a key role in the history and life of GreenSpirit, thanks to Alan Shepherd, who started it and who for two decades continued working tirelessly to make books on green spirituality available to readers all over the UK. Many of our members were first introduced to GreenSpirit through the Book Service.

The mail order catalogue, which is regularly updated, contains many unusual and hard-to-obtain titles. And as well as mail order, the Book Service has a stall at all major GreenSpirit events and at many other public events and festivals throughout Great Britain. There is also a secondhand section and a free search service for rare and out-of-print titles. All proceeds from the Book Service are divided between two charities: the Schumacher Society and GreenSpirit, and this has been a wonderful boon to the organization throughout all the years of its existence.

Our website, as well as being our main, online presence, includes a large treasury of educational information which we call the 'Resource Pack,' and which receives an impressively large number of 'hits' every week from all over the globe.

The local groups extend our influence beyond our membership, introducing others to our ways of celebrating the seasons and special moments of the year, and drawing people in from local communities. Our activities touch souls, with devotional time, talk time, art and creativity. Always, our connection with Nature (and our deepening acceptance and understanding of our own *human* nature) is what nourishes our souls.

"We watched, fascinated, as Hilary set up her loom. She selected the warp threads with care: bright blues and purples, delicate greeny mohair. When the intricate construction of the warp was complete, the weaving proper proceeded apace and soon a beautiful braid was taking shape.

In the same way our wild week was woven out of diverse threads. Old stagers ... bright new threads friends from other worlds, new to the shores of Lake Padarn, and the magical realm of the storyteller.

And what a realm. The roundhouse with its Celtic carved entrance and elegantly curving thatch: the welcoming barn, place of cooking and sharing of food, conversation, company and the passing of the talking stick around the circle: the comfortable straw bale Hogan: the beautifully ecological 'loo with a view': the log house with its beautiful interlocking ceiling: the comfortable chalet and the stunning 'cob cottage.' All this set in the fairytale landscape of pools and waterfalls and ancient oaks ... the fabric wove itself—from simple, element based, rituals, swimming in the lake, inspired meals offered by one individual after another, making contact through talk—whether sharing about our lives or grappling with the great questions, drumming, singing and dancing round the evening fire. And all this culminating in the last day's grand ritual.

...We gathered at the end of the week to express our gratitude, to each other and the land and the place. Our faith in humanity—and the potential of humanity for transformation in the face of the ecological challenge—renewed, and some powerful new energy generated for GreenSpirit to meet that challenge. We departed well pleased with the fabric we had woven."

– *Isabel Clarke*

So GreenSpirit is my 'sangha'. The people who make up GreenSpirit are the congregation with whom I join in person, from time to time, to do ritual, to learn, celebrate and share. Beyond them, my sangha widens out to include all those others around the country and around the world with whom I can now commune through the magic of modern communication technology. My image of this is the one that Joyce Edmond-Smith spoke of in her chapter on Buddhism: "The jeweled net of Indra, where at every intersection there is a clear jewel and where the jewels all reflect each other's images, appearing in each other's reflection ad infinitum." We are all jewels in that net. And since it is green spirituality that we share, I suppose that means we are emeralds.

For comprehensive, up-to-date information about GreenSpirit as an organization, contact details for other countries, and a wealth of information and resources pertaining to green spirituality, please visit our Website: www.greenspirit.org.uk

Mailing Address:
137 Ham Park Road
Forest Gate
London E7 8LE

Telephone: +44 (0)208 552 2096

30. The Theory of Anyway

Sharon Astyk and Pat Meadows

We are obligated to live rightly, in part because of what living rightly gives us: integrity, honor, joy, a better relationship with our deity of choice—and peace.

So let's talk about joy and peace.

Chasing status and material goods (or the Almighty Dollar) clearly does not lead to either joy or peace. Look around you at the people you know who are engaged in these pursuits. Do you think they are really happy? Do they seem to have joy in their lives? I don't think so. The status- or dollar-chasers whom we have observed seem to be quite unhappy for the most part, and some are clearly nervous wrecks.

"His Holiness, the Dalai Lama describes two kinds of selfish people: the unwise and the wise. Unwise selfish people think only of themselves, and the result is confusion and pain. Wise selfish people know that the best thing they can do for themselves is to be there for others. As a result, they experience joy."[1]

In 1971, Frances Moore Lappé's seminal book *Diet for a Small Planet* [2] was one of the first to point out that the details of our daily lives matter; they make a difference to the world. Wow! We found that a very empowering concept (and still do).

We cannot all give up everything and go to the Sinai Desert to be contemplative nuns or monks. We cannot all be relief workers in Africa. But we can all make a difference nevertheless, just by the choices we make in every day life.

It is also very empowering to realize that this is an ongoing lifetime commitment and not a one-shot deal. If you mess up today...well, you get more chances to make decisions and choices tomorrow, and hopefully they will be more skillful decisions and choices than those of today.

So one needs at least to try and make one's everyday choices (as well as the larger, life-changing decisions) in accord with this idea. Life keeps getting in the way, of course, as it does for all of us, in the form of family responsibilities, the need to earn a living, and ill health; sometimes we have more success than at other times. It is an ongoing journey: one that continues for life.

With specific reference to 'peak oil' preparations, there is a terrific psychological difference determined by the frame of mind in which one takes certain actions. Supposing, for example, you are going to cover your windows with clear plastic in winter, to save on energy. Well, you can think of yourself as being forced into this act by peak oil, by global warming, or for economic reasons. There is not much joy in taking defensive actions.

But if you can think of it as contributing to 'the repair of the world,' then you have a totally different view of the action. Now you can really be happy about it; you have made a difference, however small, by this action. You have conserved resources for those who desperately need them (especially if you contribute the money that you save to a charity), you have lessened your contribution to global warming and to air pollution. Wow! This is a good thing.

Over time, these points of view have an effect on your personality and character. The defensive or 'forced to do this' motivation tends to harden and close you, shutting you away from others. The 'repair of the world' motivation tends to awaken compassion in you, to soften you towards others.

"A human being is a part of a whole, called by us 'universe', a part limited in time and space. He experiences himself, his thoughts and feelings as something separated from the rest... a kind of optical delusion of his consciousness. This delusion is a kind of prison for us, restricting us to our personal desires and to affection for a few persons nearest to us. Our task must be to free ourselves from this prison by widening our circle of compassion to embrace all living creatures and the whole of nature in its beauty."

Albert Einstein

At least five of the world's great religions (Judaism, Buddhism, Christianity, Islam and Hinduism) stress 'the repair of the world.' Judaism probably says it most clearly. The Hebrew expression is '*Tikkun Olam*' (the repair of the world) and this is an obligation of observant Jews.

In Buddhism, the same idea is beautifully expressed in 'The Bodhisattva's Vow,' by Shantideva, written in the eighth century CE which contains this line: "For as long as space endures and for as long as living beings remain, until then may I too abide to dispel the misery of the world." [3]

Christianity has Jesus' exhortation to his followers: "Do unto others as you would have them do unto you." This can be extended to environmental causes, and Peak Oil since, obviously, others would enjoy clean air and sufficient resources to enable them to live decently.

Hinduism states "This is the sum of duty; do naught onto others what you would not have them do unto you,"[4] and Mohammed spoke to Islam saying "Hurt no one so that no one may hurt you."[5] The Bahá'i faith teaches "Ascribe not to any soul that which thou wouldst not have ascribed to thee, and say not that which thou doest not. Blessed is he who prefers his brother before himself." [6]

However, as citizens of this planet, 95 percent of what is needed to resolve the coming crisis in energy depletion, or climate change or whatever, is what we should do *anyway*. Which is why we call this 'The Theory of Anyway.'

Living more simply, more frugally, using less, leaving reserves for others, reconnecting with our food and our community, these are things we should all be doing because they are the right thing to do on many levels. That they also have the potential to save our lives is merely a side benefit (a big one, though).

This is a deeply powerful way of thinking because it is a deeply moral way of thinking. We would like to think of ourselves as moral people, but we tend to think of moral questions as the obvious ones: "Should I steal or pay?" "Should I hit or talk?" The real and most essential moral questions of our lives are the questions we rarely ask of the things we do every day: "Should I eat this?" "Where should I live and how?" "What should I wear?" "How should I keep warm/cool?" We think of these questions as foregone conclusions: I should keep warm X way because that's the kind of furnace I have, or I should eat this because that's what's in the grocery store. The Theory of Anyway turns this around, and points out that what we do, the way we live, must pass ethical muster first. We must always ask the question "Is this contributing to the repair of the world, or its destruction?"

So if you announced, tomorrow, that the peak oil issue had been resolved, we would still keep gardening, hanging our laundry to dry in the sun instead of using a dryer, cutting back and trying to find a way to make do with less. Because even if we found enough oil to power our society for 1000 years, there would still be climate change, and it would be wrong of us to choose our own convenience over the security and safety of our children and other people's children.

And if you said tomorrow that climate change had been fixed, that we could power our lives forever with renewables, we would still keep gardening and living frugally. Because our agriculture is premised on depleted soil and depleted aquifers, and we are facing a future in which many people will not have enough food and water if we keep eating this way. To allow that to happen would be a betrayal of what we believe is right.

And if you declared that we had fixed that problem too, that we were no longer depleting our aquifers and expanding the dead zone in the Gulf of Mexico, we would still keep gardening and telling others to do the same, because our reliance on food from other nations, and our economy impoverishes and starves millions of poor people and creates massive economic inequities that do tremendous harm.

And if you told us that globalization was over, and that we were going to create a just economic system, and we had fixed all the other problems, and that we didn't have to worry anymore, would one then stop gardening?

No. Because the nurture of a piece of land would still be the right thing to do. Doing things with no more waste than is absolutely necessary would still be the right thing to do. The creation of a fertile, sustainable, lasting place of beauty would still be right work in the world. We would still be obligated to live in way that prevented wildlife from being run to extinction and poisons contaminating the soil and the air and the oceans. We would still be obligated to make the most of what we have and reduce our needs so they represent a fair share of what the Earth has to offer. We would still be obligated to treat poor people as our siblings, and you do not live comfortably when your siblings suffer or have less. We are obligated to live rightly, in part because of what living rightly gives us: integrity, honor, joy, a better relationship with our deity of choice—and peace.

There are people out there who are prepared to step forward and give up their cars, start growing their own food, stop consuming so much and stop burning fossil fuels…just as soon as peak oil, or climate change, or government rationing, or some external force makes them. But that, we believe is the wrong way to think about this. We cannot wait for others to tell us, or the disaster to befall us. We have to do now, do today, do with all our hearts, the things we should have been doing 'anyway' all along.

Notes

1. Chodron, P. *When Things Fall Apart* (Shambhala, 1997) p. 88
2. Lappé, F.M. *Diet for a Small Planet* (Ballantine, 1971)
3. Ven. Geshe Ngawang Dakpa (from 'Tse Chen Ling Buddhist Lectures,' 2000)
4. from the *Mahabharata*, (5:15:17) (ca. 500BCE)
5. in *The Farewell Sermon* (c. 571–632 CE)
6. *Tablets of Baha'u'llah* 6.71.

31. Simplicity, Activism and the Fourfold Way

Marian Van Eyk McCain

More than half a century has passed since that Sunday morning when I skipped church to sit under a tree and think about what 'God' is, or is not.

The honeysuckle is blooming in the hedges and its scent fills the lanes. Meadowsweet too, its creamy flowers a-hum with bees. How well those two fragrances combine. One savory, like fresh-milled grain, the other sweet as its namesake honey. I sniff them in turn—savory first, then sweet. Like a meal. My nose takes and binds their duality into a different, greater whole.

I am walking down the lane towards our cottage, with four books under my arm.

As I turn the corner, I reflect, as always, on how I love this home of ours, this tiny, simple house of mud and stone which has nestled here against the hillside, keeping the rain off people, and probably their companion dogs and cats too, since 1733.

No cats or dogs live here now. But we share shelter with a host of other creatures, seen and unseen. Spiders, daddy-long-legs, dozing moths who wake at dusk to dance in the lamplight—and sometimes mice. (Though we do have a benign relocation system for those whenever they start raiding the larder). Through the hollows in its old, worn flagstones the house breathes, and inside and outside don't seem entirely separate. I like that.

I make myself a cup of green tea and climb the steps beneath the hawthorn tree to my favorite sitting place, between the wisteria and the runner beans. It is a small patch of grass, no more than six feet by eight: a lawn for a leprechaun. But it is enough for me.

Everything here is enough. We have no car, no TV, no washing machine, no microwave oven, no central heating, and no shower stall, just an old bathtub. Yet we lack nothing. Sitting here, with my bare feet in the warm grass, the bees working the beans and marigolds, birds singing and the sun on my skin, I feel richer than I have ever felt in all my long life.

But the books on my lap weigh heavily. I have to review them for a magazine, but they don't offer happy reading. One is about the awful politics of dioxin.[1] That is one of the most deadly, persistent chemicals ever, and it is everywhere. It kills people, deforms unborn babies, devastates wildlife, and makes lots of money for its manufacturers. Which of course is why it is everywhere and will continue to be everywhere, wreaking havoc, for centuries. The second is an exposé of the evils of the modern food industry, from the nightmare of the chicken factory to the 'just in time' ordering system that has turned our already choked motorways into mobile warehouses and forces casual, immigrant workers to live in rat-like squalor on Spanish rubbish tips or to be squashed by gangmasters six to a room in East Anglian shacks.[2]

Beside me, these beans, on their poles, are festooned with scarlet flowers. We grow most of our own food, buy organic, and buy local. I have only been into the supermarket twice since we came to live here, and both times it was for an anti-GM demonstration. I feel myself detaching, feeling smug. Yes it is awful, but at least I am not part of it.

But that's not true. Of course I am part of it. We all are. It is one world and we are all fragments of it. There is no escaping that.

The next book scores a bull's eye. It is on climate change and carbon rationing.[3] Here is a list of all the excuses people make for the carbon emissions they cause. "What about folks like me who have loved ones in other countries?" someone protests. "We *have* to fly in airplanes, even if that does put more carbon dioxide— and other bad things—into the air than a year's worth of car driving. There has to be an exception for *us.*"

Wrong. There are no exceptions. Not if we want our planet to stay green, to stay alive. My justifications are crumbling. I think about my grandchildren on the other side of the Atlantic and the airplane tickets in an envelope on the sideboard. I feel the Earth under my feet and the pain of conflict rising in my heart. Here is a pair of opposites I cannot reconcile. I can only live with it, here in this place of tension between guilt and yearning.

It does not matter that I belong to Greenpeace and Friends of the Earth. It does not matter that I recycle almost everything that I cannot compost or that I write letters, sign petitions, pull up genetically engineered maize with my own hands or scramble up and down wooded hillsides at dusk in the hope of springing a cattle farmer's badger traps. It is not enough that I am vegetarian, use eco-friendly products and write books and blogs about how to live simply and lightly on the Earth. There is more. There is always more. I cannot do it all. I also know I cannot tear up those plane tickets.

Sometimes I feel angry. I feel angry with rich people, wasteful people, people who drive around in oil-guzzling monster vehicles and shop till they drop and don't seem to care and or even to think about these things, let alone agonize over them. And then I feel angry with myself for being so dreadfully judgmental.

Sometimes I just ache. I ache for the bone-thin people, the starving children with the wistful eyes, and the mothers who bore them only to watch them die. I ache for the parched, dry soil, the dying rivers, the clear-felled forests, the loss of species we shall never see again, the seeds doomed to lie forever under concrete. The more I ache, the more beautiful it seems to be here in this simple place, in this simple life that I love so much. The ache and the joy join hands inside me and I weep.

Life, said the Buddha, is pain and suffering.

He was right of course. But for me there is a deeper, greener rightness. Yes, sometimes there is pure pain. And sometimes there are moments of pure joy. And yes, in a sense they are all *maya*, illusion, a creation of the unenlightened human mind. But this embrace of duality, this fusion of aching pain and soaring joy feels to me like the most profound experience of being fully alive, embodied, in and of this world and in erotic relationship with all that is. And that feels exquisitely right. To me, anyway. This, I believe, is what June Raymond was speaking of, in an earlier chapter, when she talked about having "...a heart that is able to hold the suffering without denying love."

Freya Mathews, in her book on Panpsychism, speaks eloquently to this. She describes standing in the peaceful beauty of the moonlight and remembering the crow she saw earlier in the evening with its leg caught in a steel trap, doomed to suffer all night and to die in the morning.

"When you stand beneath the moon and commune with the One, it must not be with the sentimental joy of one who is blind to its dark face. You must hold the crow and the moon together in your heart. You must live within the unresolved space of this paradox." [4]

Maybe it was motherhood which first taught me, at a deep, cellular level, about this two-stranded nature of full aliveness. The words of Judith Wright's poem to her soon-to-be-born child have lingered in my mind for 40 years:

"Today I lose and find you
whom yet my blood would keep—
would weave and sing around you
The spells and songs of sleep."[5]

One's whole life feels like that in many ways. A longing to birth each new moment, each new experience, and yet to hold on, to stay safe, to protect ourselves, our loved ones, our lifestyles, while all the time knowing that there is no such thing as safety, no such things as security, certainty or hiding places. To be human, to have eaten from the tree of knowledge, is to be doomed to full, painful—plus joyful—awareness.

> "The foxes have holes and the birds of the air have nests but the son of man hath not where to lay his head."[6]

So all our culture's bolt holes are illusory. No TV, computer games, overwork, alcohol nor 'retail therapy' can protect us completely from feeling the agony of mortality—of loving and dying—nor the despair of knowing what a mess our species is making of the planet. They can, however, prevent us from experiencing the fullness of joy. Without that sweet delight in being alive, despair is corrosive. That is why, for me, living as simply and lightly as I can is essential. It keeps that joy flowing.

The two—the joy and the aching—do not always blend. But they are always linked. The more joy one feels about being part of the Earth, the stronger the agony about what is happening to it, and the more danger there is of being destroyed by unalloyed despair.

There are many things which have helped me to avoid that danger. One is a comment by Peter Russell that there are two possible scenarios ahead of us. The first predicts that human consciousness will change in time to prevent total, ecological collapse. So to help create that change we all need to do a lot of inner work and cultivate detachment, caring and compassion. The other scenario is that the collapse will inevitably happen. In which case there will be chaos, and in order to deal with the chaos we shall need to do a lot of inner work and cultivate detachment, caring and compassion. Therefore, since our tasks are the same whatever happens, we may as well just get on with them.[7] (There's the 'Theory of Anyway' again.)

Which brings me directly to another helpful thing.

This is a teaching I received nearly 20 years ago from the cultural anthropologist and Basque shaman, Angeles Arrien. She calls it the Fourfold Way.[8]

From her cross-cultural research into shamanic traditions, Angeles discovered four archetypal patterns that assist people's creative expression, health and adaptation to change. These are: The Way of the Warrior, with its rule, *"Show up, choose to be present"*: The Way of the Healer, which exhorts, *"Pay attention to what has heart and meaning"*: The Way of the Visionary which insists, *"Tell the truth without blame or judgment,"* and The Way of the Teacher which tells us to, *"Be open—rather than attached—to the outcome."*

This translates into a simple formula, applicable to any and every situation. There are just four rules to follow.

- *Show up*
- *Pay attention*
- *Tell the truth*
- *Don't be attached to outcomes*

So I showed up this morning to collect these books. I try always to show up when there is work I can do, whether it is signing petitions, trashing GM crops, publishing articles or rescuing badgers.

As I read these books that are on my lap, I shall pay careful attention to their authors' words. Right now, I am paying attention to the birds, the bumblebees, the marigolds, and the scent of the meadowsweet and the honeysuckle. I am paying attention to the sun that caresses my body with its shining fingers and to the way the grass blades tickle my bare toes. I try to pay attention to my limitations, also, and to honor my body's need for consideration as I move into old age and my soul's need for rest and play and time out from angst and activism.

I am telling the truth of my joy, my pain, my anger and judgments, my carbon dilemma and the experience of living in the tension of paradox. And I shall try not to be attached to your response to this book.

I have done my best to describe here, through my own words and through the writings of others, the many-stranded fabric of a twenty-first century green spirituality that could, when fully lived and practiced by everyone, birth a new consciousness. Now, as this task ends, I must let go fully into a sense of trust. For as Thomas Berry reminds me:

"If the dynamics of the universe from the beginning shaped the course of the heavens, lighted the sun and formed the Earth, if this same dynamism brought forth the continents and seas and atmosphere, if it awakened life in the primordial cell and then brought into being the unnumbered variety of living beings ... and guided us safely through the turbulent centuries, there is reason to believe that this same guiding process is precisely what has awakened in us our present understanding of ourselves and our relation to this stupendous process. Sensitized to such guidance from the very structure and functioning of the universe, we can have confidence in the future that awaits the human venture."[9]

Notes

1. Allen, R. *The Dioxin War* (Pluto Press, 2004)
2. Lawrence, F. *Not on the Label* (Penguin, 2004)
3. Hillman, M. *How We Can Save the Planet* (Penguin, 2004)
4. Mathews, F. *For Love of Matter* (SUNY, 2003) p.160
5. Wright, J. "Woman's Song" in *Woman to Man* (Angus & Robertson, 1949)
6. Matthew 8:20
7. Grof, S.& Russell, P. *The Consciousness Revolution* (Element, 1999)

8.   Arrien, A. *The Four-Fold Way* (HarperSanFrancisco, 1993)

9.   Berry, T. *Evening Thoughts* (Sierra Club, 2006) p.169

Adapted from an essay first published in the Winter 2004 issue of the GreenSpirit Journal.

About the Contributors

Sharon Astyk is the author of three books: *Depletion and Abundance: Life on the New Home Front* (2008) *A Nation of Farmers: Defeating the Food Crisis on American Soil* (2009) and *Independence Days: The Power of Full Pantry to Transform Nearly Everything* (2009) all from New Society Publishers. In her copious spare time, she and her husband raise produce, goats, chickens, fruit, children and havoc on her small farm in upstate New York. She's been fortunate enough to know her co-contributor Pat Meadows now for a full decade.

Grace Blindell, born in 1921, studied at the Institute in Culture and Creation Spirituality. She writes from the abundant richness of her life: having trained as a nurse during World War II she has lived and worked in France, Malaya (now Malaysia), Nigeria, the UK and (after 'retiring') the Gaza Strip. Her spiritual path, from Christian origins, now leads her to choose to have no label, unless it might be 'Creation-Centered Universalist.'

Jean Bee has a background in physics and has taught and written about complexity theory over the last ten years. She also works with organizations undergoing change, so is able to bridge the gap between theory and practice.

Meryn Callander was born in Australia in 1952. A graduate of Monash University in Melbourne, she worked as a social worker with children in crisis and as a passionate planter of native gardens, until a journey to Europe and the US in search of a deeper understanding of wellness led to her partnering with John Travis in 1979. She became co-director of Wellness Associates, a non-profit educational organization dedicated to personal and planetary wellbeing. Together, they published *Wellness For*

Helping Professionals: Creating Compassionate Cultures (Wellness Associates Publications, 1990), and *A Change of Heart: The Global Wellness Inventory* (Arcus Press, 1993) and are currently working on a new book: *Why Men Leave*, which addresses the phenomenon of men who leave their wives and new babies shortly after the birth of the child. Meryn is co-founder of the Alliance of Transforming the Lives of Children. She and John and their daughter, Siena live in subtropical northern New South Wales, Australia, where they are busy planting rainforest trees on their 2-acre creek frontage land just outside the bustling village of Mullumbimby.

Chris Clarke was Professor of Applied Mathematics and Dean of the Faulty of Mathematics at the University of Southampton, where his research was on Astrophysics, Cosmology and the physics of the brain. Since then he has worked freelance in the area of quantum theory and consciousness. In addition to about 80 technical papers and three technical books, he has written the more popular books *Reality Through the Looking Glass* (Floris Books, 1997) and *Living in Connection* (GreenSpirit Press, 2003). He has served as on the editorial boards of two international physics journals and the journal *Ecotheology,* and has been chair of the Council of the Scientific and Medical Network as well as twice Chair of GreenSpirit.

Isabel Clarke is a Consultant Clinical Psychologist, working for the UK National Health Service. She is currently psychological therapies lead in an acute mental health hospital. She has an interest in using insights gained from her study of psychology, and her practice as a therapist, to understand fundamental questions about the nature of spirituality, and the individual and relationship, including relationship with the Earth. Her latest book, *Madness, Mystery and the Survival of God* (O Books, 2008) explores these themes. Details of this and her other publications and activities can be found on her website: www.isabelclarke.org/

Michael Colebrook is a retired marine ecologist and author/co-author of over 70 scientific papers and subsequently a number of books and essays, most recently *The Green Mantle of Romanticism* with Christine Avery and *How Things Come to Be*, in the GreenSpirit pamphlet series. He was for many years the Production Editor of the GreenSpirit Journal and remains a regular contributor to its pages.

Cormac Cullinan is a senior environmental lawyer and adviser on institutional, policy and regulatory reform in the fields of environment and natural resource management. His work in pioneering a legal philosophy that restores an ecological perspective to governance systems (Earth jurisprudence) is internationally recognized and in 2008 led to his inclusion in *Planet Savers: 301 Extraordinary Environmentalists*. He was admitted as an attorney in March 1989 and has specialized in environmental law since 1992 when he completed a Masters degree in environmental law at the University of London. He is an expert on international and South African environmental law and policy and acts for a wide range of public sector, private sector and NGO clients. Cormac is also a director of *En*Act International, an honorary research associate of the University of Cape Town, and a member of the IUCN Environmental Law Commission. He has worked on these issues in more than 20 countries, including ten in sub-Saharan Africa. In the academic field he has lectured and written widely on governance issues related to human interactions with the environment and is the author of *Wild Law* (Green Books, 2003) as well as of several works commissioned and published by the Food and Agriculture Organization of the United Nations.

Tania Dolley, after completing a degree in environmental studies, spent time travelling and studying in India and teaching English in Thailand. Her desire to understand the links between environmental problems and human behaviour led her to train as a Hakomi body-centred therapist and teach an MSc module in Ecopsychology. She currently works as a counselling psychologist and ecopsychologist and lives in Wales, where she is also involved in local community initiatives to promote sustainable living.

Neil Douglas-Klotz directs the Edinburgh Institute for Advanced Learning (www.eial.org) and co-founded the Edinburgh International Festival of Middle Eastern Spirituality and Peace (www.mesp.org.uk). His books include *Prayers of the Cosmos* (HarperOne, 1993), *Desert Wisdom* (Harper Collins, 1995), *The Hidden Gospel* (Quest, 2001), *The Genesis Meditations* (Quest, 2003), *The Sufi Book of Life* (Penguin, 2005) and *The Tent of Abraham* (Beacon Press, 2007, with Rabbi Arthur Waskow and Sr Joan Chittister). Information about his work can be also be found at the website of the Abwoon Resource Center, www.abwoon.com/

Joyce Edmond-Smith has been a member of the Network of Engaged Buddhists—of which she is the Chair—for 15 years. Her Buddhist practice is Chan (Zen). She was born and grew up in Hackney, East London. Early adulthood was spent in Paris, after initially going there as an au-pair, with two years in Martinique in the French Caribbean. She encountered Buddhism when she moved to Brighton , England as a mature student. Joyce has 'engaged' politically and socially all her life. She taught in Further Education for 25 years and was also an elected member on Brighton Council for 20 years. She has always had a passion for the environment and sustainability and has campaigned for many years on these issues, especially on climate change and considers this to be an integral part of her Buddhist practice. She also works with several local groups and is presently member of the Brighton & Hove Transition group, as well as the Brighton & Hove Food Partnership, and she is a member of the Committee of the Brighton & Hove United Nations Association.

Matthew Fox has devoted his life to recovering the mystical tradition of the West and relating it to the East and to Native traditions as well as to science and the struggle for social, gender, ecological and racial justice. He calls this movement 'Creation Spirituality.' He has encountered fierce opposition from the Vatican, which silenced him for a year and later expelled him from the Dominican Order, of which he had been a member for 34 years. Fox believes that by re-inventing education, work and worship, we can effect a non-violent revolution. Toward that end, he has established alternative schools and educational programs, including the University of Creation Spirituality and YELLAWE, a project for inner-city high school students. He is currently a scholar in residence with the Academy of Love and Learning in Santa Fe, New Mexico. He lectures, teaches, writes, and serves as president of the non-profit organization he created in 1984: Friends of Creation Spirituality. Matthew is the author of 28 books, including *Original Blessing* (Tarcher, 2000), *Creativity* (Tarcher, 2004) and *The Hidden Spirituality of Men* (New World Library, 2008). He lives in Oakland, California. His website is www.matthewfox.org/

Petra Griffiths was coordinator of the Centre for Creation Spirituality from 1988 to 1993. Petra's early career was in social policy and action (with Shelter and the National Consumer Council). She was a co-founder of the national organization, Cancerlink, and is now Director of The Cancer Resource Centre in Battersea, which has pioneered the development of a number of forms of psychosocial and spiritual support for people affected by cancer, including the multi ethnic communities of south London.

Stephan Harding is Co-ordinator of the MSc in Holistic Science at Schumacher College in Devon, England, and is a regular contributor to the college short courses. He is the resident ecologist, giving talks on Gaia Theory and Deep Ecology to most course groups, and helping students wishing to undertake credits projects. He also works with Gaian scientist James Lovelock on Gaian computer modeling. Stephan is the author *of Animate Earth: Science, Intuition and Gaia* (Green Books, 2006) www.schumachercollege.org.uk/

Jean Hardy was, with Michael Colebrook, the first Editor of the GreenSpirit Journal from 1999-2006 and continues to write for it. She has been a university teacher for most of her working life, teaching sociology, social policy, political philosophy and also transpersonal psychology, writing several books and many shorter pieces. Her best known book, still selling after 22 years and translated into five other languages, is *A psychology with a soul* (Arkana, 1990). She lives in Devon and is closely involved with the work of the Dartington Hall Trust, particularly as it pertains to holistic ecology, and to Schumacher College. She has been a member of GreenSpirit since the 1980s and served for some years on the Council.

Maddy Harland is the editor of *Permaculture Magazine: Solutions for Sustainable Living* and a co-founder of Permanent Publications, a publishing company specializing in developing our understanding of permaculture. www.permaculture.co.uk/

Don Hills was born, one of non-identical twins in 1936 in London's East End. Because of the Blitz, his family was obliged to move to the outskirts. Even there, they experienced bombing raids, air-raid shelters, and all of the associated sights and smells. He grew to hate military might, and enlisted as a conscientious objector for his National Service. His early idealism led him into evangelical Christianity, but by his middle twenties he had become disenchanted with it. He felt a calling to teaching (for seven years) and then to educational psychology (for 20 years). Spiritually, he became drawn to the GreenSpirit movement, and was for many years a Council member. For the last three years he has been Co-Editor of the GreenSpirit Journal, and in 2007 self-published his first book, *Moving On*. His special interests are Ecopsychology, and all aspects of rivers, seas and oceans. He lives with his wife Helen by the coast at Combe Martin, North Devon.

Jenny Johnson was born in Bristol in 1945 and educated at The Red Maids' School, the oldest girls' school in England. At the age of five, she began to write poems; at 50, she joined a circle dance group; at 60, she began to create her own dances and to illustrate some of her poems for the *GreenSpirit Journal*. Jenny is also a Reiki healer and practices at a centre that offers complementary therapies to those on low incomes. She lives in Exmouth with her husband, Noel Harrower, and has a married son working in Nottingham. See www.jennyjohnsondancerpoet.co.uk/

Rabbi Jamie Korngold, 'The Adventure Rabbi,' is the author of *God in the Wilderness: Rediscovering the Spirituality of the Great Outdoors* (Doubleday, 2008).

Contact details: Rabbi Jamie Korngold 303.417.6200 ext 10 jamie@adventurerabbi.org

www.GodInTheWilderness.com/

David C. Korten is board chair of the Positive Futures Network, president of the People-Centered Development Forum, and author of the best seller, *When Corporations Rule the World* (1996). His other books are *The Post Corporate World: Life After Capitalism* (2000) and *The Great Turning: From Empire to Earth Community* (2006) All three books are published by Berrett-Koehler.

www.davidkorten.org/

Satish Kumar has been Editor of *Resurgence* magazine for more than thirty years. He is also Director of Programmes at Schumacher College (a residential international centre for the study of ecological and spiritual values) and an internationally-known speaker, teacher and broadcaster. His autobiography, *No Destination,* has sold 50,000 copies and is published by Green books, as are his four other books, *You Are, Therefore I Am: A Declaration of Dependence* (2002), *The Buddha and the Terrorist* (2006), *Spiritual Compass* (2007) and *Earth Pilgrim* (2009).

In July 2000, Satish was awarded an Honorary Doctorate in Education from the University of Plymouth and the following year he received an Honorary Doctorate in Literature from the University of Lancaster. In November 2001, he was presented with the Jamnalal Bajaj International Award for Promoting Gandhian Values Abroad. www.resurgence.org/

Marian Van Eyk McCain is a retired transpersonal psychotherapist and health educator, now enjoying her incarnation as a free-lance writer. She is the author of *Transformation through Menopause* (Bergin & Garvey 1991), *Elderwoman: Reap the wisdom, feel the power, embrace the joy* (Findhorn Press, 2002), *The Lilypad List: 7 steps to the simple life* (Findhorn Press, 2004) and several works of fiction. She is also Co-Editor of the GreenSpirit Journal, editor of two newsletters, a blogger, columnist and book reviewer. A keen gardener, hiker and lover of all things green, she lives in rural Devon with her soulmate and partner, Sky, and assists him in the running of the Wholesome Food Association (www.wholesome-food.org.uk) Marian welcomes visits to her websites: www.elderwoman.org/ and www.lilypadlist.com/

Pat Meadows has been trying, with varying degrees of success, to 'live simply that others may simply live' for more than 35 years. Frances Moore Lappé's *Diet for a Small Planet* first gave her idea that daily choices made by ordinary people matter to the entire planet. Eknath Easwaran and Thich Nhat Hanh have also been important to Pat's view of the world. Now retired, she considers herself incredibly fortunate to be living and gardening in Pennsylvania's beautiful northern Appalachians with her husband. She and her co-contributor Sharon Astyk have been online friends for ten years.

Susan Meeker-Lowry is the author of *Economics as if the Earth Really Mattered* (1988) and *Invested in the Common Good* (1995)— both from New Society Publishers—and numerous articles. She lives in Maine, USA, where she publishes a newsletter, 'Gaian Voices: Earth Spirit, Earth Action, Earth Stories.' She can be contacted through her website: www.gaianvoices.com/

Ruth Meyers qualified as a primary school teacher in Southampton in 1972. Since then, she has worked in a variety of settings with children including inner city schools and playgroups. At present she is spending her time harvesting some of those experiences through her writing as well as undertaking grandparent duties to her three grandchildren.

Emma Restall Orr is a teacher, philosopher, poet, priest and author of a dozen books, including *Living Druidry* (Piatkus, 2004), *Living With Honor: A Pagan Ethics* (O Books, 2007), and *Kissing The* Hag (O Books, 2009). Joint Chief of the British Druid Order for nine years, she is now Head of the international Druid Network, in 2002 founding Honoring The Ancient Dead, a group advocating for the respectful treatment of ancient human remains. http://druidnetwork.org/

June Raymond is a sister of Notre Dame. She lives and works in Liverpool doing healing with the Bach Flower Remedies.

Brian Swimme is a mathematical cosmologist on the graduate faculty of the California Institute of Integral Studies in San Francisco. He received his Ph.D. (1978) from the University of Oregon specializing in gravitational dynamics, mathematical cosmology and singularity theory. Swimme was a faculty member in the Dept. of Mathematics and Physics at the University of Puget Sound in Tacoma, Washington from 1978–1981. He was a member of the faculty at the Institute for Culture and Creation Spirituality at Holy Names College in Oakland, California from 1983–1989. Brian Swimme's central concern is the role of the human within the Earth community. Toward this goal, in 1989 he founded the Center for the Story of the Universe, a production and distribution affiliate of the California Institute of Integral Studies. Brian's published work includes *The Universe is a Green Dragon* (Bear and Company, 1984), *The Universe Story* (Harper San Francisco, 1992) written with Thomas Berry, and *The Hidden Heart of the Cosmos* (Orbis, 1996). His books have been translated into eight different languages. He has been featured in several television series and has produced a 12-part DVD series 'Canticle to the Cosmos' (Tides Center, 1990). He lectures worldwide and has presented at conferences sponsored by the American Association for the Advancement of Science, The World Bank, UNESCO, The United Nations Millennium Peace Summit, and the American Natural History Museum. www.brianswimme.org/

John W. Travis, M.D., M.P.H., was born in Ohio, USA and educated at Tufts and later at Johns Hopkins University. He has been a leading figure in the wellness movement since 1975. His Wellness Inventory program is widely used as the foundation for wellness programs in both corporate and healthcare environments and by wellness coaches.

His publications include: *The Wellness Workbook*, coauthored with Regina Ryan (Ten Speed Press, 1981, 1988, Celestial Arts,

2004), *Simply Well: Choices for a Healthy Life,* coauthored with Regina Ryan (Ten Speed Press, 1990, 2001), *Wellness For Helping Professionals: Creating Compassionate Cultures,* co-authored with Meryn Callander (Wellness Associates Publications, 1990), *A Change of Heart: The Global Wellness Inventory,* co-authored with Meryn G. Callander (Arcus Press, 1993), *The Society of Prospective Medicine's Handbook of Health Assessment Tools* (SPM Press, 1999). He is co-founder of the Alliance of Transforming the Lives of Children. John now lives with his wife, Meryn Callander and their daughter Siena in northern New South Wales, Australia. www.thewellspring.com/

Sandra White is a Jungian counselor and ecopsychologist. Her special interest is in the application of principles and practices of depth psychology to our society's response to climate change. With others, she develops programs which foster greater imagination and root people more in their bodies while they contemplatively, playfully, artistically and practically engage with Nature. Like everyone involved in green spirituality and green activism, she is asking: how can we introduce attractive, fast and far-reaching change to the dominant, mainstream culture which believes that its models bring out the best in and for humankind and seems blind to the level of destruction its methods are wreaking, both for humankind and the rest of life on our beautiful planet? On the Council of GreenSpirit, Sandra also loves sharing with friends stories, food, and walking on Hartham Common near her home in Hertford, long distance paths and Lake District hills and valleys. She, too, is journeying towards greater sustainability.

Acknowledgments

As well as the 29 contributors, without whom this book could not have existed, and the various GreenSpirit members and others whose words have found their way onto these pages, there are some other people to whom special thanks are due.

To New Society Publishers, of Gabriola Island, B.C., Canada, for permission to use Sharon Astyk's material on 'The Theory of Anyway.'

To Jacana Press, of Johannesburg, South Africa, for permission to reprint the beautiful anthem 'Claim to the Country.'

To Alan Shepherd, for the seed from which this book first sprang.

To Don Hills, for your never-flagging keenness to see that seed germinate.

To Ian Mowll, for all your encouragement and practical help.

And to all my colleagues on the GreenSpirit Council, whose enthusiasm and support for the project has made it into a work of joy for me.

Thanks to Michael Colebrook and Jean Hardy, whose long years of producing the GreenSpirit Journal brought forth so much excellent writing both from within and beyond the membership of GreenSpirit.

To all the members and supporters of GreenSpirit, wherever you are, and to all those others spread across Indra's international net of emeralds, including Matt Henry and all the members of CS Communities in the USA and elsewhere, and all the people who were part of The Climbing River Foundation in Australia during those heady years, especially David Bathgate, thank you for being part of this wonderful tribe of humans witnessing for the Earth.

My heartfelt thanks also go to all those wise teachers, past and present, whose visions of green spirituality have inspired us all, above all the late Thomas Berry, whose blessing on this book given just a few months before he died, has meant so much to me. I hope we have represented you well. In particular, thank you Brian Swimme, not only for your contributions to this book, both direct and indirect, but for being one of the most inspirational teachers in whose class I have ever been privileged to sit.

And to the numerous individuals who have played a part in opening my eyes to those visions, all down the years, thank you for being in just the right place at just the right time.

Sue Worley, my sister with the eagle eyes, thank you for applying your transcription and proof-reading skills to this project. And to John Hunt and colleagues at O-Books, I want to say that it is a pleasure to be part of a team with such green, innovative and cooperative ways of working. You truly are publishers of the twenty first century and I hope many others adopt your model in the coming years.

And to Sky, my life's partner, without whose gentle reminders I might never have remembered to stand up from the computer and stretch (and without whose tireless tending of our ancient stove I would probably have frozen to death at my desk this winter), my undying love and gratitude, as always.

BOOKS

O is a symbol of the world, of oneness and unity. In different cultures it also means the "eye," symbolizing knowledge and insight. We aim to publish books that are accessible, constructive and that challenge accepted opinion, both that of academia and the "moral majority."

Our books are available in all good English language bookstores worldwide. If you don't see the book on the shelves ask the bookstore to order it for you, quoting the ISBN number and title. Alternatively you can order online (all major online retail sites carry our titles) or contact the distributor in the relevant country, listed on the copyright page.

See our website **www.o-books.net** for a full list of over 500 titles, growing by 100 a year.

And tune in to myspiritradio.com for our book review radio show, hosted by June-Elleni Laine, where you can listen to the authors discussing their books.

mySpiritRadio